Keynesianism and the Keynesian Revolution in America

Keynesianism and the Keynesian Revolution in America

A Memorial Volume in Honour of Lorie Tarshis

Edited by

O.F. Hamouda

Professor of Economics, York University, Toronto, Canada

and

B.B. Price

Senior Lecturer at the School of Humanities and Social Science, Cambridge, USA
and
Professor of History, York University, Toronto, Canada

Edward Elgar
Cheltenham, UK • Northampton, MA, USA

© O.F. Hamouda and B.B. Price, 1998

Published by
Edward Elgar Publishing Limited
Glensanda House
Montpellier Parade
Cheltenham
Glos GL50 1UA
UK

Edward Elgar Publishing, Inc.
6 Market Street
Northampton
Massachusetts 01060
USA

A catalogue record for this book
is available from the British Library

Library of Congress Cataloguing in Publication Data
Keynesianism and the Keynesian revolution in America : a memorial
    volume in honour of Lorie Tarshis / edited by Omar F. Hamouda and
    Betsey B. Price.
        Includes bibliographical references and indexes.
        1. Tarshis, Lorie.   2. Keynesian economics.   3. Economics—Study
    and teaching—United States—History.   I. Tarshis, Lorie.
    II. Hamouda, O.F.   III. Price, B.B. (Betsey Barker), 1951–
    HB99.7.K373   1998
    330.15'6—dc21   98–5816
                                                                                         CIP

ISBN 1 85898 559 5

Typeset by Manton Typesetters, 5–7 Eastfield Road, Louth, Lincolnshire, LN11 7AJ, UK
Printed and bound in Great Britain by Bookcraft (Bath) Ltd.

Contents

List of tables

List of contributors

O.F. Hamouda is Associate Professor of Economics at York University, Toronto, Ontario, Canada. **B.B. Price** is Associate Professor of History at York University, and Visiting Professor at Massachusetts Institute of Technology, Cambridge, MA, USA. As close friends and former colleagues of Lorie Tarshis at Glendon College, it was their wish to honour his memory with a collection of essays from his friends, colleagues and students. They extend their thanks to all who have helped to realize this project.

Sir Alec Cairncross is Emeritus Fellow at St Anthony's College, Oxford University, England. He met Lorie Tarshis in the summer of 1936, at their college, Trinity, in Cambridge. At the time, Cairncross' PhD was conferred for his treatment of the interaction of home and foreign investments along Keynesian lines, published later in a collection of his early studies (1953). In his last conversation with Tarshis, during a visit to Scarborough College, they shared their long interest in interpreting Keynes, in connection with the aggregate supply function and with international economics.

David Colander is Christian A. Johnson Distinguished Professor of Economics at Middlebury College, Middlebury, Vermont, USA. He has been deeply interested for at least a decade in the contributions of Lorie Tarshis as one of the founders of Keynesian economics. His recent publication with Harry Landreth, *The Coming of Keynesianism to America* (1996), includes his 1986 biographical interview with Tarshis. Although Tarshis died before he could review his oral history, the book serves as a wonderful informal story of how he remembered the events.

Robert W. Dimand is Professor of Economics at Brock University, St Catharines, Ontario, Canada. He counts himself among the many students much indebted to Lorie Tarshis, after Tarshis served on his Yale dissertation committee, along with supervisor James Tobin and Katsuhito Iwai. When Dimand returned to Canada, proximity afforded him frequent visits with Tarshis. His scholarship is dedicated primarily to the history of economic thought, ranging from publications on the ideas of Marshall, Fisher and Keynes to the early history of game theory.

Sheila C. Dow is Reader at the University of Stirling, Stirling, Scotland. An avowed and well-published Keynesian, she has long respected the intellectual position of Lorie Tarshis on economic issues. Her contribution to this volume reflects her concern for the situation of global fiscal relations and her appreciation of Tarshis' analysis of Third World debt resolution. Some of her most recent publications specifically address the role of money in the economic process, with an infusion of Keynes' own perspective.

John Kenneth Galbraith is Emeritus Professor at Harvard University, Cambridge, MA, USA. The eminent economist has throughout his life espoused views shaped by the era of John Maynard Keynes. His description of Lorie Tarshis as an especially 'ardent and effective' member of the Keynesian revolution applies equally well to himself. His contribution here is a reprint of a belated review of the *General Theory*, when in 1965, the *New York Times Book Review* realized they had never reviewed it.

Richard M. Goodwin was, upon his death on 8 August 1996, Emeritus Professor of Economics at both Cambridge University, England and the University of Siena, Italy. Renowned for his novel contributions to a theoretical understanding of economic fluctuations and a notion of complex-system economics, he shared many positions in economics sympathetic with Lorie Tarshis, such as those expressed in his introductory comments to Part IV. Less well known were, perhaps, their shared love of life (and the rewards of a long one), and their fondness for painting and Tuscany.

Franque Grimard is Assistant Professor at McGill University, Montreal, Quebec, Canada. He represents almost the last generation of undergraduates that Tarshis taught at Glendon College after returning to Canada in 1971. During graduate work at Princeton, he maintained contact with Tarshis, his Keynesian mentor, and more recent work at the World Bank and the Centre de Recherche en Developpement Economique in Montreal fostered an interest in world debt, an issue of acute concern to Tarshis in his later years.

Franklyn D. Holzman is Professor Emeritus at Tufts University, Somerville and Fellow at Harvard Russian Research Center, Harvard University, Cambridge, MA, USA. He met Lorie Tarshis in 1942 while working as a junior economist on the Board of Economic Warfare in Washington, DC. In his memoir Holzman recounts his sustained friendship with Tarshis well after their respective government service. Holzman's subsequent academic career was as a world-famous scholar of Russia in the 20th century.

Charles P. Kindleberger is Emeritus Professor of Economics at Massachusetts Institute of Technology, Cambridge, MA, USA. While not long ago he published his own story, *The Life of an Economist: An Autobiography* (1991), his more recent concerns are a return to the stories of others, particularly through the issue of 'social intangibles relevant to economic processes' (the actual title of a 1993 publication). It is in this context that his intellectual connection to the Keynesianism of Lorie Tarshis is more than obvious.

Harry Landreth is Boles Professor of Economics at Center College, Lancaster, Kentucky, USA. His interest, active for at least the last decade, in the contributions of Lorie Tarshis as one of the founders of Keynesian economics, stems from a symposium on the Keynesian revolution, held in 1988 at Middlebury College and attended by Bob Bryce, Lorie Tarshis and Paul Sweezy. One extended result of that symposium, and a visiting professorship at Middlebury College, was his collaboration with David Colander on *The Coming of Keynesianism to America* (1996).

Charles R. McCann, Jr, of Pittsburgh, Pennsylvania, USA, has, since obtaining his doctorate, collaborated with Mark Perlman on several projects. He is an econometrician with a strong interest in the history of economic thought. He has published *Probability Foundations of Economic Theory* (1994), which treats the introduction of probability analysis into economics by focusing in particular on Keynes' *Treatise on Probability*. It is currently being translated into Japanese.

David McQueen is Professor of Economics at York University, Toronto, Ontario, Canada. He first knew Lorie Tarshis as the published Keynesian economist and from 1982 on as his colleague at Glendon College. His contribution, while focused primarily on the career of his professor, W.A. Mackintosh, does not neglect to hint at the possible connections between the two policy advocates, and certainly uses his numerous conversations with Tarshis as a touchstone. A former Principal of Glendon College, McQueen prized the presence of Tarshis among the faculty.

Donald E. Moggridge is Professor of Economics at the University of Toronto, Toronto, Ontario, Canada. Since 1972 he has become known as one of the principal editors of the *Collected Writings of John Maynard Keynes*, published by Cambridge University Press for the Royal Economic Society. His contribution in this volume is a reprint from Michel Cottrell and Allan Lawlor (eds) (1995), *New Perspectives on Keynes*, a special issue of *HOPE*, Vol. 27.

Ian Parker is Professor of Economics at the University of Toronto, Toronto, Ontario, Canada. His arrival at Scarborough College coincided with the late 1970s period when Lorie Tarshis served there as Professor and Administrator. Personal respect for Tarshis has come to be coupled with an increasing interest in the history of thought, particularly in Keynes. Working back from research in the economics of communication, Parker has turned to implications of Keynesianism and the *Treatise on Probability* on modern information-and-uncertainty theory.

Mark Perlman, Emeritus Professor of Economics, of the University of Pittsburgh, Pittsburgh, Pennsylvania, USA, is a much respected member of the economics 'establishment' whose acquaintance with and admiration for Lorie Tarshis goes back many years. His openness to virtually every strain of economic thinking and his willingness, in a position of editorial power, to give them voice, are testimony to his sympathy for those considered at times by some to be well outside the mainstream. His article here deals with the contrasting roles of Keynes and Knight in perceptions of uncertainty.

Melvin W. Reder is Emeritus Professor of Urban and Labor Economics at the University of Chicago, Chicago, IL, USA. His contribution reflects his close friendship with Lorie Tarshis, stemming from their 22 years as illustrious colleagues at Stanford University. During the 1950s and 60s they also 'co-authored a semi-annual report on the American economy for the London and Cambridge Economic Service (later taken over by the *Financial Times*)' where, Reder notes, he grew in appreciation of both Tarshis' expository skill and his Keynesian5 erspective.

Walter S. Salant is Senior Fellow, Emeritus of The Brookings Institution, Washington, DC, USA. Co-author with Lorie Tarshis, he was one of the non-signing participants in *An Economic Program for American Democracy* (1938) and a signing author of *US Balance of Payments in 1968* (1963). He met Lorie Tarshis at Harvard University in the early years of its Fiscal Policy Seminar. His contribution here is quite appropriately a previously unpublished paper about the early years of the Seminar which he had written in celebration of its 50th anniversary in 1988.

Paul A. Samuelson is Emeritus Professor of Economics at Massachusetts Institute of Technology, Cambridge, MA, USA. His sustained energy and enthusiasm for economics are as renowned as his impressive contributions. A self-described admirer of Lorie Tarshis, his contribution here and other recent articles reflect his firm desire to set the history of the 'economics textbook' straight. His fondness for both Tarshis and an accurate historical record are expressed at once. Success, for him, of both Tarshis' and his textbooks was a measure of the whole profession's past Keynesianism.

James Tobin is Professor at the Coles Foundation for Research in Economics, at Yale University, New Haven, CN, USA. He responded to the invitation to contribute by praising Lorie Tarshis as 'a fine economist, a wonderful person and a good friend'. The same can certainly be said of him. His relationship with Tarshis was both indirect, as a student of Richard Gilbert, an earlier co-author with Tarshis on *An Economic Program for American Democracy* (1938), and direct, for when serving on President Kennedy's Council of Economic Advisers, he engaged Tarshis in 1962.

Acknowledgements

This volume is a tribute to one of the most faithful, true Keynesians, one who read, thought, dreamt and promoted purely Keynes: Lorie Tarshis (22 March 1911–4 October 1993). Honouring the native Canadian who lived in America, this work is about his brand of Keynesianism in the making, entitled thus *Keynesianism and the Keynesian Revolution in America*. Keynesianism is far more than a theory or doctrine; it has become a way of political thinking. In the case of America, even the current quarrel between the Clinton Administration and the US Congress is about the positive and negative interpretations of Keynesian policies. Keynesianism having reached these proportions, it is important to understand how it evolved over the years so as to shape US economic policies. This volume is about the early stages of that process. Lorie Tarshis was among the first generation of participants. His own and immediately succeeding generations predominantly effected the Keynesian process, and of those participants some are represented among this volume's authors: Galbraith, Goodwin, Kindleberger, Samuelson, Salant and Tobin.

Lorie Tarshis did not invent a theory, nor does any theorem bear his name. Even so, as Holzman and Reder, close friends of Tarshis, recount, his subtle contributions did not go unnoticed. Tarshis was first among Keynes' select 'Club' in Cambridge, not only witnessing, but actually participating in, the making of the *General Theory* (1936) which Keynes was formulating and polishing during Tarshis' four years in Cambridge. His 1939 article on real wages was one of only two that Keynes appended to his second edition of the *General Theory* (1939). When Tarshis returned to North America, he was among the first group to recommend government policies based on Keynes', in *An Economic Program for American Democracy* (Gilbert et al., 1938). In 1946, he wrote the first ever economics textbook integrating Keynesian ideas. Tarshis sustained active concern in the health of the US economy, notably in a collaborative study on the *US Balance of Payments in 1968* (1963). With *World Economy in Crisis* (1984), Tarshis was also the first to ring the alarm bell about global handling of the developing countries' debt.

Lorie Tarshis was a fine, decent and good economist. It is thus not surprising that our request for contributions to this volume was met with a warm reception. The editors are extremely grateful to the contributors, many of whom have taken time and effort to respond to our request despite a burdensome schedule. Some of Tarshis' closest friends predeceased him: Emile Despres, admired co-author and colleague; Bernard F. Haley, the Chair of Economics at Stanford during the vicious attacks on Tarshis' first textbook; Abba Lerner, frequent discussant during their Cambridge–LSE years and later back in the USA; and A.F. Wynne Plumptre, instructor at the University of Toronto, for whom Tarshis played 'matchmaker'. Unfortunately, however, even some of his friends and acquaintances, blessed to survive him, were for health or other reasons unable to contribute to this volume: Robert Bryce, a contemporary Canadian student of Keynes in Cambridge; Sidney Dell, senior economist at the United Nations; Evsey Domar, acquaintance from the Harvard Seminar years; Edward Shaw, who had noticed Tarshis as early as 1936 at several of Dennis Robertson's Cambridge seminars and who subsequently, as Chair of the Economics Department in 1941, hired him at Stanford; Leonard Silk, senior journalist at the *New York Times*; Alan and Paul Sweezy, also frequent discussants during their Cambridge–LSE days and later back in the USA; and Paul Wells, a student of Tarshis who became Professor of Economics at the University of Illinois, among others. The editors thank all those who provided editorial assistance, especially Robert W. Dimand, Grace Kim, Susanne Rose and the Elgar production team. The editors are particularly grateful to Edward and Sandy Elgar for their encouragement with the volume and patience with the many delays in the preparation of the manuscript. Special thanks are due to Mrs Inga Tarshis and Professor George Smith for providing leads to some of Tarshis' old friends, colleagues and students.

Introduction

Lorie Tarshis' first encounter with Keynes and Keynesianism came in 1931 with the following declaration of his third-year university professor: 'Gentlemen, I have decided that I shall not use any of these American textbooks; I am going instead to use a very decent and reliable book by a magnificent Cambridge economist, John Maynard Keynes'. A.F. Wynne Plumptre, a young Canadian instructor who had graduated from the University of Cambridge five years earlier, was to present Tarshis with his most memorable course at the University of Toronto: Money and Banking. With Plumptre's announcement, Tarshis had his first introduction to the work of the man who was to have the greatest influence on his intellectual life.

Tarshis had found his way into a university course on economics by virtue of his enthusiasm and skill for mathematics, and his schooling at the highly competitive University of Toronto School run as a 'laboratory' by the university for its education students. Although he had intended to follow in the footsteps of his father, Dr Singer, a medical doctor and Toronto City Coroner, who had died during the typhoid epidemic of 1915, he was counselled to go into economics. At the time, the study of undergraduate economics at the University of Toronto meant entering a core programme called 'Commerce and Finance'. The first year was, from the standpoint of economics, modest, focusing on economic geography and geology. In the second year, economics was more seriously undertaken, with the main courses being Principles of Economics, Industry and Trade, and Economic History.

Early in his second year of university, Tarshis' Professor of (British) Economic History, C.R. Fay, lecturer from Cambridge and close friend of Keynes, came to class one morning looking ashen and said, 'Gentlemen, I think you should know that you will remember yesterday for the rest of your lives'. Fay's pontifical tone and message did stay in Tarshis' mind: it was the day of the first big crash on Wall Street. The crash touched Tarshis and his fellow students in a very simple way. They were all involved in 'playing' the Stock Market, 'investing' in gold mines and the like which, until a few months before, had been going up and up. The students played the game competitively, but Tarshis remained unconvinced that he had learned any economics in this way. His second-year reading of Alfred Marshall's *Principles of Economics* (1890) had a different effect entirely. Tarshis had been confronted with the enjoyment of reading the actual works of great economists, even before Plumptre presented him with Keynes' two-volume *Treatise on Money*.

By 1931, with the combination of the visibly increasingly dire economic situation in Toronto, with suicides over business failures, bread lines, riots or the remains of riots around the Parliament building and the main streets, and his third-year curriculum, Lorie Tarshis had begun to take economics quite seriously. Among his third-year courses were Labour Economics, Money and Banking, and Public Finance. He found the course in Labour Economics highly interesting because the instructor, H. Cassidy, introduced his class to the leaders of the local Toronto unions of the Ladies' Garment Workers and the Amalgamated Clothing Workers, which were on strike for most of 1931. In getting to know some of the strikers, Tarshis was persuaded that the strike was fair and sympathized with them.

Keynes' *Treatise on Money*, however, was to prove the biggest stimulus to his dedication to economics to date, and Tarshis spent the greater part of his third year of university challenged by working through it. Apparently Plumptre, who had assumed the position of Tarshis' mentor, saw in him a student ripe for more intensive exposure to the dissenting opinions of Keynes, perhaps even in Cambridge itself. Tarshis may already have voiced his opinion that the orthodoxy in economics at the University of Toronto, that the Depression was a temporary phenomenon and a long-run return to normalcy would occur, did not seem sensible to him. The months were passing, and nothing seemed to be getting better. Tarshis took his observations to show a growing wedge between what was happening in the real world and what the authoritative economists said would happen, and seemed to doubt their idea that market forces would eventually take care of the economy's woes.

Tarshis had applied for a Rhodes Scholarship, but having learned it would not have sent him to Cambridge to study with Keynes, he was happy to have won instead a Massey Fellowship in 1932. He found the whole atmosphere at Cambridge favourable to dissent from the orthodoxy of his Toronto years, and in economics Keynes was certainly the example. An undergraduate for two years at Trinity College, Tarshis prepared the second part of the Economics Tripos, earning a first at the end of his second year. He was subsequently awarded the Trinity Exhibitioner Fellowship, which enabled him to stay for two more years in Cambridge to begin his doctoral work in the Faculty of Economics and Politics. While enjoying the normal student dissipations, Tarshis nonetheless recognized the importance of Keynes' lectures from the start, taking detailed notes of each one (published with others' lecture notes in Rymes (1989)).

From the first 11 a.m. lecture of his first term with Keynes (10 October 1932), Tarshis sensed the general atmosphere of excitement in the room. While waiting he wrote down in his notebook 'Theory of Money and Prices', which had been the announced title of the course Keynes was to offer. When Keynes came in, however, he began: 'Gentlemen, I have decided to change the title of my course of lectures from "Theory of Money and Prices" to "Monetary Theory of Production"'. Tarshis crossed out the old title on the front of his notebook, wrote down the new one and then began to puzzle over it. He wrote a great big question mark, his shorthand for 'what is Keynes talking about?'. None of the students had to wait long for an answer, as Keynes very quickly revealed his new ideas.

Keynes raised a question in that first lecture to which, throughout his life, Tarshis had felt society gave insufficient attention. Keynes asked: 'What would you think if you were a businessman and you were advised to treat your workers in the same way as you treat your capital assets?'. He continued:

> How would a society work if the employer treated his labour force in the way he treats his capital assets (protecting them with canvas tenting material or whatever can be got to keep the moisture off, greasing the wheels and so on), rather than as he does now, throwing them out on the street and saying 'waste away'? If you are a worker, you're simply thrown out of work; you're simply told, 'come back in two months, we may have something for you then'. The employer is the boss; if he does not have work for his workers he says goodbye and good luck. But that's the limit of his concern.

Having written the reflections down, Tarshis thought about them extensively. Keynes asserted that the situation would be very different if the labour force were treated as a capital asset; then, for all practical purposes, unemployment would disappear.

During his four-year stay in Cambridge, Tarshis had quite a lot of contact with Keynes, since – as had Plumptre, his mentor – he participated in Keynes' 'Political Economy Club' meetings, every two or three weeks on average. When Tarshis had arrived in Cambridge in 1932, an invitation from Keynes to become a member of the Club had awaited him. The Club met in Keynes' room four or five times a term on Monday nights from 7.30 to shortly before midnight. Tarshis found Keynes' Club very exciting, feeling that its discussions were on the cutting edge of economics.

Money and real wages were Tarshis' first concern as a publishing scholar. He had started thinking about the issue in his third year at Cambridge, initially in a vague way, for a thesis. In the next few years Tarshis developed his interest very concretely into his doctoral study, aimed at using the insights of microeconomics to tackle a macroeconomic problem – the distribution of wage income. Tarshis' analysis started with the firm and profit maximizing and then generalized to a collection of firms. Although he did not coin Kalecki's graceful concepts of 'mark-up' and 'degree of monopoly', the results of Tarshis' (1939) thesis, 'The Determination of Labour Income', independently echoed those Kalecki (1938) had published, where labour share depends on the degree of monopoly and the elasticity of the typical marginal cost function.

In September 1936, Tarshis assumed a teaching job at Tufts College (Medford, Massachusetts) and, despite coping with a heavy teaching load, completed his dissertation within the academic year. Under the remote supervision of Maurice Dobb and Dennis Robertson, the dissertation rested for anything really novel on the *General Theory* and the not-yet-accepted ideas of Keynes. Without agreeing with every detail of the *General Theory,* it accepted Keynes' major conclusions. Tarshis never saw any reason to reject them – but he did maintain that the *General Theory* oversimplified matters.

At the outbreak of World War II, with government demands interrupting his teaching, Keynes did not read Tarshis' dissertation. He did, however, see some of the ideas that had crystallized from it into 'Changes in Money and Real Wages' (1939), which Tarshis sent to him as a note for publication in the *Economic Journal.* Tarshis had already formulated some of his ideas on the subject in 'Real Wages in the United States and Great Britain' (1938). In the *General Theory* Keynes had written that he would not be surprised to find that in a period in which money wages are rising, real wages are falling and vice versa. The hypothesis was based, it seemed, on the notion that money wages will rise when employment is rising and vice versa; real wages will fall when employment is rising because there are rising marginal costs. Prices go up even if money wages stay the same, therefore real wages drop. Tarshis found that Keynes' hypothesis was not correct: if money wages were rising, real wages might be rising, but they might also be falling. He concluded that the picture was much more complicated than Keynes had depicted. Real wages depended on many factors, of which the level of output was only one.

Keynes immediately accepted the note, intrigued by Tarshis' findings. He even asked Tarshis to add a paragraph or two based on his comparison of changes in the level of real wages and changes in output (or unemployment, where data were available). Both economists were certainly unaware that, ever since Marshall, no data would be found to confirm the thesis. Tarshis, like Keynes, felt that his conclusion had no effect on the validity of the *General Theory*'s assertion that aggregate supply and aggregate demand between them determine price and output.

Tarshis' initial position as instructor at Tufts College afforded him both the amazing annual salary of $2500 and, in the Boston area, compatible colleagues from Harvard and Tufts. A small group began meeting regularly to discuss the economic situation in the USA, and by September 1937 had decided to write a collective book. The result, *An Economic Program for American Democracy* (1938) signed by 'seven Harvard and Tufts economists', advocated Keynesian conclusions and expressed their dismay at the failure of US policy-makers of the late 1930s to use Keynesian analysis properly. It argued that things are more complicated than they appear: while a general statement or theory might justify assumptions in academic discussion, it may not be adequate when action is required to face a particular economic situation. The message was aimed at the inconsequent economic policies of the US government, whose economists professed to have adopted the tenets of the *General Theory*. They were not aware, the book argued, of the implications of raising taxes for reasons other than fighting inflation, as Keynes recommended. The current situation was that the US government was raising taxes to finance the introduction of the Social Security programme. Taxes were thus going up not in an effort to suppress inflation, but simply to balance the budget.

Tarshis found himself at odds with some authors of *An Economic Program* on the issue of the deficit. The deficit was a great worry at the time. Having been brought up, in the midst of Toronto and Cambridge orthodoxy, to believe that a deficit was next to the devil, Tarshis was extremely surprised by the impressive beauty of the *General Theory*, in which Keynes had not concerned himself much with deficits. In fact, the atmosphere at Keynes' Club was one of suspicion in anyone's excessive concern about the deficit. Thus, early on, Tarshis had adopted an anti-anti-deficit posture. He felt that if an economy were allowed to grow, any deficit would take care of itself. Many of Tarshis' ideas on internal and external deficits were developed later in *The United States Balance of Payments in 1968* (1963), a study commissioned on the eve of an anticipated intractable US balance-of-payments deficit, and in 'The Dollar Standard' (1974).

In 1939–40 Tarshis was a Carnegie Fellow at the National Bureau of Economic Research (NBER). In 1942, although promoted to Assistant Professor at Tufts and beginning to draft chapters of an elementary economics textbook, he left in the spring for Washington to work for a year for the US War Production Board. He found himself reunited with George Housner, a Canadian boyhood friend, and making the acquaintance of Franklyn Holzman, who rapidly became his trusted book 'editor'. Having become a US citizen, Tarshis was subsequently asked by the Pentagon to join a group of young scientists as an operations analyst of bombing raids, assigned through the Air Force to Libya, Tunisia and Italy between 1943 and 1945.

In 1946 Tarshis began teaching again, now in the Economics Department at Stanford University. In that same year he signed a contract with Houghton Mifflin of Boston for a textbook of economics which, as he had continued to polish its chapters during his early years of war service, was ready for publication the following year. The primary contribution of *The Elements of Economics: An Introduction to the Theory of Price and Employment* was conceived to be the introduction of Keynes into economics teaching and of macroeconomics into introductory courses. The textbook was a serious effort to explain all the elements of modern economics and was initially well received by over 100 colleges and universities, including almost all those of the Ivy League. It began with an introductory section of three chapters describing the labour force in terms of size, gender, wages, and so on. The second section was a study of microeconomics, based on Tarshis' pedagogical conviction that a student must first understand a good deal of microeconomics before he or she can really understand macroeconomics. Tarshis' treatment of microeconomics differed from the at-the-time universally espoused Marshallian approach that assumed free competition. He also introduced, into his text, diagrams of the firm that showed both the average and the marginal revenue curves as horizontal.

Tarshis was the first writer to introduce Joan Robinson's ideas in textbook form. To these ideas he added one important original element: his own 'mark-up theory'. He guided students not simply to recognize, as Joan Robinson had insisted, that firms very often do make marginal calculations (such as marginal cost equals marginal revenue), but also to appreciate that firms will more likely use a formula approach. Tarshis offered both the evidence and a rationale for this observation: (1) in the real world, the estimate of marginal cost for a multi-product firm is based on so many assumptions, each of them of doubtful validity, that the effort of estimating hardly seems worth it; and (2) the elasticity of demand for the firm is virtually impossible to estimate when there is either monopolistic or imperfect competition. In the textbook itself, Tarshis revealed his reluctance to ignore either aggregate supply or aggregate demand.

Both political and economic attacks were laid against *The Elements of Economics*. As early as the summer of 1947, which Tarshis spent teaching at Williams College, it was being condemned for being 'communist-inspired'. A long, hostile appraisal in the *Economic Council Review of Books*, written by the conservative Rose Wilder Lane, was disseminated by the President of the National Economic Council, Merwin K. Hart, to alert anyone connected to academic institutions, as well as political figures, to the perceived dangers in the book. The malicious rumours which circulated about Tarshis' disloyalty to capitalism provoked a substantive response among some intellectuals. Others, such as Donald Tresidder, the President of Stanford until his death in January 1948, and two subsequent Presidents, felt called upon to defend Tarshis himself and the causes of academic freedom and dignity.

The economic arguments against the book were remarkably non-specific, being put forward by those who felt that monetarism ought to be used for analysing macroeconomic problems. One could say that the book was simply a casualty in the early war on Keynes, although Tarshis, throughout his life, found the battle which confused Keynes (or Keynesians) with communism (or communists) incomprehensible. As a consequence, however, of both the attack on Tarshis' character – which by 1951 included William F. Buckley, Jr's opinions in *God and Man at Yale* – and the 1948 appearance of the first edition by McGraw-Hill of Paul Samuelson's textbook, the initial sales of Tarshis' *Elements of Economics* plunged. Later in his career, as Professor at Stanford and coincident with his assuming departmental Chairmanship in 1967, Tarshis published a substantially reworked version of the textbook as *Modern Economics,* although once again his ideas were a casualty of poor timing; the text appeared just as Keynesianism was on the verge of declining.

Tarshis criticized the hypothesis of comparative costs in 'Price Ratios and International Trade: An Empirical and Analytical Survey' (1959). With data acquired on the relation of prices and costs for the production of steel plates of specific size, thickness and weight in various countries, he found that the exporting source of a product was often not its cheapest production source, and that a country (such as the US), was exporting things for which it had comparative disadvantage. Tarshis concluded that the hypothesis that trade follows comparative advantage is an oversimplification: there are many other influencing factors, such as trade ties.

Tarshis' article, 'The Elasticity of the Marginal Efficiency Function' (1961) was novel for its direction rather than for its conclusion. It maintained that the problem of assessing elasticity must be decided, not by assuming *a priori* the marginal efficiency function as more or less elastic, but by asking 'Why is it more or less elastic?'. The elasticity of any function really depends on the diversity of opinions that lie behind it. A key element in discussing the marginal efficiency of such a function would be how diverse or close to uniform are the expectations. Great diversities in expected return yield a very low degree of elasticity.

Having reached his 'first' retirement age of 60, Tarshis left Stanford in 1971 to return to Toronto. He first taught at Scarborough College, his alma mater, in 1971–78. In 1978 Tarshis assumed for two years the position of Director of Research at the Ontario Economic Council. This immersion in policy issues rekindled in him his two final passionate economic interests: the role of taxation in the health of an economy and the state of international debt. In 'Aggregate Supply Function in Keynes's *General Theory*' (1979), Tarshis maintained that an adverse shift in the aggregate supply function can help answer the question of the cause of inflation better than excess demand. Efforts to suppress inflation or to slow it down by raising interest rates or taxes are bound to make the situation worse. While he recognized that ortho-dox economics has a role to play, Tarshis firmly maintained that Keynes' (or even Marshall's) notion of the aggregate supply function was far richer than that of many of Marshall's followers.

The introduction of a new tax, especially one that heavily influences the supply of almost everything, will surely affect the position of the aggregate supply function drawn as a line that rises to the right and is not straight; it may move it up or down, alter its elasticity, and so on. The point of the article was thus that in the aggregate, where the supply functions of all firms are combined, the supply curve is not vertical. Also, as things change, the movement is not only along the curve; the slope of the curve itself is altered. Any change in policy would not necessarily cause motion on the supply curve and thus inflation. It would be very likely to affect both the demand and the supply functions. Implicit in most policy decisions is that the supply function stays the same and only demand is moved.

Tarshis' involvement in the issue of international debt, eagerly sustained during the last phase of his teaching career, at Glendon College, York University, Toronto, 1982–88, sprang from his interest in the Euro-dollar currency markets. In his *World Economy In Crisis: Unemployment, Inflation and International Debt* (1984), Tarshis introduced the notion of a banking system that is running wild and unrestrained. He maintained that if Euro-currency banking were to come into being, an individual central bank on its own could do nothing to control the negative effect of capital movement, the international lending–borrowing situation having become so uncontrolled that it has created an unprecedented strain on the less developed countries (LDCs) in terms of their international debt. In *World Economy in Crisis* and numerous subsequent articles, Tarshis advanced a method of analysis and a scheme for bringing international debt under control.

The contributions in this volume are grouped into four sections. The first is a set of chapters on the beginning and early years of American Keynesianism. The second section, tracing Tarshis' Keynesian books, particularly the rise and sudden fall of his first textbook, is a specific reflection on Tarshis as one intellectual casualty of the pre-Joseph McCarthy era. The third group of contributions is focused on how Keynesianism guided the consideration of economic policy issues in North America in general and, in the case of Lorie Tarshis, in the subjects of real and money wages and international debt in particular. Finally, the fourth part is dedicated to chapters in which the contributors choose to take a Keynesian posture and puzzle through a particular issue, such as consumer protection, uncertainty and probability.

Each set of contributions has an introduction: the first by Alec Cairncross, the second and third by extracts from Keynes' and Tarshis' writings, and the fourth by Richard Goodwin.

In 'A Brief Memoir', the first chapter, Franklyn Holzman describes his connection to Lorie Tarshis the man. In June 1940, Holzman (himself a graduate of the University of North Carolina with a Bachelor of Arts in Economics) was advised that almost no university jobs were available to students with Jewish backgrounds, and had all but given up the idea of ever working as an economist. Upon taking a civil service exam, he was, however, in December 1941 or January 1942, offered a job as a junior economist in a unit at the Board of Economic Warfare (BEW) in Washington, DC, which included, among others, a Canadian economist named McDiarmid. After having spent his first month baffled by two projects of great importance to the war effort and returning, in a tremble, to report to the United States and Canada division on his results, Holzman felt, however, most fortunate to have met Lorie Tarshis. Although Holzman worked together with Edith Hyslop, his immediate and professional superior as she had completed a few years of graduate work before the war effort began, under Tarshis' compassionate supervision, he and Holzman rapidly became close personal friends, sharing, among other things, similar 'Leftish' political and social views. Although on meeting Tarshis Holzman had not yet become either 'Keynesian' or 'socialist', Tarshis clearly sensed a close intellectual bond with Holzman. Holzman writes of Tarshis' asking him in short order if he would read the already drafted chapters, and the other chapters to come, of the elementary economics textbook Tarshis was writing. Holzman was thus one of the first to read and comment on parts of the emerging manuscript of *The Elements of Economics*, the first textbook ever to include the lessons of the Keynesian revolution.

Although Holzman would have been happy to have spent the war years at BEW, in September 1942 he was drafted into the Armed Forces. He did reconnect with Tarshis after the war ended, when he entered Harvard University's doctoral programme in economics and Tarshis was in the Boston area, teaching economics at Tufts University. By 1948 Holzman was, however, back in Washington at the US Treasury, where he reconnected with Hyslop and met her husband, Al Sherrard. The next and only communication between Holzman and Tarshis was in the mid-1950s, by which time Tarshis was teaching at Stanford and Holzman, at the University of Washington, Seattle. In 1957 Holzman was invited to teach summer school at Stanford, and since, at the same time, his wife was asked to be a consultant on a book on input–output economics that Hollis Chenery and Paul Clark at Stanford were preparing for publication, the Tarshis and Holzman families were able to spend a fair amount of time together. Although that summer of 1957 was to be their last close contact, Holzman writes of Tarshis' remaining one of his favourite people ever since their meeting in Washington in 1941.

John Kenneth Galbraith has come to be known as one of the small group of economists instrumental in introducing Keynes' ideas to America. In his now famous and oft-printed essay which pays respect to many others who pioneered the Keynesian revolution in America, 'How Keynes Came to America', Galbraith tells the story from the publication in 1936 in both Britain and the United States of *The General Theory of Employment, Interest and Money* by John Maynard Keynes, the most influential book on economic and social policy in the 20th century, to the commonplace acceptance of Keynesian policies by the administrations of Presidents Kennedy and Johnson. Galbraith praises the Keynesian revolution – and Tarshis as one of those who experienced it – as one of the great modern accomplishments in social design for its effecting fiscal policies which followed both Keynes' argument that neither wage movements nor changes in the rate of interest have, necessarily, benign effect, and his proposed remedy of supplementing private with public expenditures to bring aggregate demand to a level where all willing workers could be employed.

Although from 1920 to 1940 Keynes, in Cambridge and London, was sought out in person by students such as Lorie Tarshis and intellectuals from all over the world, Galbraith ties Keynes' influence in the United States most closely to the *General Theory*'s having fallen on fertile ground among the intellectuals in Cambridge, Massachusetts, and in turn in Washington, DC, and to the extremely difficult book's having received an accessible 'translation' there. In addition to Harvard's large community of young unemployed economists who snapped up the book with great excitement in the late 1930s, Marriner Eccles, Lauchlin Currie and Simon Kuznets, already in public positions, were warm to a presentation of conclusions similar to those they had reached themselves. It is to Alvin H. Hansen's exposition of Keynes' ideas in books, articles and lectures, and his application of them to the American scene, to which Galbraith attributes most credit for their 'translation'. Bureaucrats and politicians took Hansen's ideas, and perhaps even more so his sense of conviction, from Harvard to Washington, to the National Planning Association, the NBER, the Federal Reserve Board, the Work Projects Administration (WPA), the Treasury and the Legislature with the Employment Act of 1946. Before the Keynesian revolution was to effect the commonplace policy of the 1960s, however, Galbraith reflects on some of its hurdles bespeaking a counter-revolution. With the focus on Harvard, Galbraith has not taken on the task of exposing the worst of those who nurtured thoughts of a Keynesian conspiracy or plot in America, but identifies the nefarious pressure exerted by Harvard's graduates for an investigation of its Department of Economics through the annual review of the Visiting Committee. He draws that episode, and virtually his whole story, to a close with the ironic historical twist that Clarence Randall, head of a hostile reviewing Committee, once he became assistant and adviser to President Eisenhower (along with Arthur F. Burns), adopted Keynesian policy to overcome the recession of 1958, to the extent of incurring a deficit of $9.4 billion in the national income accounts.

D.E. Moggridge notes at the outset of his chapter, 'The Diffusion of the Keynesian Revolution: The Young and the Graduate Schools', that Samuelson, Schumpeter and even Keynes offered oft-repeated characterizations of the spread of Keynesian (and other) ideas. His article, reprinted from a special issue of *HOPE*, sought to add to existing reflections on the diffusion of Keynesian ideas some statistical information, particularly with reference to graduate education in economics, the last matter being of special interest because, by the early 1950s, the notion of a 'core' of economic theory intended to bind together the profession and enable communication among every type of economist had entered academic economics. The core of the chapter is thus a bibliographical and biographical study of the 392 articles and authors which appeared between the beginning of 1936 and the end of 1948 and were recorded either in classes 2.30, 2.31, 2.320, 2.322 or 2.325 of the *Index of Economic Journals* or in the surveys of post-*General Theory* developments in the first two revisions of Gottfried Haberler's *Prosperity and Depression* (1946). Moggridge chose the *post quam–ante quam* dates for two reasons: the *General Theory* appeared in February 1936, and the 1948 appearance of both Patinkin's 'Price Flexibility and Full Employment' and the first edition of Samuelson's *Economics* could be taken as marking by way of terminus the widespread acceptance of a basic 'Keynesian' model and message at both the professional and undergraduate levels.

Through tables, the author surveys the characteristics of the authors of the articles examined, that is, their scattering over birth years, age at first article and, in terms of their graduate training, the universities where their highest degree was granted, and the place, date and number of accepted doctoral dissertations for American-trained economists. The high ranking at the time of the graduate schools at the University of Chicago and Harvard University (and, for that matter, at the London School of Economics (LSE)) was, Moggridge argues, probably symptomatic of the fact that they provided the best analytical training in economics available in the late 1930s and 1940s. By way of contrast, as far as can be determined, the theoretical training of economists at Columbia left much to be desired. Oxford and Cambridge did not yet figure, largely because they were not well-organized centres of graduate instruction in economics. To consider who the key individuals were, Moggridge tabulates the statistics of published acknowledgements and journal citations, noting with interest that among the most cited books and articles are all the expected classics from the early discussions of the *General Theory*: Lange's 1938 piece for *Economica*, Haberler's 1946 *Prosperity and Depression*, Hicks' 1937 formulation of IS–LM for *Econometrica* and 1939 *Value and Capital*, Robertson's 1940 *Essays in Monetary Theory*, and Hawtrey's 1937 *Capital and Employment*.

Moggridge reaches the conclusion that Keynesian ideas were diffused to particular individuals through the strong association between the discussion

of Keynesian ideas at a limited number of centres of learning and the persuasive recruitment of students to them by their instructors and peers.

In 'Harvard's Fiscal Policy Seminar: The Early Years', Walter S. Salant
surveys the importance of the early years of that Harvard Seminar, which
began in September 1937 when the Graduate School of Public Administration first opened and Alvin Hansen of the University of Minnesota took up his
appointment as Professor of Economics at the Littauer School. The Seminar's
beginnings, Salant notes, coincided with the American economy's going into
a sudden tailspin and followed the publication of Keynes' book, *The General
Theory of Employment, Interest and Money* by little more than a year. In the
Seminar devoted to policy, Keynes was consequently to be intensively discussed, initially in terms of the consumption function and the multiplier,
problems deemed to be in need of theoretical clarification. Salant traces the
Seminar's main policy foci through the economic outlook and planning for
the post-war period, with special attention given to the problem of European
recovery and the Marshall Plan. His article is especially valuable as no
official archive of the papers given at the Fiscal Policy Seminar seems to
exist, nor even any complete list of the speakers and papers presented within
the first several decades of its existence.

The Seminar was conducted jointly by Hansen and Professor John Williams,
first Dean of the Graduate School of Public Administration. Salant considers
their first year of the Seminar to have been among its most important, for
several reasons. First, the impression was created during that year that Hansen
was the more active of the two organizers, an impression Salant attempts to
alter by considering the relatively neglected role of Williams, characterizing
him as having been a very valuable critic, especially in the field of international finance and the role of capital movements. Second, during the first year
was also set the two-part *modus operandi* that was to be followed in subsequent years, with one part a student-faculty 'Seminar members' discussion
meeting, and the other a gathering for a formal talk by an outside speaker;
this method altering later only with respect to the frequency of meetings and
the combination of meetings with the Littauer School. Third, 1937–38 formed
an important part of the professional training and experience of the earliest
School of Public Administration graduate students. To support his claim for
the importance of the early year(s), Salant describes: (1) the Seminar as
having provided a place for fledging economists to try out ideas by presenting
papers and getting criticisms through discussions, as, for example, the early
papers by Paul Samuelson on the interactions of multiplier and accelerator
and Evsey Domar on the burden of internally held government debt; (2) the
efforts of the senior members of the Seminar to find theoretical answers to
baffling policy problems as a valuable stimulus; and (3) the debate it stimulated among the economist participants outside its meetings, as took form, for

example, in *An Economic Program for American Democracy* (Gilbert et al., 1938), which Tarshis co-authored and Herbert Stein called 'the first manifesto of the young Keynesian school' (1968, p. 164).

The second section of the volume deals with the intellectual aspects of Tarshis' books which reflect his Keynesianism and especially the circumstances which surrounded the reception of his first textbook, *The Elements of Economics* (1947). James Tobin, author here of 'Lorie Tarshis: An Early Keynesian Herald in America', identifies each of Tarshis' books in chronological order. He himself first became aware of Lorie Tarshis as 'the Tufts economist' whose *An Economic Program for American Democracy* (1938), published with six Harvard economists named as co-authors, excited and rallied young New Dealers and Keynesians such as himself. Tarshis was at the time proving to be especially important in the transmission of Keynesian doctrine from the old Cambridge to the new. Tobin identifies Tarshis' named co-authors, talented theorists and teachers all: Richard Gilbert, Paul Sweezy and his wife, Maxine, George Hildebrand, Arthur Stuart and John Wilson (who were moving Harvard economics towards Keynes and Roosevelt), as well as several others: Emile Despres, Walter Salant and Alan Sweezy, who 'because of their present connection with various branches of government service, did not feel free to affix their signatures to recommendations on questions of policy' (Gilbert et al., 1938, p. vi).

Tobin sees *An Economic Program* as a diagnosis of America's economic crisis as 'secular stagnation', without using those words of Alvin Hansen. The 1937–38 recession had been an important spur to the dissemination of its message and, according to Tobin, *An Economic Program* was, perhaps for practical reasons, overly charitable in its assessment of the New Deal. In the following two or three years, economic mobilization for war gave the economy a Keynesian boost far greater than Tarshis and his co-authors, Hansen or anyone else had contemplated. Perhaps because of its timing, *An Economic Program* did not make much of a splash outside the Boston area.

From the first Tarshis work he read, Tobin proceeds to characterize Tarshis' other books, from *The Elements of Economics* (1947) to his second textbook, *Modern Economics: An Introduction* (1967) and his co-authored *The United States Balance of Payments in 1968* (1963). *Elements*, published by Houghton Mifflin and edited by Edgar S. Furniss at Yale, is a volume whose copies are now somewhat difficult to locate. It was at publication the first elementary college textbook featuring Keynesian theory, essentially the novel multiplier analysis. Although at the time Keynesian macroeconomics was its distinctive feature, most of the *Elements*' nearly 700 pages were devoted to microeconomics: theories of the firm and industry, and micro-foundations of the basic Keynesian propensities to consume, invest and hold money. Tobin writes of having been impressed most by Tarshis' evident and enthusiastic urge to tell *Elements'* readers, if not everything he knew, at least everything he believed they could and should know. Although it was a pioneering book, essentially the first post-war post-Depression introductory text, excelling in quantity and quality in terms of international economics, it attracted very few professional reviews. Nonetheless, Keynesianism became a targeted approach. Sales of Tarshis' text were damaged by scurrilous right-wing attacks on it, and Paul Samuelson's *Economics: An Introductory Analysis* (1948) soon stole the market.

Although near the end of his life, Tarshis invited Tobin to Toronto on several occasions, their closest association came in 1962 when Tobin was a Member of President Kennedy's Council of Economic Advisers, and the Council engaged Despres, Salant and Tarshis – three comrades from the old Harvard days – to help out, with others, in analysing the US balance-of-payments deficit problems. Out of that request ensued Tarshis' 1963 co-authored book, *The United States Balance of Payments in 1968*.

Paul A. Samuelson intended in his chapter, 'Requiem for the classic Tarshis Textbook that First Brought Keynes to Introductory Economics', his tribute to Lorie Tarshis' *Elements of Economics*, not only to set the record straight about which elementary textbook first introduced Keynesian macroeconomics, but also to report impressionistically on the tragic, sordid treatment 'this pioneering tour de force' received from 1947–50, largely at the hands of vicious pre-Joseph McCarthyites from the extreme and uninformed Right, such as Rose Wilder Lane, Colonel Narn and William Buckley, Jr. Samuelson concludes the paper with a reminder that the wisdom and warmth of Tarshis in his intellectual concerns and persona were undeserving of the later fate.

Samuelson's second purpose was to look back, from a perspective which almost half a century of distance affords, upon the merits and shortcomings of the mid 1940s textbook expositions of both Tarshis and Samuelson, whose Keynesian macroeconomics he notes as fundamentally similar. Attributing his extended *Nabelbetrachtungen* to a peculiarity in economics of necessarily studying one's previous imperfections, Samuelson uses the metaphor of the evolving early Ford automobile, from Model T to pre-World War II Model A, as a measuring stick. The textbooks of Tarshis and Samuelson both reflect Model T Keynesianism: a bare-bones version, albeit supplemented by discussions of banks and money, of the paradigmatic Kahn–Keynes 1931–33 multiplier model of one equation in the one unknown of income. He goes on to assert, however, that both the 1947 Tarshis and 1948 Samuelson expositions are consistent, under their surfaces, with Model A Keynesianism of the Harrod–Hicks–Hansen I–S and L–M diagrams, already in the background of Keynes' 1936 *General Theory* and Joan Robinson's 1937 *Introduction to the Theory of Employment*. It is truly post-*General Theory* salutary alterations in Keynesianism which Samuelson identifies as those he and Tarshis might have included in their textbooks to render them more up-to-date, closer to James Tobin's and Franco Modigliani's 'wealth effects' and Milton Friedman's and others' long-run shifts in permanent-income saving propensities, perhaps to the imminent 'slab-sider' Ford model of 1949. Samuelson nonetheless counters anachronistic queries as to why more of a Robert Lucasian neoclassical perspective did not figure in Tarshis' and his textbooks. He notes that, although in some longer-run processes of M and P growth, the possibility that an increase in spending might go only to change the $P(t)$ price level in $P(t)Q(t)$ while leaving real output levels invariant had indeed been noticed, the authors' holding to both the idealized convention of 1933–36 which considered the P price level as virtually constant (or slowly rising) until a proximity to 'full employment' was reached, and the 1938 empirical studies of Tarshis and John Dunlop which cast doubt on the empirical validity of the neoclassical law of diminishing returns and its entailed rise in P/W as Q shows short-term growth, was an accurate reflection of the lag in the mid 1940s economics culture.

In the following chapter, David Colander and Harry Landreth continue the examination of the Keynesian textbook revolution and its interaction with the Keynesian policy revolution. In an earlier publication (1996), they argued that the Keynesian revolution in economics involved a three-part interrelated process: a policy, a theoretical, and a textbook revolution. In 'Political Influence on the Textbook Keynesian Revolution: God, Man and Lorie Tarshis at Yale', they examine the pertinence of their taxonomy to the 1947 publication by Tarshis of an introductory text which incorporated, among recent developments in economics, especially Keynesian economic thought and ideas of monopolistic and imperfect competition. They begin the background to the Tarshis work in 1936, when Lorie Tarshis and Robert Bryce came to Cambridge, Massachusetts from Cambridge, England, where they had been enthusiastic students of J.M. Keynes. Tarshis began disseminating Keynesian ideas in the US through published works with an initial policy book, *An Economic Program for American Democracy* (Gilbert et al., 1938) and then through the quite usual route of academia. An excellent writer and expositor, he was recruited in 1946 by Edgar Furniss, the Provost of the graduate school of Yale and an advisory editor to Houghton Mifflin, to write an introductory economics textbook. Tarshis' book was 699 pages long and was substantially different from previous texts, the biggest difference being perhaps its policy sensibility.

Initially Tarshis' book was well received, but soon after publication it was harshly represented as Leftist in a review by Rose Wilder Lane. In the face of her and other attacks, Tarshis' academic home, Stanford, stood firm and, despite risk to its alumni financing, refused to budge from supporting the right of free expression by its professors. The schools which had adopted

Tarshis' book were, however, not so firm, and sales soon dwindled. Tarshis was especially upset by an attack, comprised of sloppy workmanship and misleading partial quotations, by William Buckley, Jr in *God and Man at Yale* (1951), in which he criticized Tarshis and the authors of several other economics textbooks used at Yale. Anyone who knew Tarshis knows that it was impossible to dislike him personally; he was one of the most charming, caring and pleasant economists ever – hence Colander and Landreth surmise that his differences with Buckley in particular could only have been due to a clash of ideologies, conservative vs liberal. Buckley was so very openly committed to the free market that, faced with his favourable ideological preconception, even a non-ideological assessment of the costs and benefits of government policy would be considered suspect. Yet in Tarshis' mind there was nothing inconsistent in being pro-market and pro-government action, and he was very clear that he felt his own views were pro-market. Tarshis was, however, also consistent with favouring a variety of policies which would be considered 'collectivist', and his book espoused that ideological view as being science. The Colander–Landreth chapter concludes that the result of the campaign by Lane, Buckley, and others was both the death of Tarshis' book and the sanitization of economic textbooks from much of the controversy that makes economics exciting.

The chapter by Melvin Reder, 'Lorie Tarshis: Left-Wing Keynesian', forms a fitting end to this second set of contributions. Reder knew Lorie Tarshis for over 40 years, 22 (1949–71) as a colleague at Stanford. While recognizing Tarshis' wide-ranging interests, covering art, literature, music and politics, he restricts his chapter to Tarshis' concern with conventionally defined economics. To Reder, Tarshis was the exemplar *par excellence* of an endangered intellectual species, the Left-Wing Keynesian. He questions whether Tarshis' notion of the proper functions of an economist were formed in Cambridge, England, or whether his experience there merely reinforced what he had brought from Toronto; in either case, the attitude he found at Cambridge towards the subject matter and functions of the economist dominated his performance throughout his professional life. Although he did not scorn the journal-filling activities of most of his colleagues, Tarshis felt strongly that the primary objective of economics was to supply tools for economic improvement and thus that the proper objective of a university education in a social science, economics or otherwise, was to equip the student to understand and – most importantly – to improve the world. Like the Cambridge dons he admired, the students Lorie prized most were bright undergraduates eager to make their mark in the real world, preferably in influencing or creating economic policy. For Tarshis and many others of his academic generation, the example *par excellence* of useful theory was the *General Theory*, and its author the exemplar of the economist. Like Keynes and most

Keynesians, Tarshis viewed the main function of economics as the provision of a set of policies that would enable the state to function satisfactorily. For Keynes, civil servant that he was, this condition was sufficient as well as necessary.

When concern with unemployment became a major focus of political debate, Keynes realized that 'classical' economic theory was an impediment to the search for a sound policy. For Keynes, the attainment of (nearly) full employment was a necessary condition for political stability; but to Tarshis, and many other Left-Wing Keynesians of his generation, both in Britain and the US, it was more: the process of attaining nearly full employment was an opportunity to transform the economy to provide economic security to all members of society, together with a fair sharing of the social product. Though it is likely that his left-leaning followers exerted some influence on Keynes' views, both on economics and social policy, it is uncertain how far this influence would have gone had World War II not intervened. In effect, as a by-product of war finance, Keynes had, willy-nilly, come to propose the virtual socialization of saving and investment for an indefinite period.

Tarshis was a man of the Left, yet in a sense, to demarcate Left-Wing Keynesians sharply from other Keynesians is to create a breach in what could be considered a continuum. Keynesians of all shades share a belief in the competence of the state to make desired changes in the structure and functioning of the economy, and in the essential role of properly trained economists and other social scientists in effecting them, and in this Tarshis was not an exception, but a noble exemplar.

Keynesianism in America is often understood as Keynesianism in the USA, but should more appropriately be seen as a North America-wide phenomenon. Keynesian ideas greatly influenced the Canadian economy through a generation of instrumental civil servants and academics. David McQueen gives an example of this impact in 'Another Canadian Keynesian: W.A. Mackintosh'. While strong lines of intellectual exchange can easily be evoked between specific Canadian civil servants, that is, William Mackintosh and Robert Bryce, and A.F.W. Plumptre and Louis Rasminsky (as well as the direct relation of each pair with Keynes), McQueen acknowledges that a direct intellectual connection between Mackintosh and Tarshis is harder to evaluate. Apparently Tarshis and Mackintosh never spent a great deal of time together, unlike the case with the others, but this, of course, does not rule out the potential for a considerable amount of intellectual cross-fertilization. Indeed Mackintosh, a former professor and personal acquaintance of McQueen, played a significant part as a prominent Canadian proselytizer of Keynesian ideas.

Macintosh, a Queen's University man to the core, not to mention a sometime Queen's Principal (1951–61), was generally regarded as one of the two most prominent figures in the original Canadian 'staples' school of economic history, as it flourished in the 1920s, 1930s and 1940s. In addition to his historical work, Mackintosh was best known for his grasp of the essentials of the Keynesian, macro approach to matters both domestic and international, and for his contributions to the making of Canadian economic policy during and after World War II. McQueen's chapter purports, in no sense, to be a stand-alone piece, if only because in addition to Keynes himself, three other figures – Robert Bryce, Wynne Plumptre and Louis Rasminsky – in particular must have played a major role in turning pragmatically inclined Mackintosh into an important, if somewhat qualified, Keynesian. In the 1930s and 1940s, both the economics profession and the volume of serious economics publications were orders of magnitude smaller than they have become, but, not just to economists but to nearly everyone, World War II, through its extraordinary transforming action on the Canadian economy, had demonstrated that the Depression, or at any rate its length and depth, had been unnecessary, and that, for reasons political and social as well as economic, it must not be repeated. Sheer force of circumstance made the times uniquely propitious for the adoption, both nationally and internationally, of Keynesian ideas.

McQueen asserts that what did much to move Mackintosh towards Keynes was the manifest usefulness of the Keynesian macro–policy apparatus for the purposes of the wartime economic management and post-war planning in which Mackintosh was so intimately involved, including notably creating the new national accounts, primitive though these still were. In the Queen's University graduate programme in economics as of 1947–48, Mackintosh taught one of two required courses in a small basement room in Kingston Hall: 'Problems of the Canadian Economy'. It included, naturally, a fair content of Canadian economic history, with a particularly good empathy for western Canada which, more than any other part, had experienced many of the features of life in a 'globalized' economy generations before that term would come into popular use. Inevitably, however, the most stimulating parts of the course bore on more recent macroeconomic developments, although Mackintosh never romanticized government or his involvement in the corridors of power.

The story of Lorie Tarshis' interest in policy decisions regarding real and money wages is told in part by Robert W. Dimand in his chapter 'Keynes, Tarshis, Real and Money Wages, and Employment'. The detailed examinations of Tarshis in 1938 and 1939 of changes in real and money wages in Britain and the United States, together with research by John Dunlop, caused John Maynard Keynes to draw back from the account of money wages, real wages and employment presented in Chapter 2 of the *General Theory*. Keynes had argued that the 'classical theory of employment', as presented by Pigou, Keynes' colleague at King's College, was based on two fundamental postulates, under which demand for labour would equal the supply of labour and there would be no involuntary unemployment: 'I. The wage is equal to the marginal product of labour. II. The utility of the wage when a given volume of labour is employed is equal to the marginal disutility of that amount of employment'. Such views were held more generally than by just Pigou, and although it has been shown that Pigou did not draw the policy conclusion of wage-cutting as a remedy for unemployment as Keynes thought he implied, Edwin Cannan, Professor Emeritus at the LSE, did in his Presidential Address to the Royal Economic Society (1932).

Keynes first presented his account of the two classical postulates on 16 October 1933 in his lecture series on 'The Monetary Theory of Production', and in offering objections to the second postulate of the classical theory, he specifically expressed interest in seeing the results of an enquiry into the actual relationship between changes in money wages and changes in real wages. Having attended four terms of Keynes' lectures at Cambridge (1932–35) and participated in Keynes' Political Economy Club, Tarshis began the predictably interesting statistical analysis of changes in real and money wages. Dimand recounts how Tarshis (1938) constructed and graphed monthly series for average nominal and real hourly earnings for 89 manufacturing and 14 non-manufacturing industries in the United States apparently from January 1932 to January 1938, observing that changes in the volume of production of American industry appeared to have had no great significance for the level of real wages. Tarshis did further statistical analysis, directly related to the first classical postulate, and in 1939 gave a presentation of the data underlying his earlier article, bringing evidence to bear on Keynes' supposition that real and money wages would change in opposite directions. Dunlop, also at Cambridge, England, before his career at Harvard, found that annual data for Britain from 1860 to 1937 (excluding 1913–19) showed that real wage rates and money wage rates tended to increase together. Within three years of its publication, the theory of money wages, real wages and employment in Chapter 2 of the *General Theory* was severely shaken by the empirical findings of Tarshis and Dunlop. Keynes replied by 1939 that recasting Chapter 2 and discarding the first classical postulate would only strengthen his theory, since an expansion of effective demand could then increase employment without depressing real wages. Dimand notes, however, that dropping the first classical postulate would leave the *General Theory* without an explanation of how a change in equilibrium income, due to a change in aggregate demand, would translate into changes in employment and hence output, rather than just changed prices.

Much later, in 1984, Lorie Tarshis published *World Economy in Crisis: Unemployment, Inflation and International Debt* through the Canadian Institute for Economic Policy. Tarshis' concern with international debt was a direct consequence of his devotion to Keynesianism. He thought that, if the USA as the leading developed economy in the world could find a way of alleviating the burden of the debt to the Third World, then Keynesian analysis for raising the effective demand at the national level could also be applied to the international level.

In 'Keynesian Monetary Theory and the Debt Crisis', Sheila Dow gives a brief account of the ideas expressed in Tarshis' work, focusing on those specifically addressed to his passionate policy concern of the problem of soaring international debt. Tarshis had addressed simultaneously the problems of soaring inflation, unemployment and debt. He identified the cause of growing Third World debt as being the payments imbalances arising from the 1973 oil price shock, and the efforts of international banks to recycle petrodollars from oil exporters to oil importers. Since one of the primary aims for the International Monetary Fund (IMF) was to prevent the recurrence of the experience of the 1930s which Tarshis well remembered, he set out a three-point programme for IMF reform designed to increase the institution's effectiveness and to restore exchange stability. Tarshis' analysis of the debt crisis also focused on the functioning of the international financial system whose lending activity had facilitated it. Accordingly, he set out six proposals for addressing the immediate problem of the debt overhang, which was threatening bank solvency, and for reforms to make the Eurocurrency market less fragile and less capable of replicating the credit explosion of the 1970s.

The 1980s saw the eventual introduction of a range of measures designed to avert the full realization of a debt crisis, that is, to prevent a widespread debt moratorium and extensive incidence of bank failure. Following Mexico's default in 1982, the IMF identified the need for structural adjustment in debtor countries to improve their capacity to service debt. However, this approach failed to improve the situation, other than preventing actual bank collapses. The Baker Plan was announced in 1985 to address this worsening situation, advocating a significant increase in bank lending to debtor countries, with this lending being contingent on IMF conditionality, that is, on agreement to structural adjustment. In the meantime, the banks were evolving market-based solutions to restructure their portfolios in order to reduce their risk exposure. A new plan, the Brady Plan of 1989, reflected a shift in understanding the nature of the crisis, with a recognition that not all the debt might be serviceable, that is, that there was an element of insolvency. In the meantime, the Bank for International Settlements had been addressing the general issue of uncontrolled international credit, notably in the Eurocurrency market.

Dow notes that Tarshis' proposals for reform held much in common with Keynes' ideas for a world central bank, for equal pressure on surplus countries to adjust along with deficit countries, for control of short-term capital flows, and for debt forgiveness. Yet while experience with the international banking and monetary system in the last decade has reinforced the importance of Tarshis' Keynesian arguments for a fundamental change in institutions and practices, and while there was some shift towards his ideas with the Brady Plan, no solution to the debt crisis has comprehensively incorporated the concerns set out in Tarshis' *World Economy in Crisis*.

The chapter by Franque Grimard, 'A Case Against Muddling Through: Lorie Tarshis' Proposal and the International Debt Problem', takes a second look at Tarshis' contribution to the literature on the 'Third World debt crisis'. The 'debt crisis', a troubled situation triggered by Mexico's announcement in August 1982 that it could no longer meet its debt-servicing payments, was the specific context that Lorie Tarshis addressed in *World Economy in Crisis*. Grimard provides a further review of the causes of the crisis and the difficulties that have impeded its satisfactory resolution. Despite the initial profitability of predominantly US bank loans to LDCs, that situation reversed itself in the 1980s, due first to the Volker–Reagan shock that by creating the recession of the early 1980s led to a drastic reduction in demand for LDC exports, and second to the sharp increase in interest rates starting in 1978.

Tarshis stressed that the international financial system's troubles stemmed from most large banks being overexposed to bad LDC loans, but the crisis was first confronted as if it were a short-term liquidity problem with debt rescheduling as the solution. By 1985, some conditions had indeed improved, but mere debt rescheduling did not lead to a lasting end to the crisis. By 1988, despite two years of growth in the developed world and structural adjustment in the developing world, the Baker Plan, calling for more lending, had failed. The next attempt to solve the debt crisis was the Brady Plan of swapping old debt for new terms. By 1992, ten years after its start, the debt situation was in fact no longer one of 'crisis' and the international financial community felt renewed optimism for a resolution of Third World debt. This optimism came, however, to a halt in December 1994 with the devaluation of the Mexican peso, a brutal reality check. The situation of LDCs in the early 1990s had given false hopes that growth could resume in these countries and contribute to improvement in their living standards.

Tarshis' proposal of 1984 had stressed the need for debtor *and* creditor countries to forgive some proportion of the debt. He believed that debt forgiveness should be done according to particular global, egalitarian, incentive-producing principles. By 1987 he presented his ideas as 'a monetary solution to a monetary problem – too much credit extended by the commercial banks'. While Tarshis was aware that his proposal would encounter difficulties, by 1990 he was emphasizing its advantages. One other scheme proposed around the same time was the International Debt Discount Corporation (IDDC) by Kenen. Neither the IDDC nor the Tarshis Plan was adopted by the international financial community, although there seems to be an answer to why not.

Tarshis' proposal is seen to have suffered specifically from several problems related to those which any comprehensive debt reduction plan has to address: it neglected the problem of moral hazard and precedence; it saw serious need for reforms of the international monetary system, including supervision of an exchange rate system by a newly empowered IMF; and it encountered the unwillingness of surplus countries to participate in a system in which they might encounter costs, this latter being interestingly the same problem confronted by Keynes' *bancor* proposal.

While all the chapters in this collection honour the memory of Lorie Tarshis as a careful and not uncritical student of Keynes, most treat ideas within Keynes which Tarshis himself pursued. In the fourth set of chapters, however, the authors address an issue of particular concern to Keynes, such as consumer protection, uncertainty or probability, to which Tarshis himself did not direct any lengthy attention. In model Tarshis fashion, however, the authors worry their issues through to interesting and stimulating conclusions. In '*Caveat Emptor*, Investor, Depositor', Charles P. Kindleberger tackles the issue of the government's possible role in protecting the consumer, investor and/or depositor in an environment of economic theory in which at least one founding father, Adam Smith, has been cited as saying that honesty is not always the best policy and the tradition of *caveat emptor* rules. While the theory of *laissez-faire* would work, he writes, either if consumer, investor and depositor were wary in protecting their interests or if sellers and bankers were uniformly competitive and honest, but neither is consistently the case. Instead those who ought to be wary are vulnerable due to their lack of intelligence or stupidity, their lack of information or ignorance, and/or their lack of judgement or credulity, none of which can be completely corrected for by family or schooling; and those who ought to be honest and fair cannot maintain high standards, whether individually or in groups, perhaps, Kindleberger ponders, due to having missed the early childhood experience of an ethical environment or later strict professional guidelines. Observing that there are some private sector checks in the form of outsider directors for companies and computer trading monitoring for stock exchanges, as well as recourse to legal suits, Kindleberger, without succumbing to any easy rule, nonetheless supports rather the legacy of economic history that a government presence through tight regulatory practices is needed to patrol the nature of private economic transactions initiated by promoters and salespeople in the market, as well as the honest fulfilment of contracts with innocent and/or ignorant consumers, investors and depositors.

Ian Parker has chosen Keynes' theory of probability, expectations and uncertainty as his focus, although it is only since the early 1980s, and particularly in the last decade, that it has received much attention. Undeniably this aspect of the *General Theory* did not weather the passage across the Atlantic well, and Parker seeks out some explanation for its limited degree of early transmission to North America, either as integral to the argument of the *General Theory* or as a basis for macroeconomic theory. He discovers that: (1) many of the subtleties of Keynes' approach to probability, expectations and uncertainty were lost or suppressed in the process of its diffusion; (2) aspects of the *General Theory* other than its treatment of probability and so on were emphasized; (3) 'teachable' interpretations and glosses of Keynes' *General Theory*, notably those of Hicks and Hansen, rapidly emerged, in which Keynes' concept of uncertainty and its economic role were effectively eliminated; and (4) various versions of '"Bayesian" cardinal subjective-probability theory', presupposing that a *cardinal* measure of the probability of the occurrence of each of certain, somehow well-defined, states of the world actually exists, even if it is only subjectively in the mind of the beholder, were hegemonically incorporated into the core of the contemporary mainstream analysis of 'decision-making under risk or uncertainty'.

The primary focus of Parker's chapter is on the theory of probability and expectations, presented in the *Treatise on Probability*, Keynes' compendium of a wide range of issues in the logic of partial belief, or probability, broadly defined. Keynes published the *Treatise* in 1921, although much of it had already appeared by 1908 in his second, successful, fellowship dissertation; during the extended hiatus of over a decade, he had made significant additions only to Part V on 'The Foundations of Statistical Inference'. Originally, it was Moore's *Principia Ethica* (1903) to which Keynes was indebted, and Whitehead and Russell's *Principia Mathematica* (*c*. 1910) which he was confronting. Parker elucidates these influences in a brief sketch of some of the major features of the *Treatise on Probability* itself and then turns to his main objectives: (1) to indicate some of the shortcomings in R.B. Braithwaite's and related appraisals of the *Treatise*; (2) to suggest that what Braithwaite in particular views as Keynes' partial 'capitulation' to Frank Ramsey's approach is rather more semantic than substantive; (3) to apply principles drawn from the *Treatise* to Ramsey's 1931 framework for probability analysis, in order to suggest that on the criteria Keynes set out, Ramsey's own account of probability is seriously limited; and (4) to suggest the essential relevance and implications of the *Treatise on Probability* not only for a full interpretation of Keynes' approach to economics as regards the significant elements of continuity between the *Treatise* and Keynes' later economic writings, but also for the future development of economics.

Charles R. McCann and Mark Perlman introduce their chapter dedicated to the discussion of 'Keynesian Economics and the Meaning of Uncertainty' with direct reference to Keynes, as it were, denying that he had been willing to 'throw over all my fundamental economic principles when I come and study fluctuations'. This passage was quoted by Lorie Tarshis in 'The Aggregate Supply Function in Keynes's *General Theory*' (1979), and, noting that Tarshis was specifically interested in Keynes' concern with 'fundamental economic principles' in the context of theoretical models of economic fluctuations, the authors address a more basic sense in which they see Keynes as unwavering. The central element which, the authors assert, all followers seem to agree is important for understanding the modal Keynesian model, despite the fact that their interpretations differ, is Keynes' postulation of a nonstationary environment. McCann and Perlman note that Keynesians, in relegating Keynes' economics to the determinism of the formal model stipulated in the *General Theory,* ignore the import of uncertainty and expectations, while modern post-Keynesians, in their desire to endogenize uncertainty, seek actively to discuss uncertainty and expectations within a 'Keynesian' framework and New Keynesians introduce the concept of *hysteresis* to do so. Like these interpreters, for example, Coddington, Davidson and Cross, respectively, the authors attempt to reconcile aspects of Keynes' works to the single theme of his need to incorporate the concept of fundamental uncertainty.

Of special relevance are three of Keynes' works: his *Treatise on Probability* (1921), with its emphases on subjective apprehensions of the individual to external environmental stimuli and on an account of rationality which holds that non-logical behaviour is not inherently irrational; his *General Theory* (1936), in which focus shifted to a concern with the identifiable disruptive 'macroeconomic' problems of inflation and unemployment; and his *QJE* article, 'The General Theory of Employment' (1937), where, by pursuing a practical remedy, Keynes attempted to address the problem of the *GT* form of analysis, that is, that, despite the fact that once one has a well-defined aggregate as the basis of economic argument, it cannot be true that the study is any longer concerned with *knowledge* and rational *behaviour*. While the main philosophical argument of the *General Theory* centred on the fundamental notion of uncertainty and the manner in which expectations are engendered in dealing with an unpredictable environment, the manner in which Keynes handled the problem was to treat it as essentially external to the model. His subsequent solution involved the reconsideration of three techniques, each of which he had employed in varying degrees in the *General Theory*: (1) 'ignore the prospect of future changes about the actual character of which we know nothing'; (2) accept the '*existing* state of opinion' as correct, 'unless and until something new and relevant comes into the picture'; and (3) fall back on '*conventional* judgement'. While, in the *General Theory* and following, Keynes invoked 'conventions' as merely a means of handling uncertainty within the confines of the social collective (ostensibly for purposes of the model), the authors note the obvious political implications. McCann and Perlman see the difference between the *Treatise on Probability* and the *General Theory* as slight and due to Keynes' concern with employing the appropriate rhetoric for his need to persuade a non-academic, political audience to accept his policy prescriptions in the time and the environment in which the *General Theory* was written. Tension between the works is thus superficial.

O.F. Hamouda
B.B. Price

Lorie Tarshis' major writings

Tarshis was diagnosed near the end of his life with Parkinson's Disease which in its course gravely affected his memory. Further, he never did keep a good running record of his published writing. This, in combination with his life-long modesty, meant not only that much of his writing has not been catalogued, but much of it never saw nor probably ever will see publication. Despite their relatively small number, we think inspiration can yet be found in those writings in which his ideas did circulate formally. The following is certainly only a sample, but the only one known to us:

(1938), 'Real wages in the United States and Great Britain', *Canadian Journal of Economics and Political Science*, 4 (August), 362–75 (with discussion by Robert B. Bryce, pp. 375–6).

(1938), with R.V. Gilbert, G.H. Hildebrand, Jr., Arthur Stuart, M.Y. Sweezy, P.M. Sweezy and J. Wilson (E. Despres, W.S. Salant and A.R. Sweezy who, though participants, remained unnamed as they were employed by the US government), *An Economic Program for American Democracy*, New York: Vanguard Press.

(1939), 'Changes in Real and Money Wages', *Economic Journal*, 49 (March), 150–54; (rpt 1946) in William Fellner and Bernard F. Haley (eds), *Readings in the Theory of Income Distribution*, Philadelphia/Toronto: Blakiston, pp. 330–35.

(1941), 'Real and Money Wage Rates: Further Comment', *Quarterly Journal of Economics*, 55 (August), 691–7.

(1947), *The Elements of Economics: An Introduction to the Theory of Price and Employment*, Boston: Houghton Mifflin Publishing Co.

(1955), *Introduction to International Trade and Finance*, New York: Wiley/London: Chapman & Hall.

(1959), 'Price Ratios and International Trade: An Empirical and Analytical Survey', in M. Abramovitz et al. (eds), *The Allocation of Economic Resources: Essays in Honour of B.F. Haley*, Stanford: Stanford University Press, pp. 237–44.

(1961), 'The Elasticity of the Marginal Efficiency Function', *American Economic Review*, 51 (5), 958–85.

(1962), 'Retained Earnings and Investment', in K. Kurihara (ed.), *Post-Keynesian Economics*, London: Allen and Unwin, pp. 345–88.

(1963), with W.S. Salant, E. Despres, L.B. Krause, A. Rivlin and W.A. Salant, *The United States Balance of Payments in 1968*, Washington DC: Brookings Institution.

(1967), *Modern Economics: An Introduction*, Boston: Houghton Mifflin.

(1974), 'The Dollar Standard', in P.A. David and M.W. Reder (eds), *Nations and Households in Economic Growth*, New York: McGraw-Hill.

(1979), 'Aggregate Supply Function in Keynes' *General Theory*', in M. Boskin (ed.), *Economics and Human Welfare: Essays in Honour of Tibor Scitovsky*, New York: Academic Press, pp. 361–92.

(1980), 'Post-Keynesian Economics: A Promise That Bounced?', *The American Economic Review Papers and Proceedings*, 70 (2, May), 10–14.

(1984), *World Economy in Crisis: Unemployment, Inflation and International Debt*, Ottawa: Canadian Institute for Economic Policy and Toronto: James Lorimer & Company.

(1987), 'Disarming the Debt Bomb', *Challenge*, May–June, 18–23.

(1988), 'The International Debt of the LDCs', in O. Hamouda and J. Smithin (eds), *Keynes and Public Policy after Fifty Years*, New York: New York University Press, Vol. 2, pp. 183–93.

(1989), 'A Return Visit to the International Debt Problem of the LDCs', in O. Hamouda, R. Rowley and B. Wolf (eds), *The Future of the International Monetary System: Change, Coordination or Instability?* Armonk, NY: Sharpe, pp. 160–69.

(1990), with M.H.I. Dore, 'The LDC Debt and the Commercial Banks: a Proposed Solution', *Journal of Post Keynesian Economics*, 12 (Spring), 452–65.

PART I

Introductory comments: 'Lorie Tarshis'

Sir Alec Cairncross

Lorie Tarshis arrived in Cambridge, England in October 1932, just when foreign students were beginning to pour into the city under the spell of John Maynard Keynes. Nearly all of them came as undergraduates (in 1931–32 there had been only two research students in economics and no living PhD). Most of them came from some part of the Commonwealth or from the United States; very few were from Europe. Six came from Toronto alone, including R.B. Bryce, who gave Harvard its first exposition of Keynesian ideas, and E.H. Norman, who later committed suicide in Cairo where he was Canadian Ambassador. Whether all six took economics I cannot be sure, but they played a distinguished part in the life of the University, both Bryce and Tarshis ending up with firsts in a year that included W.B. Reddaway, T.W. Hutcheson and V.K.R.V. Rao.

Tarshis was about a month younger than I and was attached to the same college, Trinity, where Dennis Robertson was the Economics Tutor. He was a member of Keynes' Club but, so far as I remember, did not read a paper. He was rather quiet and keen on his studies, with a slight hesitation of speech but plenty of enthusiasm for whatever he took in hand. I don't recall being much involved with him, but we were throughout on friendly terms.

Tarshis stayed on after taking his degree, putting in the further two years' residence needed for a PhD, but went to America to teach at Tufts in 1936. I remember meeting him in Trinity in the summer of 1936 when he came back for the conferment of my PhD, just as, if my memory serves me right, he was getting ready for his wedding.

He in turn was awarded a PhD in 1939, although there is some slight doubt as to the subject. In the University records his title is given as 'The Marginal Productivity of Capital', but other sources (rightly?) give 'The Distribution of Labour Income' as the title. At least this squares with the articles he wrote at the time of his 'Changes in Real and Money Wages' in the *Economic Journal* (March 1939).

Tarshis was a convinced follower of Keynes. His interests in economics developed from Keynes' writings, with amendments to some (in the behaviour of real wages in the business cycle, for example) and elaborations of others (when I last talked to him at Scarborough College he was intensely interested in the shape of the aggregate supply function). He was, above all, an admirable teacher and expositor of economic theory – an enthusiast yet temperate in argument.

1. Lorie Tarshis: a brief memoir

Franklyn D. Holzman

Let me present a few facts about myself for background. I graduated from the University of North Carolina in June 1940 with a Bachelor of Arts in Economics. I wanted to go to graduate school but was advised that almost no university jobs were available to students with Jewish backgrounds. So I looked for a job in the New York area and lived at home. Unemployment was widespread in New York, and I spent the next 18 months either unemployed or employed in menial jobs (busboy, mailing clerk in a large textile firm, typist for an accountant); my wage ranged from $6 to $14 a week. Although I hated accounting, I started studying it in night school at the City College of New York, in the hope that an uncle of mine who headed a small accounting firm would eventually hire me.

I had all but given up the idea of ever working as an economist when, after taking a civil service exam, I was offered a job as a junior economist in the Board of Economic Warfare (BEW) in Washington, DC in December 1941 or January 1942. I reported for work and met with V. Frank Coe, my new boss. We spent about an hour together, during which he outlined two projects that were to be completed within a month. The first was to estimate Nazi Germany's oil situation in mid 1944; the second was to estimate what it would cost the United States to launch a one million-man expeditionary force to Europe. Needless to say I didn't have the vaguest idea as to how to proceed on these projects and was paralysed with fear.

A month passed and I returned, trembling, to report to the States and Canada units. In addition to Lorie Tarshis and myself, there were about half a dozen others in this division. Lorie quickly put me at ease with regard to what I viewed as my 'failure' to complete Coe's projects. He said that the whole division couldn't have done a good job on such projects in only a month's time. Sensing my lack of confidence, he supervised my work carefully at first, but after a month or so left me largely to my own devices.

We rapidly became close personal friends. Several factors were responsible. We were both living as bachelors. I was unmarried, and he had moved to Washington without his wife or children. We also shared a deep love of classical music, but he was way ahead of me. My interests at that time stretched from Mozart and other early classicists to Beethoven and Schubert and even to Schumann and Brahms. His major interests were in the baroque period. He got me interested in baroque music by making me a present of Bach's wonderful *Musical Offering*.

We also shared similar 'Leftish' political and social views – what a friend of mine once labelled 'Keynesian socialist' – although, as we shall see below, I was not yet a 'Keynesian'. Finally, we were both interested in economics, my interest having been instantly revived by my job as a junior economist in Washington and my association with Lorie. In fact, about the time he took the job in Washington, he was in the early stages of writing his elementary textbook, which would be the first textbook ever to include the lessons of the Keynesian revolution. When he told me about it, I was enthusiastic. I had completed a BA in Economics without ever having read or heard lectures dealing with John Maynard Keynes. In fact, after graduating from college, I bought a copy of Keynes' *The General Theory of Employment, Interest and Money* (1936) and read it by myself. Without anyone with whom to discuss it, I got very little out of it.

Lorie asked me if I would read the chapters already drafted for his book and others that he would be writing in the future. I readily agreed; in fact I was eager to have the opportunity to refresh my knowledge. I eventually read some eight completed chapters. He often tried out ideas on me as to how to present Keynesian concepts, which was for me both challenging and exciting. I thought that his micro chapters were far superior to those that I had read in other college textbooks.

I would have been happy to have spent the war years at BEW, but in September 1942 I was drafted into the Armed Forces. I was sent first to an American Bomber Air Base in the United Kingdom and eventually to a Joint United States–Soviet Air Base in the Ukraine. While I was in England, I received a letter from Lorie telling me that he was also in the Army, stationed in Italy. He seemed to be enjoying his experiences there. He mentioned, among other things, frequenting a bookstore which, if I remember correctly, was run by a German refugee and his daughter, who, I believe, eventually became Lorie's second wife, Inga.

After the war ended, I entered Harvard University's doctoral programme in economics. Lorie was also in the Boston area, teaching economics at Tufts University. We bumped into each other a few times at Harvard seminars and met for lunch several times in the Square, where he filled me in on happenings at the Joint War Production Board after I had left, as well as problems relating to his finishing the textbook and getting it published.

Our next communication was in 1956, by which time he was teaching at Stanford and I at the University of Washington, Seattle. I was searching for a new text for my introductory course in International Economics and ran across his newly published textbook, *Introduction to International Trade and Finance* (1955). I adopted the book because I preferred its treatment of the Keynesian macroeconomics of international trade to those in alternative textbooks. My choice was undoubtedly influenced by the fact that at that time I was busy writing an article on the foreign trade multiplier. This coincidence led to a renewal of our correspondence with each other.

In 1957 I was invited to teach summer school at Stanford and, at the same time, my wife was asked to be a consultant on a book on input–output that Hollis Chenery and Paul Clark at Stanford were getting ready for publication. We spent a lovely summer at Stanford. Not the least of our pleasures was getting to know the Tarshis family in their native habitat. Lorie had told me how much he enjoyed playing chamber music (mostly recorders) and we enjoyed watching their little group perform. (Ten years later, when our children were a bit older and after I had belatedly taken cello lessons, we had our own little family quartet.)

That summer of 1957 was the last time that Lorie and I were able to spend a fair amount of time together. We were again at Stanford during the 1970–71 school year but Lorie and his family spent that year elsewhere, much to my great disappointment. We bumped into each other at the American Economics Association annual meeting in Washington, DC in December 1981. We took off from the meetings and had a long lunch together. It was the last time we saw each other.

Since we met in Washington in 1941, Lorie has been one of my favourite people. I deeply regret that our life paths did not intersect more often and for longer periods of time.

2. How Keynes came to America[1]

John Kenneth Galbraith

I believe myself to be writing a book on economic theory which will largely revolutionize – not, I suppose, at once but in the course of the next ten years – the way the world thinks about economic problems.

Letter from John Maynard Keynes to George Bernard Shaw,
New Year's Day, 1935

The most influential book on economic and social policy so far in this century, *The General Theory of Employment, Interest and Money* by John Maynard Keynes, was published in 1936 in both Britain and the United States. A paperback edition became available in America for the first time not long ago and quite a few people who took advantage of this bargain must have been puzzled at the reason for the book's influence. Though comfortably aware of their own intelligence, they could not read it. They must have wondered, accordingly, how it persuaded so many other people – not all of whom, certainly, were more penetrating or diligent. This was only one of the remarkable things about this book and the revolution it precipitated.

By common, if not yet quite universal, agreement, the Keynesian revolution was one of the great modern accomplishments in social design. It brought Marxism in the advanced countries to a total halt. It led to a level of economic performance that inspired bitter-end conservatives to panegyrics of unexampled banality. Yet those responsible have had no honours and some opprobrium. For a long while, to be known as an active Keynesian was to invite the wrath of those who equate social advance with subversion. Those concerned developed a habit of reticence. As a further consequence, the history of the revolution is, perhaps, the worst told story of our era.

It is time that we knew better this part of our history and those who made it, and this is a little of the story. Much of it turns on the almost unique unreadability of the *General Theory* and hence the need for people to translate and propagate its ideas to government officials, students and the public at large. As Messiahs go, Keynes was deeply dependent on his prophets.

The *General Theory* appeared in the sixth year of the Great Depression and the 53rd of Keynes' life. At the time Keynes, like his great contemporary, Churchill, was regarded as too candid and inconvenient to be trusted. Public

8

officials are not always admiring of men who say what the right policy should be. Their frequent need, especially in foreign affairs, is for men who will find persuasive reasons for the wrong policy. Keynes had foreseen grave difficulty from the reparations clauses of the Versailles Treaty and had voiced them in *The Economic Consequences of the Peace* (1920), a brilliantly polemical volume which may well have overstated his case and which certainly was unjust to Woodrow Wilson, but which nonetheless provided what proved to be a clearer view of the post-war economic disasters than the men of more stately views wished anyone to expect.

Later in the 1920s, in another book, Keynes was equally untactful towards those who invited massive unemployment in Britain in order to return sterling to the gold standard of its pre-war parity with the dollar. The man immediately responsible for this effort, a highly orthodox voice in economic matters at the time, was the then Chancellor of the Exchequer, Winston Churchill, and that book was called *The Economic Consequences of Mr. Churchill* (1925).

From 1920 to 1940, Keynes was sought out by students and intellectuals in Cambridge and London; was well known in London theatre and artistic circles; directed an insurance company; made, and on occasion lost, quite a bit of money; and was an influential journalist. But he wasn't really trusted on public questions. The great trade union which identifies trustworthiness with conformity kept him outside. Then came the Depression. There was much unemployment, much suffering. Even respectable men went broke. It was necessary, however unpleasant, to listen to the candid men who had something to say by way of remedy. This listening is the terrible punishment the gods reserve for fair weather statesmen.

It is a measure of how far the Keynesian revolution has proceeded that the central thesis of the *General Theory* now sounds rather commonplace. Until it appeared, economists, in the classical (or non-socialist) tradition, had assumed that the economy, if left to itself, would find its equilibrium at full employment. Increases or decreases in wages and in interest rates would occur as necessary to bring about this pleasant result. If men were unemployed, their wages would fall in relation to prices. With lower wages and wider margins, it would be profitable to employ those from whose toil an adequate return could not previously have been made. It followed that steps to keep wages at artificially high levels, such as might result from (as it was said) the ill-considered efforts by unions, would cause unemployment. Such efforts were deemed to be the principal cause of unemployment.

Movements in interest rates played a complementary role by ensuring that all income would ultimately be spent. Thus, were people to decide for some reason to increase their savings, the interest rates on the now more abundant supply of loanable funds would fall. This in turn would lead to increased investment. The added outlays for investment goods would offset the diminished outlays by the more frugal consumers. In this fashion, changes in consumer spending or in investment decisions were kept from causing any change in total spending that would lead to unemployment.

Keynes argued that neither wage movements nor changes in the rate of interest had, necessarily, any such benign effect. He focused attention on the total of purchasing power in the economy – what freshmen are now taught to call 'aggregate demand'. Wage reductions might not increase employment; in conjunction with other changes, they might merely reduce this aggregate demand. Moreover, Keynes held that interest was not the price that was paid to people to save but the price they got for exchanging holdings of cash, or its equivalent, their normal preference in assets, for less liquid forms of invest-ment. And it was difficult to reduce interest beyond a certain level. Accord-ingly, if people sought to save more, this wouldn't necessarily mean lower interest rates and a resulting increase in investment. Instead, the total demand for goods might fall, along with employment and also investment, until savings were brought back into line with investment by the pressure of hardship which had reduced saving in favour of consumption. The economy would find its equilibrium not at full employment, but with an unspecified amount of unemployment.

Out of this diagnosis came the remedy. It was to bring aggregate demand back up to the level where all willing workers were employed; and this could be accomplished by supplementing private expenditure with public expendi-ture. This should be the policy wherever intentions to save exceed intentions to invest. Since public spending would not perform this offsetting role if there were compensating taxation (which is a form of saving), the public spending should be financed by borrowing – by incurring a deficit. So far as Keynes can be condensed into two paragraphs, this is it. The *General Theory* is more difficult. There are nearly 400 pages, some of them of fascinating obscurity.

Before the publication of the *General Theory*, Keynes had urged his ideas directly on President Roosevelt, most notably in a famous letter to the *New York Times* on 31 December 1933: 'I lay overwhelming emphasis on the increase of national purchasing power resulting from government expendi-ture which is financed by loans'. Keynes visited Roosevelt in the summer of 1934 to press his case, although the session was no great success; each, during the meeting, developed some doubts about the general good sense of the other.

In the meantime, two key Washington officials, Marriner Eccles, the ex-ceptionally able Utah banker who was to become head of the Federal Reserve Board, and Lauchlin Currie, a recent Harvard instructor who was its Assistant Director of Research and later an economic aide to Roosevelt (and later still a prominent victim of McCarthyite persecution), had on their own account reached conclusions similar to those of Keynes as to the proper course of fiscal policy. When the *General Theory* arrived, they took it as confirmation of the course they had previously been urging. Currie, a brilliant economist and teacher, was also a skilled and influential interpreter of the ideas in the Washington community. Not often have important new ideas on economics entered a government by way of its central bank. Nor should anyone be disturbed. There is not the slightest indication that it will ever happen again.[2]

Paralleling the work of Keynes in the 1930s and rivalling it in importance, though not in fame, was that of Simon Kuznets and a group of young economists and statisticians at the University of Pennsylvania, the National Bureau of Economic Research and the United States Department of Commerce. They developed from earlier beginnings the now familiar concepts of national income and gross national product and their components, and made estimates of their amount. Included among the components of national income and gross national product were the saving, investment, aggregate of disposable income and the other magnitudes of which Keynes was talking. As a result, those who were translating Keynes' ideas into action could now know not only what needed to be done but how much. Many who would never have been persuaded by the Keynesian abstractions were compelled to belief by the concrete figures from Kuznets and his inventive colleagues.

However, the trumpet – if the metaphor is permissible for this particular book – that was sounded in Cambridge, England, was heard most clearly in Cambridge, Massachusetts. Harvard was the principal avenue by which Keynes' ideas passed to the United States. Conservatives worry about universities being centres of disquieting innovation. Their worries may be exaggerated but it has occurred.

In the late 1930s, Harvard had a large community of young economists, most of them held there by the shortage of jobs that Keynes sought to cure. They had the normal confidence of their years in their ability to remake the world and, unlike less fortunate generations, the opportunity. They also had occupational indication of the need. Massive unemployment persisted year after year. It was degrading to have to continue telling the young that this was merely a temporary departure from the full employment norm, and that one need only obtain the needed wage reductions.

Paul Samuelson, who subsequently taught economics to an entire generation and who almost from the outset was the acknowledged leader of the younger Keynesian community, has compared the excitement of the young economists, on the arrival of Keynes' book, with that of Keats on first looking into Chapman's Homer (1st edn., 1611). Some will wonder if economists are capable of such refined emotion, but the effect was certainly great. Here was a remedy for the despair that could be seen just beyond the Yard. It did not overthrow the system but saved it. To the non-revolutionary, it seemed too good to be true. To the occasional revolutionary, it was. The old economics was still taught by day. But in the evening, and almost every evening from 1936 on, almost everyone in the Harvard community discussed Keynes.

This might conceivably have remained a rather academic discussion. As with the Bible and Marx, obscurity stimulated abstract debate. But in 1938, the practical instincts that economists sometimes suppress with success were catalysed by the arrival in Cambridge from Minnesota of Alvin H. Hansen. He was then about 50, an effective teacher and a popular colleague. But most of all, he was a man for whom economic ideas had no standing apart from their use.

Most economists of established reputation had not taken to Keynes. Faced with the choice between changing one's mind and proving that there is no need to do so, almost everyone gets busy on the proof. So it was then. Hansen had an established reputation, and he did change his mind. Though he had been an effective critic of some central propositions in Keynes' *Treatise on Money*, an immediately preceding work, and was initially rather cool to the *General Theory*, he soon became strongly persuaded of Keynes' importance.

Hansen proceeded to expound the ideas in books, articles and lectures and to apply them to the American scene. He persuaded his students and younger colleagues that they should not only understand the ideas but win understanding in others and then go on to get action. Without ever seeking to do so or being quite aware of the fact, he became the leader of a crusade. In the late 1930s Hansen's seminar in the new Graduate School of Public Administration was regularly visited by the Washington policy-makers. Often the students overflowed into the hall. One felt that it was the most important thing currently happening in the country and this could have been the case.

The officials took Hansen's ideas, and perhaps even more his sense of conviction, back to Washington. In time there was also a strong migration of his younger colleagues and students to the capital. Among numerous others were Richard Gilbert, later a principal architect of Pakistan's economic development, who was a confidant of Harry Hopkins; Richard Musgrave, later at Princeton and other universities, and now once again back at Harvard, who applied Keynes' and Hansen's ideas to the tax system; Alan Sweezy, later of the California Institute of Technology, who went to the Federal Reserve and the Work Projects Administration (WPA); George Jaszi, who went to the Department of Commerce; G. Griffith Johnson, who served at the Treasury, the National Security Resources Board and the White House; and Walter Salant, now of the Brookings Institution, who served influentially in several federal agencies. Keynes wrote admiringly of this group of young Washington disciples.

The discussions that had begun in Cambridge continued through the war years in Washington, where most of the earlier participants were now serving. One of the leaders, a close friend of Hansen's but not otherwise connected with the Harvard group, was the late Gerhard Colm of the Bureau of the Budget. Colm, a German refugee, had made the transition from a position of influence in Germany to one of major responsibility in the United States government in a matter of some five years. He played a major role in reducing the Keynesian proposals to workable estimates of costs and quantities. Keynesian policies became central to what was called 'post-war planning' and designs for preventing the re-emergence of massive unemployment.

Meanwhile, others were concerning themselves with a wider audience. Seymour Harris, another of Hansen's colleagues and an early convert to Keynes, became the most prolific exponent of the ideas in the course of becoming one of the most prolific scholars of modern times. He published half a dozen books on Keynes and outlined the ideas in hundreds of letters, speeches, memoranda, Congressional appearances and articles. Professor Samuelson, mentioned above, put the Keynesian ideas into what became (and remains) the most influential textbook on economics since the last great exposition of the classical system by Alfred Marshall (Samuelson, 1948). Lloyd Metzler at the University of Chicago applied the Keynesian system to international trade. Lloyd G. Reynolds gathered a talented group of younger economists at Yale and made that university a major centre of discussion of the new ideas.

Nor was the Harvard influence confined to the United States. At almost the same time that the *General Theory* arrived in Cambridge, Massachusetts, so did a young Canadian graduate student named Robert Bryce. He was fresh from Cambridge, England, where he had been in Keynes' seminar and had, as a result, a special licence to explain what Keynes meant in his more obscure passages. With other Canadian graduate students, Bryce went on to Ottawa and to a succession of senior posts, ending as Deputy Minister of Finance. Canada was perhaps the first country to commit itself unequivocally to a Keynesian economic policy.

Meanwhile, with the help of the academic Keynesians, a few businessmen were becoming interested. Two New England industrialists, Henry S. Dennison of the Dennison Manufacturing Company in Framingham, Massachusetts, and Ralph Flanders of the Jones & Lamson Machine Company of Springfield, Vermont (and later United States Senator from Vermont), hired members of the Harvard group to tutor them in the ideas. Before the war they had endorsed them in a book, in which Lincoln Filene of Boston and Morris E. Leeds of Philadelphia had joined, called *Toward Full Employment* (1938). It was only slightly more readable and even less read than Keynes.[3] In the later war years, the Committee for Economic Development (CED), led in these matters by Flanders and Beardsley Ruml, and again with the help of the academic Keynesians, began evangelizing the business community.

In Washington during the war years, the National Planning Association (NPA) had been a centre for academic discussion of the Keynesian ideas. At the end of the war Hans Christian Sonne, the imaginative and liberal New York banker, began underwriting both the NPA and the Keynesian ideas. With the CED, in which Sonne was also influential, the NPA became another important instrument for explaining the policy to the larger public. (In the autumn of 1949, in an exercise combining imagination with rare diplomacy, Sonne gathered a dozen economists of strongly varying views at Princeton and persuaded them all to sign a specific endorsement of Keynesian fiscal policies. The agreement was later reported to Congress in well-publicized hearings by Arthur Smithies of Harvard and Simeon Leland of Northwestern University.)

In 1946, ten years after the publication of the *General Theory*, the Employment Act of that year gave the Keynesian system the qualified, but still quite explicit, support of law. It recognized, as Keynes had urged, that unemployment and insufficient output would respond to positive policies. Not much was said about the specific policies but the responsibility of the federal government to act in some fashion was clearly affirmed. The Council of Economic Advisers became, in turn, a platform for expounding the Keynesian view of the economy and it was brought promptly into use. Leon Keyserling, as an original Member and later Chairman, was a tireless exponent of the ideas. He saw at an early stage the importance of enlarging them to embrace not only the prevention of depression but the maintenance of an adequate rate of economic expansion. Thus in only a decade had the revolution spread.

Those who nurture thoughts of conspiracy and clandestine plots will be saddened to know that this was a revolution without organization. All who participated felt a deep sense of personal responsibility for the ideas; there was a varying but deep urge to persuade. There was a strong feeling in Washington that key economic posts should be held by people who understood the Keynesian system and who would work to establish it. Currie at the White House ran an informal casting office in this regard. But no one ever responded to plans, orders, instructions or any force apart from his own convictions. That perhaps was the most interesting feature of the Keynesian revolution.

Something more, however, was suspected, and there was some effort at counter-revolution. Nobody could say that he preferred massive unemployment to Keynes. And even men of conservative mood, when they understood what was involved, opted for the policy – some asking only that it be called by some other name. The CED, coached by Ruml on semantics, never advocated deficits. Rather, it spoke well of a budget that was balanced only under conditions of high employment. Those who objected to Keynes were also invariably handicapped by the fact that they hadn't (and couldn't) read the book. It was like attacking the original *Kama Sutra* for pornography without being able to read Sanskrit. Still, where resisting social change is involved, there are men who can surmount any handicap.

Appropriately, Harvard, not Washington, was the principal object of attention. In the 1950s, a group of graduates of mature years banded together in an
organization called the Veritas Foundation and financed a volume called
Keynes at Harvard, anonymously published in 1960. It found that 'Harvard
was the launching pad for the Keynesian rocket in America'. However, it then
damaged this highly plausible proposition by identifying Keynesianism with
socialism, Fabian socialism, Marxism, communism, fascism and also literary
incest, meaning that one Keynesian always reviewed the works of another
Keynesian.[4] Like so many others in similar situations, the authors sacrificed
their chance for credibility by writing not for the public but for those who
were paying the bill. The University was comparatively unperturbed, the
larger public sadly indifferent. The book continued for a long while to have
some circulation on the more thoughtful fringes of the John Birch Society.

As a somewhat less trivial matter, a more influential group of graduates
pressed for an investigation of Harvard's Department of Economics, employing
as their instrument the Visiting Committee that annually reviews the work of
the Department on behalf of the Governing Boards. The Keynesian revolution
belongs to our history; so accordingly does this investigation.

It was conducted by Clarence Randall, then the unduly articulate head of
the Inland Steel Company, with the support of Sinclair Weeks, a leading
zipper manufacturer, onetime senator and long a tetrarch of the right wing of
the Republican Party in Massachusetts. In due course, the Committee found
that Keynes was, indeed, exerting a baneful influence on the Harvard economic mind and that the Department of Economics was unbalanced in his
favour. As always, there was the handicap that the investigators, with one or
two possible exceptions, had not read the book and were thus uncertain as to
what they attacked. The Department, including the members most sceptical
of Keynes' analysis – no one accepted all of it and some not much – unani-
mously rejected the Committee's findings. So, as one of his last official acts
before becoming High Commissioner to Germany in 1953, did President
James Bryant Conant. In consequence of the controversy, there was much
bad feeling between the Department and its critics.

In ensuing years there was further discussion of the role of Keynes at
Harvard and of related issues. But it became increasingly amicable, for the
original investigators had been caught up in one of those fascinating and
paradoxical developments with which the history of the Keynesian (and
doubtless all other) revolutions is replete. Shortly after the Committee reached
its disturbing conclusion, the Eisenhower Administration came to power.

Mr Randall then became a Presidential assistant and adviser. Mr Weeks
became Secretary of Commerce and almost immediately was preoccupied
with the firing of the head of the Bureau of Standards over the question of the
efficacy of Glauber's salts as a battery additive. Having staked his public

reputation against the nation's scientists and engineers on the issue that a battery could be improved by giving it a laxative (as the late Bernard DeVoto put it), Mr Weeks could hardly be expected to keep open another front against the Harvard economists. But much worse, both he and Mr Randall were acquiring a heavy contingent liability for the policies of the Eisenhower Administration. And these, it soon developed, had almost as strong a Keynesian colouration as the Department at Harvard.

President Eisenhower's first Chairman of the Council of Economic Advisers was Arthur F. Burns of Columbia University and the National Bureau of Economic Research (and later adviser and Chairman of the Federal Reserve Board under Richard Nixon). Mr Burns had credentials as a critic of Keynes. A man who has always associated respectability with mild obsolescence, his introduction to the 1946 annual report of the National Bureau was called 'Economic Research and the Keynesian Thinking of Our Time'. He made his own critical interpretation of the Keynesian underemployment equilibrium and concluded, perhaps a trifle heavily, that 'the imposing schemes for governmental action that are being bottomed on Keynes's equilibrium theory must be viewed with skepticism'. Alvin Hansen replied rather sharply.

But if Burns regarded Keynes with scepticism, he viewed recessions (including ones for which he might be held responsible) with antipathy. In his 1955 report as Chairman of the Council of Economic Advisers, he said 'budget policies can help promote the objective of maximum production by wisely allocating resources *first between private and public uses*; second, among various government programs' (italics added). Keynes, reading these words carefully – government action to decide as between private and public spending – would have strongly applauded. And, indeed, a spokesman for the National Association of Manufacturers told the Joint Economic Committee that they pointed 'directly toward the planned and eventually the socialized economy'.

After the departure of Burns, the Eisenhower Administration incurred a deficit of $9.4 billion in the national income accounts in the course of overcoming the recession of 1958. This was by far the largest deficit ever incurred by an American government in peacetime; it exceeded the total peacetime expenditure by Roosevelt in any year up to 1940. No administration had ever given the economy such a massive dose of Keynesian medicine. With a Republican administration, guided by men such as Mr Randall and Mr Weeks, following such policies, the academic Keynesians at Harvard and elsewhere were no longer vulnerable. Keynes ceased to be a wholly tactful topic of conversation with such critics.

Presidents Kennedy and Johnson continued what is now commonplace policy. Advised by Walter Heller, a remarkably skilful exponent of Keynes' ideas, they added the new device of the deliberate tax reduction to sustain aggregate demand. And they abandoned, at long last, the double talk by which advocates of Keynesian policies combined advocacy of measures to promote full employment and economic growth with promises of a promptly balanced budget. 'We have recognized as self-defeating the effort to balance our budget too quickly in an economy operating well below its potential,' President Johnson said in his 1965 report.

Now, as noted, Keynesian policies are the new orthodoxy. Economists are everywhere to be seen enjoying their new and pleasantly uncontroversial role. Like their predecessors who averted their eyes from unemployment, many are now able to ignore – often with some slight note of scholarly righteousness – the new problem, which is an atrocious allocation of resources between private wants and public needs, especially those of our cities. (In a sense, the Keynesian success has brought back an older problem of economics, that of resource allocation, in a new form.) In addition, there is the dangerously high dependence on military spending and the problem of the wage–price spiral. But these are other matters.

The purpose of this essay is to pay respect to those who pioneered the Keynesian revolution in America. Very much a part of this community was Lorie Tarshis, who is celebrated in this volume. He was one of the most ardent and effective voices in the Keynesian revolution.[5] We should take pride in the men who brought it about. It is hardly fitting that they should have been celebrated only by the reactionaries. The debt to the courage and intelligence of Alvin Hansen is especially great. Next only to Keynes, his is the credit for saving what even conservatives still call capitalism.

NOTES

1. This piece was originally published in the *New York Times Book Review* (1965) when they discovered they had never reviewed *The General Theory* (1936); it was then republished in *A Contemporary Guide to Economics, Peace and Laughter* (1971, pp. 43–59).
2. Currie failed to gain promotion at Harvard partly because his ideas, brilliantly anticipating Keynes, were considered to reflect deficient scholarship until Keynes made them respectable. Economics *is* very complicated.
3. I drafted it.
4. The authors also reported encouragingly that 'Galbraith is being groomed as the new crown prince of Keynesianism [*sic*]'.
5. Since, alas, Tarshis is one of the several omitted in the original publication of this chapter, these two sentences are added to address the presence of the article in this volume in memory of Lorie Tarshis.

3. The diffusion of the Keynesian revolution: the young and the graduate schools

Donald E. Moggridge

Experience seems to show that people are divided between the old ones whom nothing will shift and are merely amazed by my attempts to underline the points of transition so vital in my own progress, and the young who have not been properly brought up and believe nothing in particular. ... I have no companions, it seems, in my own generation, either of earliest teachers or of earliest pupils.

Keynes to Harrod
30 August 1936

The *General Theory* caught most economists under the age of 35 with the unexpected virulence of a disease first attacking and decimating an isolated tribe of South Sea islanders. Economists beyond 50 turned out to be quite immune to the ailment. With time, most economists in between began to run the fever, often without knowing or admitting their condition.

Paul A. Samuelson
'Lord Keynes and The General Theory' *(1946)*

The division of professional opinion cannot be described in the same terms for every country: in some it amounted to no more than a ripple on the surface. But in England and the United States it went deep, and here a phenomenon asserted itself unmistakably that deserves passing notice. Keynesianism appealed primarily to young theorists whereas a majority of the old stagers were, more or less strongly, anti-Keynesian. One aspect of this is too obvious to detain us and has, in addition, often been emphasised: *of course* it is true that part of the resistance which every novel doctrine meets is simply the resistance of arteriosclerosis. But there is another. The old or even mature scholar may be not only the victim but also the beneficiary of habits of thought formed by his past work. ... And in a field like economics, where training is often defective and where the young scholar very often simply does not know enough, this element in the case counts much more heavily than it does in physics where teaching, even though possibly uninspiring, is always competent.

Joseph A. Schumpeter
A History of Economic Analysis *(1954)*

Keynes, Samuelson and Schumpeter have provided the profession with oft-repeated characterizations of the spread of Keynesian (and other) ideas. They are, however, characterizations that have been followed up only informally. There have been, it is true, 'reviews of the reviews' of the *General Theory*, not to mention surveys of the various controversies that the book generated (Klein, 1947, Ch. 4). There have also been studies of aspects of what followed, such as the invention and adoption of IS–LM and the reactions of various individuals or institutions to the new work (Asso, 1990; Collins, 1981; Durbin, 1985; McCormick, 1992; Stein, 1968; Young, 1987; Young and Lee, 1993), and there have been memoirs (Brown, 1988; Kregel, 1988). The purpose of this chapter is to add to the existing literature by providing more information about the diffusion of the ideas in question, partially with reference to graduate education in economics.

This last matter is of some interest because in the early 1950s, just after the end of the period under consideration, the notion of a 'core' of economic theory 'which should bind the profession together and ... enable economists of all types and persuasions to communicate with one another' entered academic economics (Bowen, 1953, pp. 42–3).[1] That core included a widely accepted version of Keynesian economics that had emerged in the years immediately after publication of the *General Theory* (Patinkin, 1990).

The core of this chapter is a bibliographical and biographical study of the 392 articles that appeared between the beginning of 1936 and the end of 1948 and were recorded either in classes 2.30, 2.31, 2.320, 2.322 and 2.325 of the *Index of Economic Journals* or in the surveys of post-*General Theory* developments in the first two revisions of Gottfried Haberler's *Prosperity and Depression* (1946).[2] These 392 articles were by some 180 different authors, for 147 of whom we have biographical data. This bibliographical and biographical information has been supplemented by an examination of some graduate prospectuses for some American and British universities. It could be further supplemented by an examination of what actually happened in various classrooms (either through students' or lecturers' notes), or of comprehensive examinations and of dissertation titles, but it is probably impossible to recapture the extent of student interaction and mutual stimulation at universities with large graduate programmes in economics.[3]

The dates were chosen for straightforward reasons: the *General Theory* appeared in February 1936, while the 1948 appearance of both Don Patinkin's 'Price Flexibility and Full Employment' and the first edition of Samuelson's *Economics* could be taken as marking the widespread acceptance of a basic 'Keynesian' model and message at both the professional and undergraduate levels. The end date could, of course, be extended to encompass more of the post-war period – and incidentally more of the early publishing careers of the post-war Keynesian establishment – but we are not convinced that anything other than perhaps conformity with the dates in the last column of Table 3.3 would be gained thereby.

Let us begin with a discussion of the characteristics of the authors of the articles examined. These are set out in Tables 3.1 and 3.2. From Table 3.1 it is clear that the authors we are concerned with were more likely than not to have been 35 or under when the *General Theory* appeared, for 109 of the 147 have birth years of 1901 or later. They also tended to publish 'young', in that the 'age' of authors at time of first publication in the field was likely to be under 35.

Table 3.1   Characteristics of authors

Birth year	No. of authors	'Age' at first article*	No. of authors
Before 1883	4	≤25	18
1883–90	11	26–30	34
1891–1900	23	31–35	37
1901–5	27	36–40	22
1906–10	31	41–45	11
1911–15	30	46–50	10
1916–20[a]	18	≥51	15

*   Difference between the year of birth and the year in which the first article in the sample appeared.
[a]   Three individuals were born after 1921.

Table 3.2   Top ten sources of authors' highest degrees

University	No. of authors
Harvard	26[a]
Cambridge	17
London School of Economics	16
Chicago	12
Columbia	9
Oxford	7
Berkeley	4
Berlin	4
Wisconsin	4
Vienna	3

[a]   In addition, there were two degrees from Radcliffe.

In terms of their graduate training, Tables 3.2 and 3.3 set out what we know about the authors and American-trained economists more generally. The authors are likely to have been educated, at least in part, outside the United States: 79 of the 147 individuals for whom we have information have an American degree as their highest degree. If we compare the origins of those whose highest degree was from an American institution with what we know more generally about American PhDs in economics, those in our sample are much more likely to come from Harvard or Chicago than the general run of American-educated economists. The representation of Columbia and Berkeley is roughly what one would expect, while Wisconsin and the remainder of the top ten universities are under-represented. Outside the United States, Oxbridge and the London School of Economics (LSE) dominate, although

Table 3.3   Doctoral dissertations accepted in American universities

(those with 3 per cent of total dissertations or above named)

Institution	1925/6–1934/5		1935/6–1944/5		1945/6–1950/51	
	No.	%	No.	%	No.	%
Berkeley	59	5.1	57	4.4	...	...
Brookings	40	3.4	—	—	—	—
Chicago	73	6.5	75	5.8	95	6.3
Columbia	112	9.6	150	11.5	132	8.5
Cornell	82	7.0	94	7.2	68	4.5
Harvard	122	10.5	121	9.3	257	17.1
Illinois	79	6.8	73	5.6	66	4.4
Iowa	...	...	...	...	46	3.1
Minnesota	35	3.0	51	3.9	48	3.2
New York	...	...	56	4.3	46	3.1
Northwestern	...	...	39	3.0	...	...
Ohio State	...	...	51	3.9	47	3.1
Pennsylvania	76	6.5	...	...	...	...
Stanford	36	3.1	...	...	...	...
Wisconsin	99	8.5	91	7.0	92	6.1
Total for US	1166		1317		1501	

Symbols: — does not have graduate programme; ... has graduate programme but produced less than 3 per cent of successful PhDs in the period in question.

Source: Bowen, 1953, pp. 209–10.

the Diaspora of the 1930s is evident in the number of individuals with their highest degrees from Berlin and Vienna.

The ranking of American graduate schools (and, for that matter, LSE) is, however, probably symptomatic of something else. It could be argued that Chicago, Harvard and LSE, which awarded the highest degrees for 38 per cent of those aged 35 or under in 1936, provided graduate students with the best analytical training in economics available in the late 1930s and 1940s. At Harvard, there had been the changing of the guard that brought Schumpeter, Leontief, Haberler and Hansen to the department. Unusually, none of its 1930s students gained permanent appointments (Mason, 1982, p. 420). At Chicago, the department's existing strength, epitomized by Knight and Viner, was augmented by the arrival in 1939 of Oscar Lange (who provided graduate teaching at the frontier, as it then was) and in 1943 of the Cowles Commission for Research in Economics under Jacob Marschak, which included among its members Trygve Haavelmo, Leo Hurwicz, Lawrence Klein and Tjalling Koopmans (Patinkin, 1981, p. 8). At LSE, the arrival of Lionel Robbins as Professor of Economics in autumn 1929 and his attempt, over the objections of the Director, to make the school a centre of economic theory began a period of 'creative tension and excitement' that affected both older appointees such as John Hicks and new ones such as R.G.D. Allen, Evan Durbin, E.A. Hayek, Nicholas Kaldor, Abba Lerner and Ursula Webb (Kaldor, cited in Kregel, 1988, p. 14). There were, as well, links between the younger faculty and the graduate students at LSE and Cambridge through the joint London and Cambridge Economic Seminar that arose from an attempt by Lerner and some of the other younger LSE people to reduce the intellectual gap between the two institutions. There was also the *Review of Economic Studies* to provide a similar link. Even though LSE was to lose many of those named here to other institutions after 1935, Robbins was able to repeat his exercise of the 1930s after the war and rebuild the economics group, albeit in a different intellectual mold – one created in part by his own change in view which began before the outbreak of, and continued during, the war (Robbins, 1971). Hayek himself left LSE in 1949.

By way of contrast, as far as we can tell, the theoretical training of economists at Columbia left much to be desired. C.P. Kindleberger, who was there as a student, reports that in the 1930s 'economics education at Columbia ... was not exciting' and that 'there was no core of economic theory' (1991, p. 31). A reading of the announcements of the graduate-level offerings of the faculty of political science (which included economics) for the 1930s confirms this. George Stigler, on the faculty from 1947 to 1958, has more to say in its favour. This is perhaps not surprising since the post-war period saw a large infusion of new blood and curricular reforms that swept away many of the traces of institutionalism. However, even Stigler reports: 'when I returned to

Chicago from Columbia I reckoned it a gain that I was coming to an institution where seniority would not be considered an adequate substitute for research' (1988, p. 46). He then tellingly compares the Chicago of the 1950s with LSE in the 1930s, of which he had some experience. Wisconsin shared many of Columbia's problems in the period we are discussing.[4]

As yet, we have not mentioned Oxford and Cambridge, largely because they were not well-organized centres of graduate instruction in economics. Both offered doctoral degrees, but the taking of such degrees in economics was a very new phenomenon in the 1930s (and one confined largely to foreigners for several decades), and neither ancient university then offered formal instruction in economics designed specifically for graduates.[5] In these institutions, graduate work really meant learning from the literature, your supervisor, your fellow students and sympathetic faculty, but it was very much a matter of luck and circumstances, as A.J. Brown's 1988 memoir of his period at Oxford shows. It is true that graduates of overseas universities regularly went to Oxbridge as affiliated students doing a second BA. In the process, many became quite well-trained economists, as did many of the Oxbridge graduates in our list who left with an undergraduate degree, but the training acquired was a by-product of a system designed for another purpose.[6]

We have briefly considered who the individuals were and where they were educated. We have yet to say anything as to where they published, whom they acknowledged and whom they cited. Let us take the matter of acknowledgements first, if only because it was not all that common: only 64 (16 per cent) of the articles examined contained any acknowledgements; only two individuals[7] published three articles with acknowledgements, and only seven individuals[8] published two articles with acknowledgements. Of those acknowledged, only 14 individuals' names appeared twice or more. The most acknowledged economist was Alvin Hansen with five; Milton Friedman, Abba Lerner and Dennis Robertson came in with four apiece; and Oscar Lange, Jacob Marschak and Paul Samuelson came in with three each.[9] All held posts at Cambridge, Chicago, Harvard, LSE or Oxford during the decade under consideration. Apart from the fact that all of Alvin Hansen's acknowledgements came from Harvard-educated or -employed economists, there is no clear pattern.[10]

Of course, acknowledgements recognize only one possible source of stimulus or assistance. There is also the straightforward citation of the work of oneself and of others. In the articles we examined, there were citations of 897 other individual pieces of literature. The most cited item was Keynes' *General Theory*, with 144 mentions. With that number of citations for the one book, it is not surprising that Keynes was the most cited author, with 248 citations. Nobody else reached 100, and only five individuals, including

Keynes, exceeded 50. The 38 people with ten or more citations appear in Table 3.4; the 26 publications with ten or more citations appear in Table 3.5.

It is interesting to note that among the most cited books and articles we get almost all the classic items we would expect from the early years of the discussions of the *General Theory*: Lange's 1938 piece for *Economica*, Haberler's 1946 *Prosperity and Depression*, Hicks' 1937 formulation of IS–LM for *Econometrica* and his 1939 *Value and Capital*, Robertson's 1940 *Essays in Monetary Theory* and Hawtrey's 1937 *Capital and Employment*. Perhaps the only oddities arise from the low level of citation of the other papers closely associated with the initial formulation of IS–LM: Meade's 1937 piece for the *Review of Economic Studies* and Harrod's 1937 article for *Econometrica*, both of which received only three citations, two fewer than Modigliani's classic 1944 article for *Econometrica*. But this merely provides an example of the power of a simple diagram in the profession.

The dominance of Oxford, LSE, Harvard, Chicago and Cambridge continues in the citations. Only four of the 20 most cited living authors did not hold

Table 3.4   Authors' citation rankings (ten or more citations)

Name	No. of citations	Name	No. of citations
Keynes, J.M.	248	Wicksell, K.	18
Hicks, J.R.	82	Klein, L.	18
Pigou, A.C,	65	Knight, F.H.	17
Robertson, D.H.	64	Dunlop, J.T.	16
Lerner, A.	53	Kuznets, S.	15
Lange, O.	43	Hayek, F.	14
Hansen, A.H.	39	Fisher, I.	13
Robinson, J.	38	Woytinsky, W.S.	13
Haberler, G.	35	Angell, J.	13
Ohlin, B.	32	Smithies, A.	13
Harrod, R.F.	29	Kahn, R.F.	12
Hawtrey, R.G.	29	Viner, J.	11
Kaldor, N.	27	Frisch, R.	11
Kalecki, M.	26	Tinbergen, J.	11
Samuelson, P.	26	Shackle, G.L.S.	11
Clark, C.	21	Leontief, W.	10
Marshall, A.	21	Lutz, F.	10
Schumpeter, J.	20	Myrdal, G.	10
Clark, J.M.	19	Wright, D.M.	10

a post at one of those universities at some time between 1936 and 1938. Within the overall rankings, however, the European Diaspora prevented those five institutions from dominating the educational experiences of those most frequently cited. Nevertheless, if one considers the 'young' within this group,[11] 70 per cent took their highest degree at either Oxford, LSE, Harvard or Cambridge.[12]

The journal citations recorded in Tables 3.4 and 3.5 also point to another characteristic of the literature: its general supportiveness of the Keynesian

Table 3.5　Individual publication citation rankings (ten or more citations)

Publication	No. of citations
Keynes (1936) *General Theory*	144
Lange (1938), *Econometrica*	28
Haberler (1946) *Prosperity and Depression*	27
Hicks (1939) *Value and Capital*	26
Hicks (1937), *Econometrica*	22
Keynes (1930) *Treatise on Money*	21
Ohlin (March 1937a) and (June 1937b), *Economic Journal*	21
Keynes (June 1937a), *Economic Journal*	20
Harrod (1936) *Trade Cycle*	17
Lerner (1938), *Economic Journal*	17
Robertson (September 1937), *Economic Journal*	16
Hicks (1936), *Economic Journal*	15
Robertson (1940) *Essays*	14
Robertson (1936), *Quarterly Journal of Economics*	13
Marshall (1890) *Principles*	12
Hawtrey (1937) *Capital and Employment*	12
Hansen (1941) *Fiscal Policy*	12
Pigou (1927a) *Industrial Fluctuations*	11
Kahn (1931), *Economic Journal*	11
Clark (1937) *National Income*	11
Wicksell ([1898]1936) *Interest and Prices*	10
Lerner (1936), *International Labour Review*	10
Pigou (1937), *Economic Journal*	10
Dunlop (1938), *Economic Journal*	10
Kalecki (1939) *Essays*	10
Klein (1947) *Keynesian Revolution*	10

Note:　For full bibliographical details, see the bibliography.

position, with most of the support coming from the 'young'. If one goes to the individual publications of living authors recorded in Table 3.5, leaving Keynes himself to one side, 14 might be considered as supportive of his position and seven as critical. The age factor also comes out clearly in Table 3.5, with 11 of the supportive authors born in 1901 or after, and all of the critics having been born before 1900. If one goes by the living authors in Table 3.4, again leaving Keynes to one side, the ratio of support to opposition would be much closer. However, the same pattern appears: the overwhelming majority of 20 'supporters' were born in 1901 or after, while, among the critics, the figures are just as strongly reversed.[13]

Interestingly enough, the pattern of journal citation differed from that of journal publication, with the *American Economic Review* and *Review of Economic Statistics* less cited than published in, and *Economica*, the *Economic Journal*, *Econometrica* and the *Quarterly Journal of Economics* more cited. Rankings appear in Tables 3.6 and 3.7.

It can thus be said that the evidence suggests a strong association between the discussion and diffusion of Keynesian ideas and a limited number of centres of learning. One of these centres, Cambridge, was the source of the ferment as well as of significant criticism. Another, Oxford, had disciples (Harrod and Meade) who had been intimately involved in the creation of the ideas and, in the Institute of Economics and Statistics, an active and a growing research enterprise (Chester, 1986, Ch. 10; Young and Lee, 1993, Ch. 5). Neither centre provided formal graduate instruction in economics. That was characteristic of the other three centres – Harvard, Chicago and LSE – of which the last two were also sources of significant criticism as well as support.

Table 3.6   Most cited journals

Journal	No. of citations
Economic Journal	182
Quarterly Journal of Economics	132
Econometrica	100
American Economic Review	95
Review of Economic Statistics	92
Economica	79
Journal of Political Economy	52
Review of Economic Studies	36
International Labour Review	17
Oxford Economic Papers	11

Table 3.7 Original journals of publication

Journal	No. of articles
American Economic Review	43
Review of Economic Statistics	37
Quarterly Journal of Economics	34
Economic Journal	32
Econometrica	22
Review of Economic Studies	17
Journal of Political Economy	16
Economic Record	13
Economica	11
Indian Journal of Economics	8
Southern Economic Journal	8

How did the ideas get diffused to particular individuals? Here some notions of Albert Hirschman's might prove useful:

New ideas have two principal intellectual effects: the persuasion effect and the recruitment effect. The persuasion effect is the obvious one of attracting followers from among specialists already labouring in the particular discipline where the idea makes its appearance. The recruitment effect is more important and ambiguous. As a result of the intellectual excitement generated by the new idea and the ensuing debates, intellectually able and ambitious recruits are newly attracted toward the field where the discovery has been made, where its scientific merits remain to be evaluated, and where its ramifications are yet to be worked out. This phenomenon was extremely important in the United States with its vast university system. (Hirschman, 1989, p. 356)

Good examples of 'persuasion' there certainly are. At LSE one need think only of Abba Lerner and Nicholas Kaldor – and, perhaps, Evan Durbin. Before 1936 Lerner had established himself as an active publisher in microeconomics and international trade, but had made no contribution to macroeconomics. However, as the result of persuasion from Joan Robinson and Richard Kahn, he spent some of his Leon Fellowship year in 1934/35 in Cambridge where the ideas were taking their final shape, was persuaded of their utility, and became a prolific and fervent advocate, first at LSE and from 1937 in America.[14] Kaldor started his academic career as a devotee of Robbins and Hayek, yet under the influence of John Hicks, whose reading was more catholic, he was 'put on the track of (among others) the younger Swedish economists, particularly Myrdal, who made me realise the shortcomings of the ... approach of the Austrian school ... and made me such an easy convert to Keynes after the appearance of the General Theory' (Kregel, 1988, p. 14).

By that time Hicks had already left LSE for a post in Cambridge, not because he had become a Keynesian 'which in a sense I was', but because of an invitation from Pigou and friendship with Dennis Robertson (Hicks, quoted in Kregel, 1988, pp. 4–5). While in Cambridge, of course, he formulated IS–LM. This became an important instrument of persuasion itself. It was first used for such purposes in print by Kaldor in his critique of Pigou's 1937 paper in the *Economic Journal*, which served as a substitute for a Presidential address to the Royal Economic Society (Kaldor, 1937). Durbin occupied an intermediate position: politically he was more aligned with Labour, but in economic theory he was intellectually influenced by, if critical of, Hayek. Durbin's most important theoretical publications preceded the appearance of the *General Theory*, but from his political views and his correspondence it is clear that he moved part way towards Keynes (Durbin, 1985, esp. Part 3; McCormick, 1992, pp. 71–5).

The classic, and by far the most important, American case of persuasion was that of Alvin Hansen. The exact dating of the conversion between his two reviews of Keynes' *General Theory* and his first full academic year at Harvard in 1937/38 is uncertain (Barber, 1987, p. 200). Gottfried Haberler recalled Hansen's presence at the Geneva seminar organized to discuss the draft of *Prosperity and Depression*, where 'he did not take a very Keynesian position' (Haberler, 1976, p. 11). He calls the Hansen conversion 'sudden', but does not know how it came about. Neither, it seems, does anyone else. But Haberler suggests that for Hansen, theory was not an end in itself but rather 'a means to derive prescriptions for effective policy' (Haberler, 1976, p. 11). In this context he suspects that Hansen was persuaded because Keynesian policies were 'the obvious cure for mass unemployment and Keynes provided a rational theoretical justification, while many orthodox economists strongly rejected the obvious remedy' (Haberler, 1976, p. 11). William Barber's discussion of the causes of the conversion, which he dates slightly later, is basically consistent with Haberler's explanation (Barber, 1987, pp. 204–5).

Examples such as these were important because they had direct effects in the classroom, as both the LSE calendar list of graduate courses with suggested reading and memoirs of the Hansen/Williams seminar tellingly indicate. the *General Theory* is in the course syllabi of Durbin, Kaldor and Lerner in the 1936/37 academic year, and it remained there.[15] It even enters the undergraduate curriculum of the school in 1937/38 in P.B. Whale's course 'Theory of Money and Credit' and in 1938/39, albeit in Hicks' IS–LM form and clearly labelled supplementary and more advanced reading, it is in Robbins' 'General Principles of Economic Analysis'.[16]

There was also the persuasion and recruitment of students by their peers. The classic case here is R.B. Bryce, the 'missionary' to Hayek's seminar at LSE, who proceeded, full of the Keynesian message, to Harvard in autumn 1935.[17] His Harvard paper, based on his LSE seminars (see note 14), turns up in Schumpeter's papers as the theoretical justification for Bryce's 'Memorandum of Work Proposed' of 1 October 1935 (Harvard University Archives, Schumpeter Papers, HUG(FP)47, Box 2; published in 1977). Bryce also reported that he used the same notes in discussions with his fellow students (Bryce, quoted in Patinkin and Leith, 1977, pp. 40–41). It is not surprising that a group of Harvard students around Bryce ensured early access to the *General Theory* by arranging for the shipment of 30 copies directly from London. Inevitably, there was a study group, organized at Harvard by Seymour Harris, to see what the new work contained (Tsuru, cited in Kregel, 1988, p. 185). Among the students who arrived with Bryce at Harvard in autumn 1935 were Paul Samuelson, Robert Triffin and Shigeto Tsuru. With Abram Bergson, John Kenneth Galbraith, Richard Musgrave, Paul Sweezy and Wolfgang Stolper already in residence and more to follow, it is not surprising that Triffin recalled, 'I learned as much or more, as an economist, *student colleagues* of mine in the most brilliant class that Harvard probably ever had ... than I did from the professors whose classes I attended' (quoted in Kregel, 1988, p. 151).

The process of recruiting was well under way – and it would continue for no little time.

But let us go back to the beginning and the hypothesis associated with the three quotations from Keynes, Samuelson and Schumpeter. It is clear that publication of the *General Theory* affected the young more than the old, although, for example, the conversion of Alvin Hansen (born 1887) and the use of IS–LM in *Employment and Equilibrium* (1941) by A.C. Pigou (born 1877) (Solow, 1986) show the speed with which the virus could significantly infect the work of scholars over age 50 in varying degrees – in both cases, within five years. The cut-off of 35, with the qualifications about ultimate acceptance, is arbitrary, given that there were a number of people aged just over 35 who played an important role in diffusing the ideas – Gottfried Haberler, Roy Harrod, Jacob Marschak and M.E Timlin – and a number of people in the 35 to 50 age range in 1936 who were never reconciled to the ideas: A.W. Marget and J. Rueff, for instance. But the generational emphasis of the hypothesis, which is not new – it is, after all, a part of Thomas Kuhn's (1962, Ch. 12) discussion[18] of the process in which scientific revolutions are resolved – is well borne out. However, at least in the context of this body of literature, what might be called the Keynes/Schumpeter hypothesis of 'the young who have not been properly brought up' or have been defectively trained does not seem to be well sustained. If it were as likely as not that those involved in the discussion of the *General Theory* and its implications for economics, especially the young, were more likely than normal to have been the recipients of the best training available at the time, including that in Schumpeter's own department, then one must think again. Such training, with its renewed openness to Continental influences, might for Keynes, a Marshallian to the end, have seemed like a less than 'proper' upbringing. But it should hardly have been such to Schumpeter, the champion of Walras and almost all things Continental.

Finally, it is clear that in an important sense, as Nathan Rosenberg (1975, pp. 475–6) has emphasized, the decade following publication of the *General Theory* saw the ideas in the book refined, elaborated and modified so that the profession could make them operationally useful. This process of 'critical revision', which aided the diffusion of the ideas themselves, was itself helped by complementarities between Keynes' ideas, the development of econometrics and the development of national income accounting.

All of this might only echo David Bensusan-Butt's comment that 'the *General Theory* fell among the economists of the day with a very big bang indeed. Nothing, *for any of them*, was ever quite the same again' ([1967] 1980, p. 35; emphasis added).

NOTES

1. As defined by Bowen, the core in economic theory was 'the field as it is generally accepted in the profession at the time'. The emphasis was to be 'fairly conventional but up-to-date and integrated' and 'should acquaint the student with some of the important modern literature and with current intellectual issues in the field' (Bowen, 1953, p. 109).
2. This is a reprint of the third edition. The first edition was published by the League of Nations in 1937. A second edition, with an additional Chapter 8, followed in 1939, while the 1943 edition had an additional Chapter 13. It is interesting to speculate on the form of what became Haberler's *Prosperity and Depression* (1946) and of what, perhaps, the whole process of Keynesian diffusion might have taken had the survey been done by the person to whom it was first offered – Dennis Robertson (Nuffield College, Oxford, Loveday Papers, Box 66, Diary, entry for 2 November 1933).
3. For an indication of such programmes in the United States, see Table 3.3 (p. 21). Note that, if one restricted the use of the term 'large' to those programmes producing an average of ten or more PhDs in economics per annum, the field would be much smaller, including only Columbia and Harvard in the first two periods and adding only Chicago, Wisconsin, Cornell and Illinois in the third period.
4. Of course one could do worse. Evsey Domar reports of his undergraduate career at UCLA, which did not produce any PhDs in economics before 1945 (Bowen, 1953, p. 209): 'But 1936 was the year of *The General Theory*. It was hotly debated in the journals, and yet all that I learned about Keynes by my graduation in 1939 was that such an economist existed; and even this information came not from my professors but from a fellow student' (quoted in Szenberg, 1992, p. 119).
5. The Oxford B.Phil. was first examined in June 1948, but the small number of candidates (four in 1950) limited the amount of formal teaching provided for some years. The

Cambridge M.Phil., which followed almost three decades later, had formal instruction from the beginning.

6. For memoirs of Oxbridge undergraduates during the period surrounding the creation and publication of the *General Theory*, see Brown, (1988, esp. pp. 18–31) and Bensusan-Butt ([1967] 1980, esp. pp. 26–35); for affiliated students see, for example, the notes by Bryce, Salant and Tarshis in Patinkin and Leith (1977, pp. 39–64); see also Rymes (1987, 1989).

7. Abba Lerner and Harold Somers.

8. Trygve Haavelmo, Alvin Hansen, Lawrence Klein, H.M. Oliver, Melvin Reder, Paul Samuelson and Henry Wallich.

9. Those with two mentions were W.M. Crum, W. Fellner, R.B. Goode, A.G. Hart, L.R. Klein. W.W. Leontief and A.C. Pigou.

10. Among those with two acknowledgements, only Crum's and Pigou's were restricted to graduates of, or colleagues in, their own institutions.

11. Because they were both born in 1900, Harrod and Haberler would not count as 'young' in Samuelson's sense. Both probably did in Keynes' and Schumpeter's.

12. One other. Lawrence Klein took his PhD at MIT; Lange had been at LSE and Harvard without taking a degree, while moving towards Chicago. Samuelson, whose undergraduate career included graduate courses, might be said to leave a trace of Chicago on the record (Samuelson, 1972).

13. A rather rough look at the list of all publications by authors for whom we have sufficient biographical data suggests a similar dominance of the young among Keynes' supporters. If one divides the articles into three classes – supportive, opposed and unknown – for authors born in 1900 or earlier, the numbers are 14:38:11, as compared with 67:27:24 for those born in 1901 or after.

14. McCormick (1992, p. 167) credits Lerner for inviting R.B. Bryce from Cambridge to give a lecture on Keynes' ideas to his LSE seminar. Unfortunately, the paper in question was discussed at four meetings of Hayek's seminar, as Bryce's letter of 5 July 1935 makes clear (in Keynes, 1979, *CW*, Vol. 29, p. 131). McCormick's study is full of such minor errors, which means it must be used with care.

15. The three courses were initially called 'The Modern Purchasing Power Controversy', 'Problems of the Theory of Economic Dynamics' and 'The Theory of Index Numbers'. Kaldor's course later became 'Advanced Problems of Economic Theory (Statics and Dynamics)', while Durbin's became 'Modern Trade Cycle and Monetary Theory'. Lerner's departure from the school meant that he never gave his graduate lectures on 'Unemployment in Theory and Practice' advertised in the 1937/38 calendar.

16. In a recent letter to the author, Tom Wilson remembers Robbins' graduate seminar in the same year:

> I was never his pupil at LSE but I used to attend the great graduate seminar in 1938/39 which he chaired. We watched with fascination the terrific battles between Hayek and Kaldor which Kaldor usually won. What was particularly interesting was to watch Robbins himself gradually shift his position towards Keynesianism. He did not move all the way, of course, but he shifted closer to Keynes than to Hayek.

In a sense this is not surprising, since Robbins' behaviour during his term in the Economic Section of the War Cabinet Office as a member and later director when he provided active support to the campaigns for national income accounting and employment policy, would not make much sense in any other terms (Cairncross and Watts, 1989, Ch. 6; see also in Keynes, *CW*, Vol. 22, pp. 326–7).

17. Bryce, an engineer by training who had only taken up economics in 1932, was technically a PhD candidate at Cambridge. His ostensible purpose in going to Harvard was (tellingly in the light of our earlier discussion) to improve his knowledge of formal economic theory for his dissertation on business cycles.

18. Cf. also Feuer (1982, pp. 308–11).

4.   Harvard's Fiscal Policy Seminar: the early years[1]

Walter S. Salant

This paper was written to help celebrate the 50th anniversary of Harvard's Policy Seminar. The early years of that Seminar were exciting and, as it turned out, important for the United States. I am concentrating on the early years because those are the ones that I know most about, having been one of the Littauer Fellows in the first year of what was popularly referred to as the Littauer School but more formally as Harvard's Graduate School of Public Administration.

The School opened for business in the autumn of 1937, but that was not the only thing that happened at that time. Another related, and very important, event was the arrival of Alvin Hansen, who came from the University of Minnesota to take up his appointment as Professor of Economics at Harvard and who, jointly with Professor John H. Williams, the first Dean of the School, developed the Seminar on Fiscal Policy, one of several seminars that constituted the School's first-year programme.

At precisely the same time the American economy went into a sudden tailspin. It had been recovering substantially since 1933. In fact, by 1937 total output had been restored to the 1929 level, although that is rarely mentioned in descriptions of the pre-war period written for the general public since World War II. The recovery had not been a steady one. There had been several minor setbacks, and during 1936 the recovery had been accompanied by a very sharp rise in prices, despite an unemployment rate that was later estimated to be nearly 17 per cent of the labour force and much unutilized plant capacity. It was just as the academic year 1937–38 began that the recovery received a sharp setback. Industrial production began a decline that developed into a 30 per cent fall in four months. I believe that is still the fastest we have ever experienced, with the possible exception of the one in 1920–21.

In addition I remind you that in September 1937 little more than a year had elapsed since the publication of Keynes' book, *The General Theory of Employment, Interest and Money* (1936). It was being read and vigorously debated. In the Harvard Economics Department, as well as throughout the profession, the book met great resistance because, on many points of theory as well as policy, it asserted views that differed from those that had prevailed, and it flatly contradicted some of them. As I have noted elsewhere, one may get some idea of the views then prevailing about problems of depression and the policies appropriate to recovery from a book of essays by senior- and middle-level members of the Harvard Economics Department entitled *The Economics of the Recovery Programme* (1934), which contained essays by Douglass Brown, Edward Chamberlin, Seymour Harris, Wassily Leontief, Edward Mason, Joseph Schumpeter and Overton Taylor (Salant, 1976). The theory of macroeconomics was in as great a ferment as the economy itself, although the term 'macroeconomics' was not then part of our vocabulary, which is significant of the fact that there was not much to apply it to.

Thus the Fiscal Policy Seminar was launched when Keynes was being intensively discussed, not to say being fought over, when a substantial but still incomplete recovery was reversed and when Alvin Hansen arrived at Harvard.

Before going further into these earliest years, let me say a word or two about the Seminar in general, or at least its first few decades.

It has always been very much a policy Seminar. If one reviews the topics on which it has concentrated, as I have tried in a casual way to do, one finds that the choice of subjects has been much influenced by what has been going on in the economy of the country and of the world at the time.

In the first years there was a good deal of discussion of the consumption function and the multiplier, problems that at the time needed theoretical clarification. Much attention was also paid as to why the recovery of capital expenditure was not more vigorous and there was much discussion of taxes – old, new and proposed – and whether any of these were responsible for the failure of capital expenditures to recover more fully.

Then when World War II broke out, much of the time of the Seminar was devoted to economic problems associated with it, such as the financing of defence and then war expenditures, the adequacy of capacity to increase output, and related problems.

As an Allied victory came to be regarded as increasingly probable and then assured, the attention of the Seminar seems broadly to have turned towards the outlook for the post-war period and the planning of economic policy. What was the outlook for the consumption function? Could accumulation of unsatisfied demands and the financing of consumption to satisfy pent-up demand be financed by the accumulation of liquid assets to a degree sufficient to offset the cut of the government's own expenditures and to employ most of the 11 million young men and women who would be returning from the Armed Forces to civilian life? What was likely to happen to the price level? What would constitute desirable wage and price behaviour and what policies would that behaviour imply? There was also a good deal of interest in the question of why the predominant view among forecasters that there would be substantial post-war unemployment turned out to be incorrect.

The Seminar also devoted attention to the problem of European recovery, and the Marshall Plan in particular. For some reason, however, no attention was paid to economic development of less developed countries until about the academic year 1953–54, although some attention had been devoted during the war years to the domestic problems of Latin America. Finally in 1953–54, two sessions were devoted to development problems and in the following year three sessions were devoted to them. This might have reflected the view that this subject was not appropriate to the general subject of the Seminar, but a more likely explanation, I have thought, is that it was not occupying much of the attention of either Hansen or Williams before that time, even though it had been put forward in January 1949 as a major policy problem in 'point four' of President Truman's inaugural address.

In the first year of the Seminar the method of operation that was to be followed in the next few years was set, and it was altered later only with respect to the frequency of meetings. In the first year the Seminar had two types of meeting. The enrolled students, along with some auditing students and young faculty members, met every Monday afternoon from 4 to 6 o'clock to hear and discuss papers by the students or to engage in discussion of subjects advanced by Hansen or Williams.

Frequently the auditors outnumbered the enrolled participants. In writing about this stage earlier, I found that the impression most vividly recalled by old alumni, second only to Hansen's famous green eyeshade, was how crowded the room was.

On Friday afternoons the Seminar also met to hear formal talks given by outside speakers. These sessions were followed by a dinner for invited members of the Seminar and the faculty. The dinner was generally followed by a more informal and lively continuation of the discussion held that afternoon. The post-dinner discussions frequently went on until 9 or even 10 o'clock. The outside speakers were usually non-academic experts, such as government officials who were working in fields of interest to the Seminar, members of faculties of other universities or people prominent in private life concerned with matters of public policy, such as well-known tax lawyers and a leader in the accounting profession.

The members of the Seminar included some recipients of the Littauer Fellowships with experience in government. They were generally older than the average graduate student and young enough to be more progressive than many of the outside speakers. At the same time they were also old enough and experienced enough not to be backward about questioning those speakers. The discussions were vigorous, and I think we gave some of the speakers a hard time.

After the first few years the Seminar met jointly with other seminars of the Littauer School when the subject to be discussed was of interest to both groups, and these joint meetings were increasingly frequent. For example, in its third year the Fiscal Policy Seminar met with a seminar on administrative processes to hear a former Fellow speak on the work of the Bureau of the Budget, and it held two meetings with the Price Policies Seminar. Then in the next year it met seven times with other seminars. After the first few years such joint meetings were increasingly concentrated on sessions with the International Economic Relations Seminar conducted by Professors Gottfried Haberler and Seymour Harris.

I get the impression that among the members of the Seminar in its first years, Hansen was regarded as the more active of the two who conducted the Seminar. He was, it is quite true, the more active promoter of Keynes, and the members of the Seminar, who were all among the younger generation, thought of him as the leader. He certainly was more active than Williams in writing and generating new ideas and trying them out in the Seminar, at least in the very early years.

Because the role of Williams has been relatively neglected, I would like to say a word about that. Williams was less frequently engaged in writing for publication, but when he was he also presented his ideas to the Seminar. To the younger graduate students in the first years he seemed to be not so well acquainted with Keynes' *General Theory* (1936), but then he began to study it more thoroughly and systematically than he had previously done. Or so it seemed to the students. In the autumn of 1947 he addressed two consecutive sessions of the Seminar on 'Reflections on Keynesian Economics'. It was characteristic of him, at least in the years that I observed him, that he advanced his ideas less vigorously than did Hansen and he raised questions about new departures which made some students think he was conventional in his ideas. The truth was that he was far from conventional about many things. He was always a sceptic, a questioner. His questioning of the *General Theory* made some people think he was very classical, but if one reads his 1951 Presidential address to the American Economic Association, entitled 'An Economist's Confessions' (1952), one will see many expressions of dissatisfaction with classical theory, and especially with the shift from concern with growth, which was old classical, to static equilibrium analysis. In this dissatisfaction he and Hansen were soulmates.

Williams had always been a very valuable critic, especially in the field of international finance and the role of capital movements. In the first few years of the Seminar he did not, as far as I know, say much about Keynes' *General Theory*, but it is clear from his 'Confessions' essay that thereafter he must have studied it quite carefully. If he was hesitant to push any positive view very forcefully, the reason presumably is epitomized in his own self-diagnosis.

In his Presidential address he said: 'If any theorist takes my remarks too much to heart, I can only say that I never get much beyond being in a quandary' (Williams, 1952, p. 23).

The relative roles of Hansen and Williams in the conduct of the Seminar are hard for anyone who was not behind the scenes to know. A participant could only deduce them from the personalities of the two men as they were seen in action and from the relations between their interests in the topics most frequently discussed. In the beginning there was a great deal of emphasis on the consumption function and the multiplier, which appeared to have been an important interest of Hansen's, and on the economic effects of the American tax structure, the public debt and banking policy, in which both men were greatly interested. One had the feeling, however, that in the first ten or so years Williams, who also bore the burden of being the first Dean of the Littauer School, was less positive and aggressive in the discussions of the theory of output. In some years his role appeared to diminish, but then he would become active again. This was probably a result in great part of variations in the intensity of his activity for the Federal Reserve Bank of New York, of which he was economic adviser during 1933–56 and a Vice-President during 1936–47, and of his work for the government in connection with planning for the post-war international monetary system and the Marshall Plan. In several years he was away from Harvard frequently, going regularly to New York and sometimes to Washington, Paris or Geneva, often returning barely in time for the Friday afternoon meetings.

Although both men were active in the Seminar, they differed greatly in temperament as well as in the early major focus of their interests. Hansen was active and persistent in looking for positive programmes that would make the economy work better, and he had definite views about what should be done, although he was always receptive to discussion and glad to hear the views of those who disagreed with him. Williams was much more the sceptic and cautious critic. I have already quoted him as saying, 'I never get much beyond being in a quandary'. It was clear to the students that the two men disagreed about a number of things, including policies that Hansen strongly advocated. Nevertheless, relations between them, in so far as the members of the Seminar could observe those relations, were excellent. They did not openly confront one another. One alumnus of the Seminar has said that he felt frustrated by the lack of confrontation or clash of ideas between the two men which deprived him of the opportunity to witness an intellectual contest which he had apparently expected to do.

But this did not prevent the Seminar from being lively. The intellectual pressure came mainly from the graduate students who were economists. (I should mention that some were not.)

Although Hansen and Williams appeared to get along very well, I think it was a surprise to most of those who saw them both in action, as it certainly was to me, to read in Williams' short tribute in Hansen's memory in the symposium to Hansen in the *Quarterly Journal of Economics* that they were very good friends, visiting each other frequently in their homes and that Williams would 'always think of Alvin as the closest friend I have ever had'.

It is clear from conversations with the early alumni, and some others too, that the Seminar was an important part of their professional training and experience. It was a centre of stimulation for the students and also for the non-student participants, at least those who were economists.

It is also clear that the Seminar had a much wider influence than its direct influence on the individual participants. It is widely referred to as an important element in the spread of Keynesian thought in the United States. Its influence is hard to distinguish from that of Keynes' book, *The General Theory of Employment, Interest and Money* (1936), partly because the Seminar itself was an important promoter of that book's influence, as well as of ideas advanced by Hansen in his many writings.

Another element in its influence was that it provided a place for fledgling economists to try out ideas by presenting papers and getting criticisms of those ideas through discussions of the papers. A number of articles that subsequently came to be regarded as classic were first presented at the Fiscal Policy Seminar. I cite only two examples. One is Paul Samuelson's articles on the interactions of the multiplier and the accelerator which I regard as valuable not only because of the substantive result, but as an early demonstration of how mathematical formulation can lead to more rigorous thinking about a policy issue. Concerning this I attribute much of the influence to Paul, despite his having said in the *Quarterly Journal of Economics* symposium and elsewhere that he merely worked out the mathematics of an idea of Hansen's.

Another example is the presentation by Evsey Domar of a path-breaking article on the burden of internally held government debt, which was the first of his celebrated articles on economic growth. The quality of the speakers to whom the participants were exposed is also indicated by the fact that in the first 28 years of the Seminar's existence, seven of the speakers who addressed it later won the not-yet-established Nobel Prize in Economic Science (Samuelson, Tobin, Frisch, Hicks, Myrdal, Stigler and Stone). I have not obtained the list of speakers who addressed the Seminar in its 29th and later years, but I am sure that more current and prospective Nobel Laureates were among them.

These articles illustrate the stimulus given to young graduate students by the efforts of the senior members to find theoretical answers to the baffling policy problems of those years. How much expansion of output could be

expected from the expansion of government expenditures? Was the increase
in the public debt caused by deficit financing which in the United States was
a major ground for opposition to it, as harmful to the economy as the oppo-
nents of that policy said?

The discussions in the Seminar also stimulated continued debate about the
same subjects among the economist participants outside its meetings. Perhaps the outstanding visible evidence of that discussion was the drafting and
subsequent publication of a tract that represented the advanced thinking of
the time, both Keynesian and New Dealish, called *An Economic Program for
American Democracy*. This tract, written in 1938 and published in 1939 as a
hard-cover book of 72 pages plus a rousing three-page foreword, was billed
as written 'by seven Harvard and Tufts economists'. (The one Tufts economist was Lorie Tarshis, author of the first successful Keynesian textbook.)
The fact is that the discussions and drafting were participated in by four
others, one of whom did not sign because he had reservations about some
points or about the style of the book, and three others who felt they must
refrain from signing because they were about to go back to or begin government jobs at the end of the academic year. Herb Stein, in his outstanding
book, *The Fiscal Revolution in America*, refers to this tract as 'the first
manifesto of the young Keynesian school'. He calls it 'Keynesian in analysis,
stagnationist in diagnosis, and all-out in prescription, going beyond deficit
spending to drastic measures of income redistribution for the purpose of
stimulating consumption' (Stein, 1968, pp. 164–5).

Stein then goes on to tell the widely circulated story that on 2 February
1939, James Roosevelt, Franklin Delano Roosevelt's son, telegraphed his
father at the White House: 'What is the name of the book you told me is such
a swell story for this business? Much love, Jimmy'. FDR replied: 'Title of
book "An Economic Program for American Democracy" by seven Harvard
Tufts economists. Father'. Stein then mentions that the notes to FDR's personal letters edited by Elliott Roosevelt, say that the book 'was a bible of the
New Dealers' (Stein, 1968, p. 487, footnote). The point to be emphasized for
present purposes is that all, or nearly all, of the authors were in some way
connected with the Fiscal Policy Seminar.

As a final bit of evidence concerning the influence of the Seminar in its
early years, let me repeat what I learned in 1975 when I prepared my paper
for the *Quarterly Journal of Economics* symposium published in 1976. Without making the research effort that would have been necessary to identify all
the people who participated in the Seminar, I can identify enough participants
who became important in formulating economic policy to back up the point,
if not to establish it rigorously.

As of 1975, one had become Chairman of the President's Council of
Economic Advisers (CEA) and three others had become members. Two other

Littauer alumni who may have attended the Seminar had become members of the Council. Four had become members of the Board of Governors of the Federal Reserve System (including one who was previously a member of the CEA). Two had become Undersecretaries of the Treasury and more did so later. By 1975 two had become Assistant Secretaries of State for Economic Affairs. Among participants who went on to less narrowly economic positions in the federal government are one who became Secretary of Defense and one who became Undersecretary of Health, Education and Welfare. Many others became directors of bureaus and other high officials of government departments. Alumni of the Seminar also include many eminent university economists and a substantial number of economic advisers and operating officers of business firms.

I have one bit of evidence that the Seminar's first year at least was a stimulating one for Hansen too. In October 1967 I went with the late Emile Despres, also a Littauer Fellow that first year, from Washington to Cambridge to attend a dinner at Hansen's home. A month later Hansen took the trouble to write to us from La Jolla, California, where he was teaching at the invitation of his former Harvard colleague, Seymour Harris, to express his pleasure that we had come. He recalled 'our little private seminar back in '37–38', and he said that 'the great thing about that year was the fact that we were all students trying to find our way about'.

NOTE

1. Talk presented 25 April 1988 at the 50th anniversary celebration of the Fiscal Policy Seminar, Harvard University.

PART II

Introductory extracts:
'Letter to Bernard Shaw, 1 January 1936'

John Maynard Keynes

'The elements of economics: an introduction to the theory of price and employment'

Lorie Tarshis

To understand my state of mind, however, you have to know that I believe myself to be writing a book on economic theory which will largely revolutionise – not, I suppose, at once, but in the course of the next ten years – the way the world thinks about economic problems. When my new theory has been duly assimilated and mixed with politics and feelings and passions, I can't predict what the final upshot will be in its effect on action and affairs. But there will be a great change, and, in particular, the Ricardian foundations of Marxism will be knocked away.

Keynes, 1936

The writer of an introductory text cannot claim that what he has written is original. Indeed I hope that what I have written is not thought to be so; for if it is, the chances are that it is wrong. It would be difficult indeed to trace the parentage of most of the ideas which this book expresses. Certainly my teachers at the University of Toronto and at Cambridge University made me acquainted with many of them, and numerous friends who were at Harvard University between 1936 and 1941 have helped me to follow recent developments. From all these, and from the works of others which I have read and studied, the pattern of my thought has been formed. To all of them I give my sincere thanks.

Tarshis, 1947, 'Preface', pp. xi–xii

In summary, then, the economist concerns himself with such problems as unemployment, inflation, and the maldistribution of income. He does so because he recognizes that only if these conditions are remedied can ordinary people have material well-being. His methods are the methods of other scientists. He frames hypotheses, reaches conclusions, and checks them by observation. Unfortunately his subject matter, and environment in which he works, do not favor analysis. Hence economics is not simple. ... Study of the economy requires the will to think without prejudice, a strong desire to observe conscientiously and carefully, and a great deal of work. But the problems which this study is directed to solving affect us all deeply enough to make this effort worth our while.

Tarshis, 1947, 'Introduction', p. 8.

5. Lorie Tarshis: an early Keynesian herald in America

James Tobin

AN ECONOMIC PROGRAM FOR AMERICAN DEMOCRACY (1938)

I first became aware of Lorie Tarshis because he was one of the 'seven Harvard and Tufts economists' whose *An Economic Program for American Democracy*, published in 1938, excited and rallied young New Dealers and Keynesians like me. I was a junior in Harvard College at the time, an eager recruit to the Keynesian revolution. A few years older were the graduate students and young instructors who were carrying the torch, some of whom we undergraduates came to know as our teachers, as tutors in the Houses where we lived, and as participants in the frequent seminars and forums where economic theories and policies were debated. Lorie Tarshis was one of that group and present at many of these encounters. Since his teaching job was not at Harvard, he was not personally known to me.

Tarshis was especially important in the transmission of Keynesian doctrine from the old Cambridge to the new. During his four years of study at Cambridge in 1932–35, he had actually attended Keynes' series of lectures every year, faithfully taking notes each time. His notes tell more of the evolution of Keynes' thought leading to the *General Theory* than those available from any other student (See Patinkin and Leitn, 1977, pp. 39–64; see also Rymes, 1987, 1989). From England he came to New England and a job at Tufts University. At nearby Harvard, Tarshis' views of what Keynes meant were quite authoritative. Moreover, Tarshis took part in the early debate on the cyclical correlations among money wages, real wages, employment and output (*Economic Journal*, March 1939). His fellow Canadian, Robert Bryce, whose notes from three years of Keynes' lectures are also important source material, was another missionary to Harvard, where he spent two years on his return from England before going back to Canada to begin a distinguished career in the civil service. Walter Salant, a one-year note-taker in 1933, also brought first-hand knowledge of Keynes to Harvard, where he was a graduate student for the next four years.

The seven authors, along with numerous contemporaries, were moving the climate of opinion in Harvard economics towards both Keynes and Roosevelt. Initially Harvard economists had been cool to the New Deal. An earlier seven-author book, essays by senior Harvard economists called *The Economics of the Recovery Program* (Brown et al., 1934) was downright hostile. As the young seven were writing their manifesto, Alvin Hansen came to Harvard as its first Littauer Professor of Political Economy. En route from Minnesota to Boston, Hansen became a Keynesian convert at age 50. Thus the young revolutionaries gained a respected and effective senior leader. Professor Seymour Harris, author of a non-Keynesian critique of Roosevelt's gold and monetary policies in the 1934 book, also switched sides and became an entrepreneur in promulgating the new economics in forums, symposia, journals and books. By the time *An Economic Program* was published in 1938, the Cambridge public was more receptive than a couple of years before.

Who were Tarshis' co-authors? Richard Gilbert was an extremely talented theorist and teacher. I have my notes of his 1937–38 lectures in 'Money and Banking', and they still read remarkably well. After a distinguished wartime career in Washington, he gravitated into business and his potential as an academic economist was never realized. The Sweezys were Marxists, to the detriment of their future academic and professional careers. Paul's course on the economics of socialism, joint with Edward Mason, was one of the best undergraduate courses I took. He and his wife were hoping to integrate Keynes and Marx, and some pages of the book reflect their influence. Arthur Stuart's professional career was cut short when he became a victim of McCarthyism. He had been associated with Harry Dexter White in the US Treasury. George Hildebrand went on to Wellesley, the Congress of Industrial Organizations, UCLA and Cornell. He was not the only one to become much more conservative than the 1938 book. John Wilson became a business economist, indeed a Vice-President of Chase Manhattan Bank. Of the seven, Tarshis was to have the most distinguished and productive career as an economist.

Besides the seven, there were 'several taking an active part in the work of preparing the book who, because of their present connection with various branches of government service, did not feel free to affix their signatures to recommendations on questions of policy' (Gilbert et al., 1938, p. vi). One of these was Walter Salant. Others were Emile Despres, Alan Sweezy and Moses Abramowitz (who may have withdrawn from conviction rather than employment). These four all went on to distinguished careers as academic economists.

An Economic Program diagnoses America's economic crisis as 'secular stagnation', though it does not use those famous or notorious Hansenian words. In the authors' view 1929 was not just a business cycle peak, but rather the end of a century and a half of expansion of American capitalism.

During that era, growth was self-sustaining, in that growth itself generated sufficient investment to absorb the nation's saving and to employ fully the rising population. Land and natural resources were plentiful, and the government generously encouraged private entrepreneurs to exploit them. It was clear to the authors that this process had come to an end. In the 1930s and ever after, continued expansion and full employment would require government expenditures financed by borrowing. The Harvard and Tufts seven urged the federal government to face these facts squarely and courageously, undeterred by fallacious worries about public debt, inflation and taxation.

The 1937–38 recession had obviously been an important spur to dissemination of this message. Prior to that shock, President Roosevelt and his New Deal had not been overtly and unequivocally Keynesian, although the budget deficits they ran to finance their pragmatic efforts to provide work for the unemployed were in effect Keynesian fiscal policies. In 1947 FDR began his second term in one of his orthodox fiscal moods. Moreover, his new Social Security system was inadvertently a contractionary shock to the economy, collecting insurance contribution taxes long before there were any eligible beneficiaries. *An Economic Program* was urging a consciously expansionary fiscal policy. It happened that Roosevelt was already moving sharply in that direction, prompted by the recession and by Lauchlin Currie, Marriner Eccles and other Keynesian advisers.

An Economic Program was, perhaps for practical reasons, overly charitable in its assessment of the New Deal. The National Recovery Administration, a corporate–state experiment encouraging cartels to raise wages and prices, was antithetical both to Keynesian economics and to sound microeconomics. So was the Agricultural Adjustment Administration. *An Economic Program* concentrated on what might be called muscular Keynesianism: expenditures on development and protection of natural resources, electrification, housing, education and health, railroads and roads. While favouring extensions and improvements of social insurance, the programme did not encourage radical redistribution of income and wealth. It advocated public ownership of railroads and of certain other natural monopolies. It favoured federal standards of wages, hours and working conditions, and vigorously supported New Deal legislation to encourage organization of labour unions and to guarantee collective bargaining.

Two or three years later, economic mobilization for war gave the economy a Keynesian boost many times greater than the seven authors or Alvin Hansen (or anyone else) had contemplated. During the war some government economists, including Hansen and colleagues at the National Resources Planning Board, prepared plans for peacetime programmes like those advocated in *An Economic Program*. The mood of Congress and the public when peace actually came was hostile. 'Secular stagnation' became a discredited diagnosis.

Cold War and welfare state combined to expand the public sector further than anyone imagined in the 1930s, and in different directions.

More than a half century later, 1929 and the years that followed look less like a drastic and irreversible change in economic regime and more like an unusually severe cyclical downturn, which governments and central banks in the USA and Europe allowed by incredible incompetence to become a Great Depression. Indeed this failure, rather than secular stagnation and a permanent need for deficit spending, is the durable message of Keynesian economics. By 1967, in his revised textbook, Tarshis was inclined to agree.

Perhaps because of its timing, *An Economic Program* did not make much of a splash outside metropolitan Boston. I located only three professional reviews. Eli Ginzberg was moderately sympathetic in the *Saturday Review*, but criticized the authors' excess zeal. Harry Gideonse was scornful in *Political Science Quarterly*. The *American Economic Review* ran a routine and non-committal notice.

THE ELEMENTS OF ECONOMICS (1947)

Tarshis' 1947 *The Elements of Economics* was the first elementary college textbook featuring Keynesian macroeconomics. Many of the themes and analyses of *An Economic Program* reappear. The textbook treats sympathetically the Hansen hypothesis of secular stagnation. It concentrates on fiscal policy as *the* government instrument to achieve and maintain full employment. It cursorily dismisses monetary policy as an effective tool of stabilization. (*An Economic Program* does not even mention monetary policy, except to suggest that if there were a capitalists' strike against ever-rising government debt, the Federal Reserve could step in and buy Treasury bonds.) Within fiscal policy, the 1947 work focuses on expenditures and scarcely mentions the possibilities of varying tax revenues. As in 1938, Tarshis' view is that there are numerous public investments which are desirable in themselves, not simply as sources of jobs and aggregate demand. Given the long list of socially desirable public outlays, one would think there is no need to invent make-work projects. However, Tarshis the textbook writer echoes the occasional preference of Keynes himself for a high-consumption economy, worrying about the 'paradox of thrift' and despairing of the powers of monetary policy to make sure potential saving can be translated into real investment.

Although at the time Keynesian macroeconomics was the distinctively novel feature of Tarshis' text, most of its nearly 700 pages are devoted to microeconomics: theories of firm and industry, micro-foundations of the basic Keynesian propensities to consume, invest and hold money. (There is surprisingly little about households, utility and all that, and about general equilibrium.) In 1995 it is easy to forget that in the 1930s the two Cambridges produced not only the Keynesian macro revolution but previously the imperfect/monopolistic competition micro revolution.

What impressed me most about *Elements* is Tarshis' evident and enthusiastic urge to tell students and other readers, if not everything he knows, at least everything he believes they can and should know. He felt economics was important and fascinating, and he wanted to convey that feeling to readers. The book surely had the capacity to do that, especially, of course, if taught by Tarshis or someone with equal enthusiasm and dedication.

The Keynesian economics in the book is essentially multiplier analysis. In Tarshis (1947), it is expounded arithmetically in many variants and applications and in its policy implications. Keynes himself would have wanted more exposition of the opposing classical model and of his reasons for challenging it.

The first edition of Paul Samuelson's *Economics: An Introductory Analysis* appeared a year later, and soon stole the market from Tarshis. By 1950–51 Samuelson led Tarshis by roughly 160–80 in institutional adoptions. Why? They are very similar books. In particular, both expositions of Keynes are pretty much confined to multiplier analysis, but Samuelson tries harder to explain why price and interest effects do not lead to full employment. Samuelson's expositions seem less complicated, more intuitive, more concerned with conceptional clarity and less cluttered by numbers. Thanks perhaps to the passage of an additional year, Samuelson seems less bound to pre-war and wartime problems, facts, examples and conventions. For example, Samuelson is, even in 1948, more open to the possibilities of effective monetary policy.

One topic where Tarshis (1947) excels in quantity and quality is international economics, but in the 1940s and 1950s students and teachers in the US were less interested in that subject than they are now and than Canadian and British students were then.

Tarshis' 1947 textbook was published by Houghton Mifflin under the editorship of Edgar S. Furniss, Professor of Social Science, Dean of the Yale Graduate School, and the about-to-become Provost of the University. In his 'Introduction', Furniss writes: 'This book contains the best the expert economist has to offer regarding the economic problems of our times, and in particular the overall problem of full employment'. Furniss refers to that subject as 'the national income as a whole'. Furniss was, with Fred Fairchild and Norman S. Buck, author of the dominant introductory economics textbook of the inter-war period, *Elementary Economics* (1924). Their text evolved from one first published in 1911 by Irving Fisher, when he was teaching the introductory course at Yale. Revisions of Fisher's book, *Elementary Principles of Economics*, appeared in 1912, 1918 and 1921. Fairchild, Furniss &

Buck (FF&B) went through five editions from 1924 to 1948. It was quite orthodox, never tainted by Keynes.

Furniss' endorsement of the Tarshis text gains heightened significance from the following story, for which I am grateful to Yale Professor Emeritus, John Perry Miller. As a young faculty member in the late 1940s, he was approached by Furniss, who said he was under pressure from his two co-authors to bring out one more revised edition of FF&B. He asked Miller whether it would make any sense to do it 'without including a major section on determination of national income as a whole', to which Fairchild and Buck were philosophically opposed. Miller confirmed Furniss' misgivings on this point. No editions of FF&B appeared after 1948.

Sales of Tarshis' text were undoubtedly damaged by the scurrilous right-wing attack upon it, led by Rose Wilder Lane, who attacked it for the right-wing National Economic Council in 1947. Radical conservatives of those times hated Keynes almost as bitterly as they hated communists. They did not like any books that suggested any positive roles, macro or micro, for government. The generic enemy was 'collectivism'. Tarshis (1947) was the most vulnerable of the textbooks of the day, probably because of the legacies of *An Economic Program* in his text.

William F. Buckley, Jr, at that time a Yale undergraduate engaged in ideological war upon his university and in particular its economics faculty, took up the fight against Tarshis in his *God and Man at Yale* (1951). Tarshis' text was used for only one year (1947–48) at Yale before it was displaced by Samuelson (1948). Buckley did not like that book either; indeed he did not like any of the economics texts in use at Yale during his four years there, except FF&B, which Buck stuck to in his section of the introductory course. Buckley assailed Furniss for his sponsorship of the Tarshis book, his desertion of his own book (FF&B) and his alleged use of his power as Provost to build a collectivist economics department.

Although it was a pioneering book, essentially the first post-war post-Depression introductory text, Tarshis' text attracted very few professional reviews. American economics journals ignored it altogether. Sar Levitan in *Political Science Quarterly* was highly favourable, and so was J. Richard Huber in *Annals of the American Academy of Political and Social Science*. In England, C.W. Guillebaud paid Tarshis the compliment of a serious and judicious review, part by part, in the *Economic Journal*. He welcomed the exposition of Keynes and highly recommended the book as a whole, subject to the caveat that 'there is some danger lest the student should be left with the impression that the final answers have now been found' (Guillebaud, 1948).

MODERN ECONOMICS (1967)

Tarshis published a second textbook, *Modern Economics: An Introduction*. This is really a very different book – more conceptual and less mechanical in its teaching of theory, Keynesian still but less wedded to the letter of the *General Theory*, and more eclectic. In macroeconomics, for example, the book was innovative in its Gurley–Shaw treatments of monetary and financial economics and in its approach to the balance of international payments. The same dedication of a teacher ambitious for readers and students to understand is abundantly evident.

THE UNITED STATES BALANCE OF PAYMENTS IN 1968 (1963)

My closest association with Lorie came in 1962 when I was a Member of President Kennedy's Council of Economic Advisers. The United States balance of international payments was a matter of great concern to the Administration. The country's official gold reserves were dwindling, and its short-term debts to foreign governments, central banks, and other institutions and individuals were mounting. Yet the US did not have a trade deficit or a current account deficit. How should the situation be interpreted? Was the dollar in danger? Within the Administration and the Federal Reserve there were considerable uncertainties and debates.

Consequently, it was decided to engage Emile Despres, Walter Salant and Lorie Tarshis – three comrades from the old Harvard days – to help out. Their idea was that the United States was acting like a world financial intermediary, borrowing short in order to lend long or make equity investments throughout the world. In this light, our balance-of-payments difficulties were more benign than many people feared. There certainly was some truth to the Despres–Salant–Tarshis theory, and it had considerable influence. A thorough study of the balance of payments, with the initial trio augmented by several other economists, was carried out by the Brookings Institution under Salant's direction and published in 1963 as *The United States Balance of Payments in 1968*. Tarshis used this financial intermediation theory in his 1967 text.

In more recent years Lorie invited me to Toronto on several occasions. The most memorable one was a day when he had enticed J.R. Hicks to visit; there was much to talk about. In these encounters Lorie and I found ourselves very much on the same sides of contemporary theoretical and policy issues. We shared intellectual legacies of the 1930s and 1960s, but Lorie was always thinking anew about new problems in new times. He was a lovely man, a seeker of truth and a doer of good.

6. Requiem for the classic Tarshis textbook that first brought Keynes to introductory economics

Paul A. Samuelson

Many believe that *Economics* by Samuelson (1948) first brought Keynesian macroeconomics into the elementary textbook. They are wrong. That honour goes to Lorie Tarshis, a Canadian from Toronto who studied at Cambridge under Keynes and taught economics in the late 1930s at Tufts University near Boston, prior to his long stints at Stanford and back to Toronto.

It is a sad tragedy that this pioneering *tour de force* was killed in its first years largely by pre-Joseph McCarthy vicious pressures from the extreme and uninformed Right. As a result, after a year of excellent sales, Tarshis' 1947 *Elements of Economics* faded out of extensive use. My own 1948 textbook, no less and no more subversive than Tarshis', inadvertently received an unfair initial boost from the anti-Tarshis censorship pressures. In its turn the Samuelson text was later accorded the dubious compliment of being attacked by the same critics, but these attacks must be deemed love pats in comparison with the poisonous accusations levelled at Lorie Tarshis. Ironically, in the course of time and during the New Left movements among students in the late 1960s and early 1970s, mine and other mainstream textbooks earned denunciations as apologetics for exploitative capitalism.

My first purpose in these pages is to report in an impressionistic way the sordid 1947–50 events as they happened. I have done no extensive library research. However, I was fairly close to the situation and my memory is pretty good on the details. The reader is warned that Lorie Tarshis was a personal and admired friend, and that no matter how hard I try to be objective, any account by me needs to be audited by less partisan scholars.

My second purpose is to look back, with the objectivity that almost half a century of distance imparts, upon the merits and shortcomings of the mid 1940s Tarshis and Samuelson expositions. This is not so much an exercise in nostalgia and complacency as a candid critique of the inadequacies of an early stage in an evolutionary science in comparison with the cumulative subsequent developments mandated for it by later economic history and later analytical findings.

Let me make clear that the salutary alterations in Model T Keynesianism (I am using the Henry Ford nomenclatures), which we associate with names such as A.C. Pigou, Franco Modigliani, James Tobin, Milton Friedman or Robert Lucas, have essentially naught to do with the stated objections and innuendoes of Tarshis' critics such as Rose Wilder Lane, Colonel Namm, William Buckley, Jr or other vigilantes of those good old days. When they termed Lorie Tarshis a Marxist-Keynesian, that was a one-word epithet like Dam-Yankee and carried the imprimatur of Herbert Hoover himself. It was not Pigou effects in Say's Law or the constancy of the velocity of money that they extolled. Rather, it was the heresy of the Mixed Economy that they objected to root and branch. The mature Buckley who found some merit in the Stockman–Kemp–Laffer Reaganomics of the 1980s supply-siders was not the *Wunderkind* of southern Connecticut who first sniffed out unGodliness and crank Keynesianism at Old Eli. The Rose Wilder Lane who lived in the little house on the prairie and came to write *Let the Hurricane Roar* (1933) was not the later bitter ideological critic of regulationism and Tarshis. These savants of the Right did not have to know journal articles by Hayek or Friedman to recognize pornography or subversion when they saw it on American campuses.

I spent an hour with the Tarshis text (1947) in preparing this tribute. My own copy of it, received free from Houghton Mifflin by virtue of my being a teacher of elementary economics courses, had long since evaporated from my book shelves: the good go fastest. Finding a copy to read was not easy. Fortunately, Franklyn Holzman, long time Chairman of the Tufts Economics Department, had bought a copy that was being remaindered by the Tufts Library. Under my solemn promise to send on the loaned copy to James Tobin at Yale, Frank credulously let me borrow the book. I had looked at it 48 years ago but had never taught from it. When my own first edition was in press with McGraw-Hill, I had not even known that Tarshis in wartime Washington was working on his text. He certainly knew nothing of my MIT mimeographed materials out of which the 1948 first edition evolved.

Still, not surprisingly, our Keynesian macroeconomics was fundamentally similar. My pages were full of diagrams, in which $C+I+G$ schedules intersected with a 45° line or, equivalently, in which SS saving schedules plotted against income intersected with II investment schedules to determine a Y equilibrium that could be at less than full employment. His was a lucid description of how an increase in 'spending' could be expected to reduce a high level of unemployment and excess capacity. Since teachers of economics are diagram-happy, Tarshis' more austere rhetoric was perhaps less commercially Machiavellian. (Indeed, years later Tarshis and Paul Baran at Stanford proposed to write a textbook on international trade. As publishers' gossip at that time had it, they were given a royalty advance. In the event Baran revealed a preference to analyse the fundamentals of Marxian developmental economics rather than work away at the trade volume; but the conscientious Tarshis persisted to fulfil his contract (1955). Those who taught in that field told me it was an excellent book. However, when a publisher asked my opinion as to whether it would kill off its own rival bestseller, my off-the-cuff guess was that, in a field where economists are particularly diagram-obsessed, Tarshis' adoptions and sales might be limited. I am not sure that my guess was wrong.)

What do I mean by Model T Keynesianism, or by its near equivalents, Ur-Keynesianism or Neanderthal Keynesianism? In its simplest form this can refer to a Kahn–Keynes 1931–33 multiplier model that is one equation in the one unknown of *Income*, Y:

$$S(Y) = \bar{I} \leftrightarrow Y^* = F(\bar{I})$$
$$O < S' < 1 \leftrightarrow dY^* / d\bar{I} = F' = 1/S' > 1 \tag{6.1}$$

Or, defining the propensity-to-consume schedule, $C = c(Y)$ as

$$Y - S(Y), \; O < c' = 1 - S' < 1,$$

we write (*l*)'s equivalent as

$$Y = c(Y) + \bar{I}, Y^* = F(\bar{I}), F' = 1 + (c') + (c')2 + \ldots = 1/(1 - c') > 1 \tag{6.2}$$

Of course, no elementary textbook of the time wrote out this petty mathematics. But that is what Joan Robinson (1937) exposited in her excellent guide for beginners, *Introduction to the Theory of Employment*, which was a simplified version of Keynes' 1936 *General Theory*.

Both Tarshis and Samuelson supplemented this bare-bones paradigm by discussions of banks and money. Investment soon ceased to be regarded as an *exogenous* parameter, $\bar{I}$. It could be altered by bank system changes in money stocks that lowered the interest rate, r, and such endogenous drops in r could raise I in $I = f(r)$, once it was postulated that $dI/dr = f'(r)$ in this marginal-efficiency schedule was negative. Also, rises in I could be induced by increases in Y itself, in some generalized version of the acceleration principle. But relative word counts of different sections of the macro expositions would, I fear, suggest that we young Keynesians were slow in getting away from 1938–like 'liquidity traps' in which vast increments in Money, M, would not lower near-zero interest rates much and would not increase either I or the price level very much in a high-unemployment economy possessed of much excess capacity.

What is the matter with that? Strong cases make good pedagogical exercises, yes. But 1947–48 was not 1933 or 1938. Our textbooks were catching up with the earlier macro literature. But that literature was only slowly catching up with the reality contrasts between the post-war high-employment scenarios and the pre-war Great Depression. We served generations of students better than they were being served by the pre-1940 textbooks of Taussig (1911), Fairchild–Furniss–Buck (1924), Benham (1941), Ely (1893; see also Ely and Wicker, 1904), and Garver–Hansen (1926). But I see clearly in hindsight that my introductory text had not served them as well as it would have had it caught up better with the revisionist Keynesianism of Modigliani, Tobin and Duesenberry. (I refer to 'wealth effects' that were already in Tobin's (1939) Harvard undergraduate honours thesis, already in Modigliani (1944) and in his gestating lifecycle-saving modelling. I refer also to long-run shiftings in permanent-income saving propensities that Simon Kuznets, Edward Denison, Milton Friedman, James Duesenberry, Franco Modigliani and even I had already done research on. After the 1939–46 virtual doubling of nominal GNP, liquidity traps had moved off the relevant stage – not to be seen again until the Japanese slump of the 1990s! And writing after Beveridge–Hansen discussions about inflationary tendencies at really high employment levels, we ought to have amplified considerably our post-war treatments of inflation (and stagflation).) Yes, half a loaf is better than none. But a 95 per cent loaf is almost twice as good as a 50 per cent one.

I linger on this matter because, peculiarly in economics, one must always study one's previous imperfections. The now recognized curse of Radcliffe Committee Keynesian orthodoxies in 1959 Britain was its stubborn living in an empirical past. Had there been later editions of the Tarshis textbook, I am confident that events would have forced the evolutions I am claiming we all needed to make. Alas, right-wing bigotry nipped in the bud economists' ability to test this conjecture.

Actually both the 1947 Tarshis and 1948 Samuelson expositions are consistent, under their surfaces, with Model A Keynesianism of the Harrod–Hicks–Hansen I–S and L–M diagrams. (I am continuing to use the Henry Ford nomenclatures, in which the Model T Ford was succeeded in 1927 by the pre-war Model A.) Model A amplifies equations (6.1) and (6.2) above to include money stock, M, and interest rate effects on C and I:

$$Y = C(Y,r) + I(Y,r)$$
$$M = Y/V(r) \text{ or } kY + L(r); \ V'(r) > 0 > L'(r). \tag{6.3}$$

Joan Robinson (1937) also has these in the background, as of course Keynes himself did in the 1936 *General Theory*. But, judiciously, we thought such simultaneous equations should be talked *about* before beginners not be seen by them. Only in later editions, and in ghetto appendices, did I go all the way with them.

'Why,' someone born in the Lucas era will ask, 'did the authors not consider more fully that an increase in spendings might go only to change the $P(t)$ price level in $P(t)Q(t)$, while leaving real output levels invariant?' In some longer-run process of M and P growth, such a possibility did indeed get noticed. But remember that over a century of US history, involving 1200 months of data, the reported changes in nominal $\varepsilon_j p_j q_j = P(t)Q(t)$ involved about twice as much monthly percentage change in Q as in P. And after the Great Depression, the New Deal recovery of 1933–36 involved limited change in P and great percentage change in Q. The idealized convention in those days was to consider the P price level as virtually constant (or slowly rising) until a proximity to 'full employment' was reached. The empirical studies of Tarshis (1938) and John Dunlop (1938) had cast doubt on the empirical validity of the neoclassical law of diminishing returns and its entailed rise in P/W as Q shows short-term growth. Actually, once the Model A Hicks system was rewritten to distinguish nominal $Y = PQ$ from real $y = Q = Y/P$, and to distinguish real money, M/P from nominal M, the realities of the post-war incipient inflation problems could have been faced up to less imperfectly. But in the first edition of innovating texts there was a cultural lag. (Indeed, some users of my text – for example Kermit Gordon of Williams College and the German trade-union translators – preferred the first edition version to its later refinements, precisely because of its unemployment emphasis.)

If prices and wages, in the US and abroad, were said to have displayed in the 1929–50 years the perfect market-clearing flexibilities taken for granted in the Say's Law macroeconomics of the pre-1930 introductory textbooks, some modern savants would say that students would have been getting 'proper micro-foundations' for their macroeconomics. I believe that a tacit supposition that real-world prices and wages operating in the real world of, say, 1929–50 had in them various rigidities and market imperfections that entailed effectiveness of alterations in aggregate money demands to alter real outputs, real consumption aggregates and real profitabilities – that paradigm better served the students and electorates of the pre-war and post-war years. The elementary classroom was not the proper place to worry about 'proper micro-foundations' in any case. Moreover, to understand even 1980s and 1990s macro movements in history, one does better, I believe, to eschew the 'real business cycles' of the new classical school in favour of an eclectic approach that explains best the 1979–95 changes in P, Q and unemployment by a mixture of demand- and supply-side economics. Posterity will debate these issues, and I await eagerly its verdicts.

When I stress the post-*General Theory* evolutions in Keynesianism, I hope not to be misunderstood. Those equipped only with pre-1930 neoclassicism are unable to understand the degree of merit and demerit in *any* of the 1990s fashionable models of macroeconomics. A great economist like Keynes is greater even than his own nominated behaviour relations. A Keynes gives us the tools to grapple with whatever the future brings.

I conclude by remembering Lorie Tarshis for the wise scholar he was. In the modern age hard-boiled economists are a dime a dozen. Fifty years ago, when scholars were more preoccupied with issues of inequality and market imperfections, Lorie stood out as one with a cool brain put in service of a warm heart.

7. Political influence on the textbook Keynesian revolution: God, Man and Lorie Tarshis at Yale

David Colander and Harry Landreth

In Colander and Landreth (1996) we argue that the so-called Keynesian revolution in economics involved a three-part interrelated process: a policy revolution, a theoretical revolution and a textbook revolution. Of these three, the least considered part of the Keynesian revolution is the textbook revolution.

In this chapter we examine one aspect of the Keynesian textbook revolution and its interaction with the Keynesian policy revolution. Specifically, we explore the reaction that Lorie Tarshis' 1947 text, *The Elements of Economics* (one of the first principles books in the US to embody Keynesian ideas) brought about in the United States and the implication of that reaction for modern economics. We begin with a brief discussion of some background relevant to Tarshis' writing of the text.

BACKGROUND OF TARSHIS' BOOK

In 1936 Bob Bryce and Lorie Tarshis came to Cambridge, Massachusetts from Cambridge, England, where they had been enthusiastic students of J. M. Keynes. Soon after arriving in the US, they started introducing Keynesian economics to Harvard, Cambridge and to the United States. Bryce was a student at Harvard and Tarshis began his teaching career at Tufts, a half hour walk from Harvard. Bryce began spreading the gospel among the heathen; Schumpeter, as reported by John Kenneth Galbraith, called Keynes Allah, and Bryce his Prophet (Colander and Landreth, 1996, p. 137). Bryce's influence in spreading the new Keynesian ideas was at the graduate school level in his student days at Harvard, and later in his distinguished career in the Canadian government.

Tarshis took a different tack and began disseminating Keynesian ideas through published works. He and other young economists from Harvard wrote *An Economic Program for American Democracy* (Gilbert et al., 1938), which applied Keynesian economic thinking to the problems faced by the US economy in 1938. That book received significant attention and, in academic circles, it closely associated Tarshis with liberal and Keynesian ideas. Tarshis states:

> Being one of the authors of the book was not altogether positive for me. The president of Tufts thought it was awful. You see, the byline of the book was, 'By Seven Harvard and Tufts Professors'. He kept sending me reminders of donors who were going to give money to Tufts but who had decided not to, because of the book. In fact, I was regarded as an absolute Red. (Colander and Landreth, 1996, p. 64)

After that initial policy book, Tarshis followed a more usual academic route. In 1939 he completed his PhD from Cambridge and, after a stint as a Carnegie Fellow at the National Bureau of Economic Research, he became an Assistant Professor at Tufts. In 1941 Tarshis took a job at Stanford but, because of the war, he did not begin until 1945. Instead, he became a US citizen in 1942 and served on the War Production Board in 1943–45.

TARSHIS' TEXTBOOK

Tarshis was an excellent writer and expositor, and in 1946 he was recruited by Edgar Furniss, the Provost of the graduate school of Yale and an advisory editor to Houghton Mifflin, to write an introductory text which incorporated recent developments in economic thinking – especially Keynesian economic thought and ideas of monopolistic and imperfect competition. Tarshis was a fast writer and he completed the book in 1947. To those who are involved with the process of writing introductory books in the 1990s – a process that involves carefully positioning oneself relative to other books and going through a long and detailed reviewing process – the development process of the Tarshis book was extraordinary. He had no reviewers, and he wrote it in reference to no other book (Colander and Landreth, 1996, pp. 66–7).

Tarshis' book was 699 pages long and was substantially different from previous introductory economics textbooks. It included a discussion of Robinson's imperfect competition and Chamberlin's monopolistic competition theories, and it provided a Keynesian view of the macro economy, whereas the standard principles book of that time discussed only perfect competition and monopoly, and had little discussion of any macroeconomic issue.

Perhaps the biggest difference between Tarshis' book and earlier books was in policy sensibility. Most earlier books had espoused classical political economy precepts – interpret as *laissez-faire* precepts – in a general way, with little or no discussion of current problems. According to those precepts, the gold standard and sound finance – interpret as balanced budget – were good and not subject to policy debate. In these pre-Keynesian textbooks these precepts were combined with a general admiration and belief in the market system and private property. The message conveyed to students by previous books was that unimpeded markets were the best way to organize an economy. Any statements to the contrary were heresy.

With the Depression of the 1930s, that view about the role of the market was changing, both in the academic and political spheres. With the success of the Western governments in World War II, there was also a change in the view of the role of government. It was within this changing ideological structure that Tarshis wrote his book. Tarshis' book conveyed a quite different policy perspective. Tarshis saw the government as an agency through which people acted collectively for the common good. That view of government was combined with a belief that the market needed government assistance to ensure full employment. Thus it was inevitable that a book presenting the new view that questioned the self-regulating nature of the economic system would provoke a reaction.

Initially, Tarshis' book was well received. According to Tarshis:

> When the book came out in – probably April of 1947 – I kept getting glowing telegrams from the publisher. I thought, 'Oh, my God, this is just beyond belief.' The publisher was very happy....
>
> I would get letters from my very conservative publisher saying Brown has adopted it, maybe Middlebury adopted it, Yale has adopted it – one place after another had adopted it. Every time I got a letter like this that indicated ten more adoptions or twenty more adoptions, I thought, 'Boy, that bank account will be picking up.' (Colander and Landreth, 1996, pp. 66, 68)

But these happy days did not last long; soon after publication Tarshis' book was harshly attacked in a review by Rose Wilder Lane. Merwin K. Hart, a successful businessman, had organized the National Economic Council which published a *Review of Books*. Rose Wilder Lane, daughter of Laura Ingalls Wilder (who authored *Little House on the Prairie*), was editor of the *Review of Books* from 1945 to 1950. Lane's review of Tarshis' book was followed by an evidently organized campaign against it, during which the administrations and trustees of colleges adopting the textbook were sent letters calling for its removal. Letter writers to Stanford's trustees and President wanted both Tarshis and his book removed (Colander and Landreth, 1996, pp. 67–70). According to Tarshis: 'It was a nasty performance, an organized campaign in which they sent newsletters to all the trustees of all the universities that had adopted the book' (Colander and Landreth, 1996, p. 68). Lane's attack was followed by others, and soon removing the Tarshis book from economics classes had become a *cause célèbre* of conservative organizations.

In the face of these attacks Stanford stood firm and refused to budge; throughout the period Stanford supported the right of free expression by its professors. Tarshis recounts:

> ... my department chairman sheltered me. I know that from time to time the University had trouble, because after the new president came in 1949, he let me see some of the correspondence. It was villainous stuff. They were after Paul Baran, who was a Marxist; they were after Ed Shaw, who was a monetarist, and me. They thought Stanford should get rid of all of us. Wallace Sterling, the president of Stanford, wasn't as vigorous as I would think the thing deserved, but he would certainly never give an inch. (Colander and Landreth, 1996, p. 70)

The schools which had adopted Tarshis' book were not so firm and sales soon dwindled; Tarshis was not to be a millionaire book author. He states:

> Merwin K. Hart organized a thing called 'The National Economic Committee.' He got Rose Wilder Lane to write a newsletter for it and he sent copies of this newsletter ... to all the members of every Board of Trustees of every university anywhere, including politicians, Republican universities and so on. Then I began to get notices from Houghton Mifflin about 'X is canceling its order; Y is canceling its order.' Before the summer was halfway through, sales had fallen just as sharply as they had risen. I was at Williams that summer, teaching, and the president of Williams, a man called Baxter – Emile [Despres] had seen to it that Williams had adopted my book and Baxter was very strongly supportive of the book – wrote a strong letter to other university presidents he knew. But sales, instead of staying at that beautiful peak, went down just like that. The book did all right – I think I sold something like 10,000 copies. But it really died in 1948 or 1949. (Colander and Landreth, 1996, pp. 68–9)

Tarshis was especially upset by an attack by William Buckley in the book *God and Man at Yale* (1951), in which he criticized the views of Tarshis and authors of several other economics textbooks used at Yale. Tarshis states:

> That bastard Buckley – I get so angry when I think of him, because, you know, he's *still* parading his objectivity and concern for 'moral values', and so on. The amount of distortion is enormous. He would pick a phrase and tack it onto a phrase two pages later, another page later, another page four pages earlier, and make a sentence that I couldn't recognize as anything I'd written – I was only able to see it when I had my book in front of me, and I could see where they came from – and make it seem as though I was no supporter of market capitalism, which I felt I always was. (Colander and Landreth, 1996, pp. 69–70)

A CLASH OF IDEOLOGIES

Anyone who knew Lorie Tarshis knows that it was impossible to dislike him personally; he was one of the most charming, caring and pleasant economists who ever existed. Thus it had to be his views, not he himself, that were being assailed. In a way, the assault on a principles of economics textbook conveying the new pro-government interventionist policy was inevitable. To see that let us consider some of the contrasting views of Buckley and Tarshis. Buckley states his position:

> ... I look upon economics as a science of adjustment between the appetites of man, which are limitless, and the resources of nature, which are limited. I am, further, committed to the classical doctrine that the optimum adjustment – private property, production for profit and by private ownership, and regulation by a free competitive economy – brings not only maximum prosperity, but also maximum freedom. I therefore consider any infringement upon the component parts of the free economy to be unsound economics. It goes without saying that I consider such infringements as militating against maximum freedom. (Buckley, 1951, p. 51)

This quotation nicely sums up Buckley's view of economics. It contains a strong commitment to the free market. From a modern perspective it is a view riddled with problems – caused by an intertwining of positive and normative issues – but at that time it was seen by many as what economics was.

Just how openly free market-committed Buckley was can be seen in his discussion of Henry Simons' *A Positive Program for Laissez Faire* (1934; 1949). He writes:

> I find this pamphlet an extraordinary document, for perhaps to a greater extent than anyone else has done in so few pages, Mr. Simons indicts the state as bearing heavy responsibility for the evils that led to the great depression (the pamphlet was written in 1934, probably in a fit of pique), but promptly outlines a program which would give to the state unprecedented power. He equates freedom with free enterprise, and proceeds to outline a sure program for the destruction of the free economy. (Buckley, 1951, p. 94)

Faced with this ideological preconception in favour of the market, even a non-ideological assessment of the costs and benefits of government policy would be considered suspect. What made a clash even more inevitable was that, although Tarshis' book was less ideologically burdened than Buckley's, Tarshis' was not non-ideological. Tarshis' view was that massive government action had been needed during the Depression. A continuation of this government action was necessary to maintain prosperity. Given the problems that the economy had in the 1930s and the success that the Western governments had in the war in defeating fascism, the Tarshis–Keynesian view was, to many, reasonable.

In Tarshis' mind, and in the mind of many observers today, there is nothing inconsistent with being pro-market and pro-government action. But the individualistic ideology of Buckley did not allow for that combination of views.

Tarshis was very clear that he felt his own views were pro-market. He states:

> It never entered my head to be concerned about this, because my whole feeling when I was in Cambridge, England, in the last couple of years (and this continued in Cambridge, Massachusetts), was that while I agreed with the aim of the Communists in the sense of 'Let's do something to get a system that works', I accepted Keynes strongly enough to feel that revolution was not the way to do it. Following Keynes, you could get it to work.
>
> So the irony of it is, I was really, by that time, in the four years in which Keynes was writing at Cambridge, very much affected by Keynes' belief that an analysis that followed his lines – not step by step his policies, that was almost an irrelevancy – an analysis that followed his lines would enable a person to develop the kind of policy that would be needed to maintain the system: not simply to restore prosperity but to keep the system going. I think Bob [Bryce] would remember – I remember quite vividly – that Keynes in those second and third years was very much influenced by what was going on in Germany (he hated it); he was influenced by what was going on in the Soviet Union (he didn't like it) and was scared to death – I can vouch for it – that the young people were turning mostly to Communism or Fascism. He wanted to get his book, his analysis, understood, in providing a viable alternative, a way of maintaining capitalism, maintaining prosperity with the property relations that he knew in a capitalist economy. (Colander and Landreth, 1996, pp. 67–8)

Consistent with this view, Tarshis favoured a variety of policies which would be considered 'collectivist', and his book espoused that ideological view as being science. For example, in the Editor's Introduction to the book, Edgar S. Furniss writes that the book reflects Tarshis' 'conviction that the major purpose in teaching economics is to enable the student to understand the urgent problems of our national economy and to participate in their solution' (Furniss, in Tarshis, 1947, p. vii). Since the classical position was that the market would solve the problem and there was nothing that individuals could do to 'participate in the solution', this was almost a direct statement of the view that the state had a role in dealing with the Depression.

Additional examples from Tarshis' book can be cited to show his views about the role of government in the economy:

> As the nature of our economy has changed and as the problems that it has been compelled to face have altered and grown in gravity, we have been compelled to call upon the government – in other words, Ourselves Incorporated – to meet these new situations. (Tarshis, 1947, p. 54)

> The 'invisible hand' postulated by Adam Smith, in accordance with which the interest of society is promoted by each person seeking his own gain, is herein

revealed. But the result is not ideal. Although the pattern is reasonably coherent – wonderfully so in view of the complexity of our economy – it does not correspond perfectly, or even closely enough, to the pattern of our requirements. (Tarshis, 1947, p. 249)

The upshot of the analysis in this chapter and the preceding one is that unemployment can be cured. It is not something like an eclipse, which can be predicted but not stopped. We can either raise employment, or, in the absence of a better remedy, we can reduce the size of the labor force. Raising employment is not easy, and the task is made more difficult because of the man-made taboos which stand in the way. (Tarshis, 1947, p. 528)

It is often alleged that we cannot afford to relieve unemployment because it costs too much to do so. This charge is difficult to answer because it is hard to understand the sense in which the term *costs* is here used. But it is easy to understand that the costs of depression are immense and avoidable, and no economic sacrifice which incidentally makes us all better off is too great if it avoids those costs.

Our knowledge of how capitalism works shows us that we can prevent that suffering. And we have certainly found no reason to conclude that we have to scrap the system to do it. (Tarshis, 1947, p. 529)

If this analysis of employment and national income suggests anything, it should make clear the following points: that we can have prosperity; that we can get out of the deepest depression if we are willing to reason instead of following maxims that came to us from an economy as different from our own as it, in its turn, was from that of the Stone Age; and that we need to know more about our economy in order to refine our controls over it. (Tarshis, 1947, p. 577)

In Tarshis we even get a poem mocking those who favour a balanced budget:

> And now the budget's balanced
> Retrenchment is the hero
> On either side is entered
> A solitary Zero.
> (Tarshis, 1947, p. 518)

These quotations give a fair representation of Tarshis' views which could be characterized as 'committed liberal'. He certainly is not a foe of capitalism, but favours significant government intervention in order to make it operate effectively. Tarshis' position is not essentially different from that of prevailing 1990s ideology, but compared with the 1930s pro-market ideology that Buckley held, there were violations of what economics was.

THE BUCKLEY ATTACK: WAS IT JUSTIFIED?

Our initial interest in this topic derived from the Tarshis interview in which
he related the conservative reaction to his textbook and his feelings towards
Buckley. Reviewing Buckley's book discloses that he did not exhibit what
one would call objective fairness in his attack on Tarshis. In one instance he
did not even quote Tarshis correctly. However, despite the sloppy workmanship and Buckley's attempts to place Tarshis in a negative light, we found no
deliberate changing of meaning; it was more a matter of Buckley's shading
the meaning and a clash of their ideologies.

First, Buckley's book does not single out Tarshis. Tarshis' book is only one
of four that Buckley considers. In fact, Tarshis does not even receive the
harshest, or the most, criticism. In terms of long quotations cited by Buckley,
Tarshis' book receives only six, whereas the others received anywhere from six
to 15. Second, Buckley starts by explicitly stating that the authors of these texts
would not call themselves socialists and that they claim that they have in mind
strengthening the free enterprise system. He cites Tarshis as stating that 'the
pattern made by the individual flows from millions of firms in our economy is
one that broadly reflects our wants' (Buckley, 1951, pp. 49–50, quoting from
Tarshis, 1947, p. 239). He articulates his particular view of economics (quoted
above) and his belief that many alumni of Yale would agree with him. His
specifically stated purpose is to let alumni know what is being taught currently
and how at odds it is with what they believe. This informational purpose is
clearly acceptable, and in the general presentation Buckley does not present an
unfair picture of Tarshis' book. However, the devil is in the details, and in those
details Buckley shades the presentation to emphasize his points and does not
present a totally objective view. Consider two passages that Buckley cites and
contrast them with the actual text in Tarshis' work.

First, consider a quotation of Tarshis in which Buckley uses the most
ellipses:

> Does our economy provide the ideal output judging it by its correspondence with
> consumer's wants? ... We have developed ... reasons for thinking not[:] ... in-
> come inequality ... is as though we gave some people 100 votes, others 50, and
> still others only 1, and in addition, permitted some tampering with the ballot box.
> (Buckley, 1951, pp. 53, 54, quoting from Tarshis, 1947, p. 246)

The complete text from Tarshis with missing sections in italics, is:

> Does our economy provide the ideal output judging it by its correspondence with
> consumer's wants? *Do we produce automobiles, gloves, bread, and so on in
> approximately the correct proportions?* We have developed *two* reasons for think-
> ing not: income inequality *means that the total vote of buyers does not reflect their*

real requirements; and the components of our total output do not reflect our total vote (which does not reflect our total requirements) when the degree of monopoly varies from one industry to another. It is as though we gave some people 100 votes, others 50, and still others only 1, and in addition, permitted some tampering with the ballot box. *Would the list of successful candidates in such an election represent the real desires of the voters? It would be very strange if it did.* (Tarshis, 1947, p. 246)

In the last quotation there seems to be little substantive change in the quotation, nor was there in the others. However, in the next quotation, we believe that Tarshis has a legitimate concern. Buckley quotes Tarshis as follows:

The government may be said to exhaust its credit only if it is unable to borrow; and, as we have just seen, its ability to do so can never be seriously in question ... **The only question, then, is whether the government can always find a lender or someone who will accept government bonds. In the final analysis this is no problem, for the simple reason that the government controls the Federal Reserve Banks and can always compel them to buy government bonds ...** There is no sign that a high debt exhausts the credit of the government of the United States. And since as a last resource 'it can borrow from itself', there need be no fear on this account ... There are no grounds for believing that a high public debt destroys the nation's credit or leads to a marked fall in the value of the dollar. (Buckley, 1951, p. 69, quoting from Tarshis, 1947, pp. 535, 541)

The problem with this quotation is that it is incorrect. Specifically, the part of the quotation in bold is not to be found at all in Tarshis. In its place is the following:

The government can always find a buyer for its bonds – the Federal Reserve Banks if necessary. Indeed, our government has no difficulty in finding private individuals and institutions who are most eager to have government bonds. (Tarshis, 1947, p. 535. Italics here and below indicate material not quoted, but paraphrased, by Buckley in bold font above)

Tarshis continues the argument by stating that interest rates have fallen, which means that individuals have a desire to hold government bonds stronger than before, and concludes that discussion with the following:

It is possible that one day the government may be unable to sell its bonds to private individuals, commercial banks, and insurance companies. But to date its experience has been just the opposite. There is no sign that a high debt exhausts the credit of the government of the United States. And since as a last resource 'it can borrow from itself', there need be no fear on this account. (Tarshis, 1947, p. 541)

The last sentence of the quotation comes from the summary of the chapter. In that summary Tarshis reiterates his earlier argument. Buckley's quotation here is from a new paragraph and has no missing part, but it fails to include the remainder of the summary in which Tarshis qualifies his earlier expressed views about public debt.

The remainder of the summary which Buckley fails to quote is:

> There are no grounds for believing that a high public debt destroys the nation's credit or leads to a marked fall in the value of the dollar. Nonetheless, the existence of a high public debt is not a matter for indifference. It may, as we have seen, create deflation, a commodity with which our economy is already too well supplied. If so, the higher the debt, the greater is the importance of financing government expenditures suitably. When the debt is high, we must be especially insistent on maintaining the national income at the maximum. (Tarshis, 1947, p. 541)

Here is definitely a case of sloppy workmanship and misleading partial quotations on the part of Buckley. But, in our view, they do not significantly mischaracterize Tarshis' views. The misquote is a paraphrase, rather than a significant change of the meaning of the text. We suspect the cause of that misquote is that Buckley did not quote from the original source, but instead relied upon the already published polemical observations of Rose Wilder Lane, book reviewer and newsletter writer for the National Economic Committee.

Had Buckley been more careful in quoting and more fastidious in maintaining fairness, we believe it would not have significantly changed the view of Tarshis conveyed to the reader. His point is that the books under his attack build macroeconomics around Keynes, and that is what the books do, although, in doing so, they do not give alternative views equal representation. Buckley asks where Tarshis examines the views of Hayek and Mises. He states: 'For the rest, neither Morgan nor Tarshis nor Samuelson ever intimates that some reputable economists have read Keynes *and disagreed with him!*' (Buckley, 1951, p. 81, italics in original). The point Buckley makes – that the economics being taught to students in the post-World War II era was substantially different from the earlier economics – is correct. And it was different in both its microeconomic and macroeconomic spheres. The new economics was not just Keynesian macroeconomic theory and policy, but also a changed microeconomics that focused more on the imperfections in markets and the corollary of greater need for government involvement in the economy. Keynesian economics was not central to the complaints; Keynesian economics was simply part of the broader changing economics that Buckley documents.

In this sense Buckley does nothing wrong. He simply states that what he is doing is providing alumni with information about what is being taught at Yale and other schools, and the information he provides is, to a large degree, correct. Students were not being taught free market economics as they had been before, and in its place they were being taught a new economics which saw the necessity of government intervention in the market. This new economics was not regarded as an ideology by its proponents but as scientific. The old *laissez-faire* view was held by its advocates also as a sound conclusion which flowed from market activities. Both positions contain admixtures of positive and normative elements, and neither Tarshis nor Buckley attempt a balanced examination of opposing viewpoints.

The difficulties Tarshis' new economics encountered were fundamentally grounded in two pillars upon which the American higher education system rests: alumnus financing and freedom of ideas. All individuals and institutions must pay close attention to the preferences of their benefactors. Few will continue to give to those who espouse ideas and actions that conflict with those of donors. Generally, conflicts between colleges and donors are minimized, not because donors believe in freedom of ideas, but because of inertia. One could explain the failure of donors to follow carefully the activities of professors in a costly information model and/or as a principal–agent model: alumni and other donors do not carefully follow what is taught, and the information they receive is shaded by college administrators to put it in a favourable light. But, given the right conditions, a catalyst and focal point, these two can clash. The probability of clash was increased by the adverse business response to the New Deal and Franklin Roosevelt. Rose Wilder Lane provided the catalyst, and Tarshis' textbook, the focal point.

While Buckley did not present Tarshis' views in an objective manner, he did not significantly distort them. It was simply that Tarshis' views clashed so fundamentally with his individualistic ideology that he could not present them in a reasonable manner. It is also clear that Buckley's response was not simply an attack on Keynesianism. Both Tarshis and Keynesian economics were focal points for a broader reaction to changing ideologies that was occurring in the 1930s. Buckley's position is better termed 'anti-collectivist' than 'anti-Keynesian'. Keynesian economics was, for him, simply one aspect of collectivism and the loss of the advocacy of individualism in the teaching of economics.

WHY TARSHIS?

The result of the campaign by Lane, Buckley and others was the death of Tarshis' book. Samuelson's textbook (1948) did not die and became the prototype of future introductory economics books. Why did Tarshis not fare as well as Samuelson? There are a number of reasons why Tarshis' book received harsher treatment than did other books. When we asked Tarshis why

Samuelson's book did not get hit by the same phenomenon, he suggested that McGraw-Hill may have been more ready to back up a book than was Houghton Mifflin, which was then new to economics. According to Tarshis, Houghton Mifflin was small stuff compared with McGraw-Hill and was very conservative (Colander and Landreth, 1996, pp. 66, 69). Our view is that this reason was probably not that important; publishers generally want profits and will publish whatever books seem to offer them the largest expected profits.

A second reason is that Tarshis' book was the first introductory textbook in America to include the new economics. It was published in 1947, and the book that won out, Samuelson's, came out in only 1948. In war, it is axiomatic that the first lines in the battle get shot, but in doing so they pave the way for the second and third lines. That seems to have been the case here.

A third reason was that Tarshis was already 'suspect' due to his participation in the earlier political book, *An Economic Program for American Democracy* (Gilbert et al., 1938). If one was looking for a focal point, Tarshis' role in authoring that book made him a natural one. Samuelson's reputation was as a scientist, and he had played only a tangential role in the spreading of Keynesian policy views prior to the publication of his introductory textbook. Tarshis' perception of Samuelson was that in the 1930s, 'Paul Samuelson was not in the Keynesian group. He was busy working on his own thing. That he became a Keynesian was laughable' (Colander and Landreth, 1996, p. 64).

A fourth reason was that Tarshis' book had more Keynesian economics and was more deeply committed to the Keynesian view of policy than were the other introductory economics textbooks. Tarshis states:

> Book Four was macroeconomics. It was very much Keynes. That part was highly successful because it was unique, and even now I run into people who say, 'You know, you introduced me to Keynes, and I've never had a better understanding of Keynes than was given me by Book Four of your textbook.' (Colander and Landreth, 1996, p. 66)

A final reason was that Tarshis' book talked more about policy issues than did the other books, and it came to more conclusions. Samuelson's book presented the analysis with more detachment, more mathematically, than did Tarshis'. Tarshis put heart into the policy discussion in his book. It was a book of passion as well as of analysis. Samuelson's work appeared to be a book of dispassionate analysis.[1]

Modern textbooks followed Samuelson, eliminating the passion from their presentation, whereas possibly economics would have been better served if Tarshis' approach had been followed but supplemented with a passionate presentation of the other side. Policy fights in economics are in large part about ideological passions. To eliminate those is to make it a dry and far less meaningful subject.

In our view, the result of this episode was to sanitize economic textbooks from much of the controversy that makes economics exciting. It helped to create a formalization of what we teach students, and in doing so it has influenced the direction of economics away from the true policy debates which necessarily involve clashes of ideology, towards a discussion of make-believe policy fights centred around technical aspects of models – debates that do not arouse the passions that the real-world ideological debates arouse.

THE BROADER CONTEXT OF THE KEYNESIAN TEXTBOOK REVOLUTION

The clash of economic ideas during the discipline's long history reveals ideological components masked as objective analysis. Adam Smith's strong arguments against the mercantilists' view ushered in a period of economic ideas where the major focus was on the beneficial results which flow from unfettered market activities. Over time, in the footnotes, qualifications and heterodox literature, a growing body of views found imperfect workings in the microeconomic sector of the economy. Later developing economies produced an economic literature which found ample roles for government to promote economic growth and development. The clash between the German historical school and early Austrians over methodology was, in many ways, a preliminary to the ideological fights of the 1930s. So also the late 19th- and early 20th-century institutionalists argued against the basically harmonious reading of the economy rendered by Marshallians.

Many ironies came from these historical periods. The German historical school banished the marginalists from the academic temples, with consequences for German economic thought. Institutionalists were relegated to the underworld of academic institutions, but captured the powers of government during the first two terms of the Roosevelt Administration. The new economics of Keynesianism at the macroeconomic level, and Pigouvian-based welfare economics at the microeconomic level, could not capture the levers of government until the minds of the electorate had been convinced, and this required a new viewpoint in introductory textbooks. These changes in views in the textbooks are inevitably accompanied by ideological fights as to which side is being ideological.

If this episode tells us anything, it is that we should be very careful in examining our own ideological biases whenever we are challenging others about theirs.

NOTE

1. Samuelson, in answer to the question 'What kind of attacks did your book get and how did
    you deal with it?', responded that:

    > For some reason that I have no understanding of, the virulence of the attack on Tarshis
    > was of a higher order of magnitude than on my book, but there were plenty of attacks
    > on my book, and there was a lot of work done by people. Also I wrote carefully and
    > lawyer-like so that there were a lot of complaints that Samuelson was playing peek-a-
    > boo with the Commies. The whole thing was a sad scene that did not reflect well on
    > conservative business pressuring of colleges. (Colander and Landreth, 1996, p. 172)

8. Lorie Tarshis: Left-Wing Keynesian

Melvin W. Reder

I knew Lorie for a little over 40 years, 22 of them (1949–71) as a colleague at Stanford. For the better part of a decade (during the 1950s and 1960s) we co-authored a semi-annual report on the American economy for the London and Cambridge Economic Service (later taken over by the *Financial Times*), where I learned to appreciate both his expository skill and his perspective on economics. Despite differences of opinion on many issues, we remained good friends to the end of his life, though I am sure that on many occasions my views sorely tried his patience.

Lorie's interests were wide-ranging, covering art, literature, music and politics, as well as economics as conventionally defined. Over much of this, our intellectual contact was minimal, and what I shall say refers only to one aspect of his mind, although it is one that he regarded as very important.

Lorie was the exemplar *par excellence* of a now endangered intellectual species, the Left-Wing Keynesian. In providing an ostensive definition of this species, one cannot do better than to describe the relevant aspects of Lorie's mind and character.

I do not know whether Lorie's notion of the proper functions of an economist was formed at Cambridge, or whether his experience at Cambridge merely served to reinforce what he brought from Toronto, but in either case, the attitude he found at Cambridge towards the subject matter and functions of an economist dominated his performance throughout his professional life.

Although he did not scorn the journal-filling activities of most of his colleagues, Lorie felt strongly that the primary objective of economics was to supply tools for the improvement of the economy. Accordingly, he deplored the secular drift of teaching, especially of undergraduates, towards the cultivation of technical refinement at the expense of critical appreciation of the functioning of institutions and the formulation of public policy. In the same spirit, he preferred teaching undergraduates, especially those concerned with 'making a difference' in society, to the instruction of graduate students who were increasingly focused upon making a difference in the bibliographies of their prospective specialties.

True to his Cambridge background, Lorie felt that the proper objective of a university education in a social science, economics or otherwise, was to equip the student to understand and – most importantly – to improve the world. Improved tools were fine, but only if they contributed to this objective: otherwise what was their use? In the same vein, Lorie believed that a good textbook that aroused the interest and improved the comprehension of under-graduates was worth more than a comparable number of pages of journal articles that served only to keep the waters boiling in professorial pots.

Like the Cambridge dons he admired, the students Lorie prized most were bright undergraduates eager to make their mark in the real world, preferably in influencing economic policy or as politicians in their own right. Scholarly graduate students whose proximate goal was to transform syllabi were (much) less valued. While he respected the rights of students to view social policy according to their own lights, Lorie clearly preferred those who were guided by his light. He appreciated raw intellectual power irrespective of its pos-sessor, but he would make greater allowance for the failings of those having the right (i.e. Left) views than for comparable deficiencies of others.

For Tarshis and many others of his academic generation, the example *par excellence* of useful theory was the *General Theory*, and its author was the exemplar of the economist. But, beyond all but a few of that generation, Lorie was privileged to have been a (prominent) member of Keynes' seminar dur-ing the critical years of gestation and birth of the *General Theory*. His involvement with this intellectual event was reflected in his fascination with the details of the *Theory* and his lifelong efforts to expound its implications for policy and to urge their implementation.

Like Keynes and most Keynesians, Tarshis viewed the main function of economics as the provision of a set of policies that would enable the state to function satisfactorily. A necessary condition of such functioning is the uncoerced acceptance of the state's authority by a sufficiently large part of its citizens so as to ensure its peaceful continuation. Briefly, in a democracy this condition amounts to the ability of a government to get re-elected.

For Keynes, civil servant that he was, this condition was sufficient as well as necessary. He was not distinguished from contemporaries of his social class by intensity of concern for the plight of the economically disadvan-taged, but was content to go with the flow so long as mass unemployment did not assume a salience in the public mind sufficient to make its elimination an issue on which elections might turn.

When concern with unemployment became a major focus of political debate, Keynes realized that 'classical' economic theory was an impediment to the search for a sound policy. *Inter alia*, the *General Theory* (1936) was his attempt to provide a guide to the political establishment in formulating a policy that could 'solve the unemployment problem'. So long as it led to an expansion of effective demand, the details of such a policy were a secondary matter to Keynes. If political considerations dictated measures with egalitarian effects on income distribution, he would accept them, but he did not demand them. His only objection to curing unemployment by lowering the rate of interest through monetary policy was that it was inadequate to the task.

But to Lorie and many others of his generation, both in Britain and the US, it was otherwise. To them, mass unemployment was not simply a malfunction of an otherwise acceptable economic order, but merely one reflection of a social order that was unjust to the poor. The *General Theory* served not only as a much-needed revolution in economic theory, but as the rationale for broad social change whose primary objective was the reorganization of society to the advantage of the underprivileged.

For Keynes, the attainment of (nearly) full employment was a necessary condition for political stability; for Lorie and Left-Wing Keynesians generally, the process of attaining nearly full employment was an opportunity to transform the economy so as to provide economic security for all members of society, together with a fair sharing of the social product.

Though it is likely that his left-leaning followers exerted some influence on Keynes' views both on economics and social policy, it is uncertain how far this influence would have gone had World War II not intervened. However, Keynes' tract, *How to Pay for the War* (1940), provided a specific proposal to implement the social philosophy which the *General Theory* (1936) had only generally suggested. In a nutshell, Keynes proposed to pay for the war, in large part, by forced loans to be repaid at the discretion of the government as economic circumstances (mainly the state of effective demand and the danger of inflation) permitted. If implemented, this would have put control of aggregate expenditure in the hands of the government for an indefinite period of time, leaving it free to engage in such expenditures and measures of redistribution as its view of the public interest directed.

In effect, willy-nilly, Keynes had come to propose the virtual socialization of saving and investment for an indefinite period as a by-product of war finance. But for his left-wing followers, what he proposed on account of the war was what should have been done in any event. That implementing the proposed scheme would probably have entailed the substantial use of direct controls on wages and product prices did not disturb them greatly.

Left-Wing Keynesians did not equate freedom of contract with personal freedom, and their doubts about the feasibility of administering direct controls were – in the 1940s and 50s – far less than what they might have entertained later. Nevertheless, the continuing predilection of Left-Wing Keynesians to venture out along the inflation–unemployment trade-off is related to their willingness to risk having to resort to 'temporary' wage–price controls to curb open inflation in the event of miscalculation.

Lorie, for one, was always eager for news of seemingly new policy gimmicks to avert what he considered to be socially undesirable consequences of market processes. As might be expected, he disbelieved in 'rational expectations' and had a greater aversion to policies that reflected that doctrine. For him, violations of Pareto-optimality were never an important consideration in judging economic policy: he felt that the main consequence of concern with Pareto-optimality was to make 'the best the enemy of the good'.

In a sense, sharply demarcating Left-Wing Keynesians from other Keynesians is to create a breach in what should, in some contexts, be considered a continuum. Yet there is a big difference in the mind-set of someone like Lorie from that of Keynes or of 'practically minded' Keynesians generally. Lorie's views on policy were driven by a concern for the plight of the underprivileged, without regard to national boundaries.[1] Though not a socialist, he was perfectly willing to accept socialism when and where he felt it necessary to achieve his broader social objectives, among which distributional equity was primary.[2] Important though he considered it, to Lorie curing unemployment was ancillary to improving distributional equity.

In short, Lorie was a man of the Left. The Keynesian element in his ideology derived from his belief that distributional equity – loosely, 'social justice' – could best be promoted by appropriately directed intervention of the state in market processes and that economics, properly taught, provided an essential means of such direction. While unemployment and war reduced the resistance to the required institutional changes, and thus provided favourable opportunities for making them, these changes had to be made in any case.

Keynesians of all shades share a belief in the competence of the state to make desired changes in the structure and functioning of the economy, and in the essential role of properly trained economists and other social scientists in effecting them. However, many Keynesians are not deeply committed as to the kinds of change they propose to effect. Within limits they are willing to serve as instruments of those with political power.

To borrow a metaphor of Keynes, such Keynesians aspire only to be honest and competent dentists who are willing to serve purposes that they do not form. But such Keynesians shade into senior civil servants, British and American, who aspire to serve but also to guide – and occasionally to manipulate – politicians who do not understand the full implications – especially economic – of the actions they propose to take. In varying degree, such civil servants have agendas of their own, which they try to promote as best they can. These, in turn, shade into left-wingers like Lorie, whose deep ideological commitments forever keep them nibbling at the fringes of authority and blurring the distinction between administration and policy-making.

To Lorie such a role was the noblest, and the most enjoyable, to which an economist could aspire. To those who did not share his moral vision, or doubted the competence of economists to aid in its implementation, the presumptions of such a role were elitist and subversive of the authority of democratically elected officials.

To such negative thoughts, Lorie gave short shrift. His ability to do this gave him the peace of mind and serenity that made his company such a pleasure, and his passing such a loss.

NOTES

1. Although Lorie was very outspoken in his concern for the welfare of Third World persons, I cannot recall discussing immigration policy with him.
2. Although I cannot recall discussing John Rawls' *Theory of Justice* (1971) with him, a reader would not be far wrong if he/she thought of Lorie as an enthusiastic adherent of Rawls' ideas on this subject.

PART III

Introductory extracts: 'World economy in crisis: unemployment, inflation and international debt'

Lorie Tarshis

The recommendations made here for dealing with this obdurate problem of stagflation and for tackling one aspect of the problem of international debt have rested upon a view of how the economy functions that is substantially different from that held by most official economists in the English-speaking world. These economists blame overspending and extravagance, especially in the public sector, and the heavy hand of the government with its stifling effect on enterprise, and a lack of discipline in the monetary sector for all these difficulties. If the economy possessed those self-stabilizing-at-full-employment features that had been the hallmark of the classical model (which seems unlikely), their views about causes and remedies would be absolutely consistent with that model. As for the problem of international debt, again the extravagance and the living-beyond-their-means of the developing countries are seen in this official view as the basic cause and sin, once again made possible by the lack of discipline of the financial sector. And for them punishment is the only cure for such sins, and it should consist in a daily dose of austerity, pulling-in-the-belt and sackcloth and ashes.

A line from William Blake's *The Marriage of Heaven and Hell* has far more validity as a general prescription: 'Damn Braces: Bless Relaxes'. Overspending is not the enemy; underspending is. An effort to improve the quality of life is not a social vice; practicing the habits of the miser is. Though this is not economics, at least it does a better job of establishing the atmosphere in which treatment can be designed.

Tarshis, 1984, 'Summary', pp. 138–9

In many years of teaching part of the graduate course in macroeconomics at Stanford University, I relied heavily on *The General Theory of Employment, Interest and Money* by John Maynard Keynes as my starting point. On the whole I found a good chunk of what came to be identified as 'Modern

Keynesian Economics' reasonably satisfactory in its treatment of Keynes's views on aggregate demand.

But it omitted one feature that I regarded as critical, though when policy issues had to be resolved in those years of comparative calm – from 1946 to 1966 – this omission hardly mattered. Keynes in his summary stated: 'Hence the volume of employment in equilibrium depends on (i) the aggregate supply function 0, (ii) the propensity to consume x, and (iii) the volume of investment D_2. This is the essence of the General Theory of Employment' ... However, its omission from theory had serious consequences later, especially after stagflation became a problem.

This explanation for stagflation and useful leads on how to cope with it can be derived from Keynes's theory brought up-to-date and, for a change, making full use of the ASF.

Tarshis, 1984, 'Appendix', p. 152.

9. Another Canadian Keynesian: W.A. Mackintosh

David McQueen[1]

As a former graduate student and personal acquaintance of William Mackintosh, I have been asked to write something about him for this collection, and to relate his work to that of some other prominent Canadian proselytizers of Keynesian ideas, such as Lorie Tarshis. Scouring memory, no doubt imperfectly, for this purpose, has been at once a pleasant and thought-provoking task, with even some contemporary relevance.

The result, however, can in no sense purport to be a stand-alone piece. Those who would seriously know more about Mackintosh and his place in the evolution of Canadian economic studies and policy must at all costs consult other writings, three in particular: Mackintosh's landmark study for the Rowell–Sirois Commission, *The Economic Background of Dominion–Provincial Relations* (1940); his published address, 'The White Paper on Employment and Income in its 1945 Setting' (1966); and the relevant passages of Jack Granatstein's book, *The Ottawa Men* (1982).[2] All that I shall attempt to provide is some extra icing on that triple-layered cake.

Very briefly, Macintosh, a Queen's University man to the core, not to mention a sometime Queen's Principal (1951–61), was generally regarded as one of the two most prominent figures in the original Canadian 'staples' school of economic history, as it flourished in the 1920s, 1930s and 1940s. The other figure was, of course, that very different personality, Toronto's Harold Innis. (My first-hand knowledge of him was only sporadic, but since one of my leading secondary sources was the teaching and conversation of the late Tom Easterbrook, who knew him well, I shall in due course hazard a couple of Innis/Mackintosh comparisons.)

In addition to his historical work, Mackintosh was best known for his grasp of the essentials of the Keynesian, macro approach to matters both domestic and international, and for his contributions to the making of Canadian economic policy during and after World War II. During the war, he served full time in Ottawa; afterwards, he returned to Queen's, but continued to consult frequently in Ottawa.

In the 1930s and 1940s, both the economics profession and the volume of serious economics publications were orders of magnitude smaller than they have since become. Consequently, it was much easier then for an economist to keep in touch with a wide range of people and ideas within the discipline. It may safely be presumed that Mackintosh knew, or at least knew of, virtually all the most prominent figures involved in bringing Keynesian ideas to North America.

It seems to me probable, however, that in addition to Keynes himself (see below), three figures in particular must have played a major role in turning pragmatically inclined Mackintosh into an important, if somewhat qualified, Keynesian. These were Robert Bryce, Wynne Plumptre and Louis Rasminsky. All were plunged, like Mackintosh, into the intellectual crucible of wartime economic management and post-war planning, and all worked with him frequently and intensively. Bryce and Plumptre had been students of Keynes at Cambridge. Rasminsky had not, but was well grounded in Keynesian thought, in part through his League of Nations work with James Meade.

The intellectual connection between Mackintosh and Lorie Tarshis is harder to evaluate. It is virtually 100 per cent certain that they knew *of* each other – that, for example, Mackintosh would have been acquainted with Tarshis' seminal articles on real and money wages (1938, 1939), and with his textbook, *The Elements of Economics* (1947). Similarly, Tarshis would certainly have been aware of Mackintosh's authorship of the Government of Canada *White Paper on Employment and Income* (1945). It is highly likely also that the two men must actually have met on occasion – for example, during Mackintosh's 1934–35 sabbatical, much of which he spent in the United Kingdom at a time when Tarshis was still at Cambridge. Lacking in the records, however, is any period of overlap between the two as prolonged and intense as those with Bryce, Plumptre and Rasminsky.[3]

But let me now focus more specifically on Mackintosh himself. It is essential to view him in the broader context of his times, which were in certain respects very different from our own. What, I wonder, would a youngish observer, strongly attuned to the predominant themes of 1990s economic policy debate, have made of the Canadian economic scene in 1947–48, when I was Mackintosh's student? For example, having run the net national debt up to well over 100 per cent of gross domestic product during the war, the federal government had recently instituted a system of universal family allowances and also offered a comprehensive package of veterans' benefits. The latter comprised such things as free university education, including living expenses, for all ex-service people who wanted it, as thousands did.

How were such things conceivable, let alone affordable, in the much smaller, lower-living-standard Canadian economy of the day? An ample literature, well worth re-examining for its enlargement of perspective on contemporary problems, is available to answer that question in detail.[4] But part of the explanation is to be found more generally, in the profound influence on both public and professional opinion of two enormous, recent events: the Great Depression and the war. How much we still lived in their shadow! How powerfully they shaped our priorities!

It seemed abundantly clear, for reasons political and social, as well as economic, that the Depression must not be repeated. For one thing, it could now be perceived, more clearly than ever, to have been a major cause of the war. Hitler had become Chancellor on a wave of mass unemployment; Japan had sought the Greater East Asia Co-Prosperity Sphere as a solution to grave economic difficulties in a world of depression and high trade barriers.

But the war, for its part, through its extraordinary transforming action on the Canadian economy, had demonstrated, not just to economists but to nearly everyone, that the Depression, or at any rate its length and depth, had been unnecessary. 'If we can make jobs and prosperity in wartime, why can't we in peacetime?', it was widely and sometimes angrily asked. Among those who, as teenagers and/or adults, had lived through the dramatic economic transition from the 1930s to the 1940s, support for government interventionism, though short of unanimous, was perhaps at an all-time high, and doctrines of the ultimate powerlessness of fiscal policy would have had a very poor sale.

Thus sheer force of circumstance made the times uniquely propitious for the adoption, both nationally and internationally, of Keynesian ideas. This does not mean, however, that the conversion to Keynes among Canadian economists came in all cases quickly and easily. Mackintosh, for one, did not find it at all easy, and even then rejected ' ... the detailed dogmatism of the Keynesians of the stricter sort' (Granatstein, 1982, p. 168; Mackintosh, 1966, p. 144). Backed by an intellectual inheritance of Scots pragmatism, his interest focused rather on a number of Keynes' central propositions which he came to believe could be conceived and propagated as plain common sense – and which, further, could be adapted and implemented in a form suitable to a very open economy and a federal state.

What I think did much to move Mackintosh a long way towards Keynes was the manifest usefulness, for purposes of the wartime economic management and post-war planning in which he was so intimately involved, of the Keynesian macro policy apparatus, including notably the new national accounts, primitive though these still were. To be sure, once the conflict was fully engaged, wartime applied Keynesianism went into reverse thrust, coping with shortage rather than superfluity of resources. But the power of the engine in reverse seemed further to confirm its peacetime potentialities in both forward and reverse.

In this connection, a key event for Mackintosh was the last day of the 1942 Commonwealth Economic Conference in London. On that day, under Keynes'

Chairmanship, the new scheme of national accounts for the United Kingdom devised by James Meade and Richard Stone was presented to the delegates. Mackintosh was deeply impressed, and on his return to Ottawa joined with others in pushing successfully to obtain for Canada this quantum improvement in macroeconomic measurement.

At this point, by way of background for a glimpse of Mackintosh as teacher, let me sketch in the Queen's University graduate programme in economics as of 1947–48. The total enrolment consisted of David Slater, Bob Thompson and myself, all MA aspirants. Access to professors was obviously no problem, and each of us possessed that invaluable browser's passport (a more powerful force for serendipity, in my opinion, than anything the computer age has yet thrown up), a library stack permit.

There were two required courses: 'Public Finance' and Mackintosh's 'Problems of the Canadian Economy'. Otherwise, we did 'Directed Special Studies' under our thesis supervisors, in my case Frank Knox, who could not have been a better guide to Brown's *International Gold Standard Reinterpreted* (1940) and other works bearing on world trade and payments in the inter-war period. Among our preoccupations were such enduringly relevant sub-topics as hot money, exchange speculation, over-leveraging and bank failures.

My only criticism of the total programme, and that a retrospective one, was the absence of a course in mathematics and statistics for economists, which we really needed more than public finance; but just how much more mathematical a direction economics was about to take was not at that time clear.

For our course with Mackintosh, we foregathered in a small basement room in Kingston Hall. Chain-smoking through a long, filtered, Franklin Roosevelt-type cigarette holder, Mackintosh spoke slowly and thoughtfully, especially when answering questions. Longish pauses were not unusual, and one waited anxiously to see whether these would be followed with just an answer, or with an answer preceded by a careful reformulation of a badly posed question.[5]

There was, naturally, a fair content of Canadian economic history, with a particularly good empathy, it seemed to me as a westerner, for that part of Canada which, more than any other, had experienced many of the features of life in a 'globalized' economy generations before that term would come into popular use.[6]

Inevitably, however, the most stimulating parts of the course bore on more recent macroeconomic developments. It is difficult to convey the degree of excitement that we felt, so peculiar was it to that moment in history. Never had economics seemed so relevant, so linked to huge, world-altering events. A new international economy was a-borning, and a new set of analytical and policy tools stood ready to assist in its birth and upbringing. And here, talking to us, was someone who had been at the centre of it all, who had debated with

Keynes, who had been present with Louis Rasminsky and other Canadians at the creation of Bretton Woods, and who had drafted virtually all of the *White Paper on Employment and Income* and much of the subsequent Green Paper proposals for presentation to the provinces.

Some might well have envisaged such a course as little more than a pastiche of anecdotes, recounted in a phase of post-war rest and recuperation. It was anything but that. Anecdotes there certainly were, but they fitted. Each session had its theme and structure. I had the impression that the course was almost as helpful to Mackintosh himself as to us, inasmuch as he seemed to be still in a process of struggling to make sense of, and fashion into academically respectable form, a mass of often highly intense experience. It was almost as though there were, had perhaps always been, two Mackintoshs: one a man of action and the other a dispassionate observer, looking critically over the first one's shoulder.

As for Mackintosh compared with Innis, two contrasts in particular occur to me. First, if Mackintosh, like Innis, had ever specifically addressed the problems of the North American pulp and paper industry, he would, I imagine, have turned out a solid, eminently readable, thoroughly researched industry study, well situated in its more immediate historical context.

What he would not have done, but what Innis did in *Empire and Communications* (1950), was to treat the industry as an intellectual launching pad into a high-orbit consideration (couched in convoluted prose making heavy demands on the reader) of the larger significance of changing means of storing and communicating knowledge down through the last several millennia. Thus came Marshall McLuhan and all that followed. The most important single thing about Innis was his extraordinary range of vision.

On the other hand, of course, Innis could never conceivably have written the *White Paper on Employment* (Government of Canada, 1945).

This leads to a second contrast, concerning the relationship between economists and government. Innis was deeply worried that the relationship was becoming too close for the good of either academe or democratic government.[7] In general, Innis had a profound mistrust of all manner of higher authority – mistrust considerably reinforced by an experience of soldiering in the trenches under World War I generalship, and also perhaps by postgraduate studies in the Economics Department of the University of Chicago, with its tradition of maintaining careful distance in advisory and other intellectual relationships with government.[8] Innis did not refuse all such contacts; for example, he testified before more than one Royal Commission. But he certainly maintained plenty of distance from the active policy-makers and wished other academics would do the same.

Mackintosh, raised in the very different Queen's University traditions, was of course deeply immersed in government policy matters, especially during

World War II, but also before and after. His close relationship with Deputy Finance Minister, Clifford Clark, his reasoning capacities and his legendary rapid-drafting skills made him a frequent 'holder of the pen', and in these and other ways, one of the most influential mandarins in wartime Ottawa, as well as an influential consultant thereafter.

Yet this involvement in the corridors of power never seemed to cost him any significant loss of prestige in the Canadian academic community as a whole; nor did he exhibit any symptoms of that too-common Ottawa malady whereby the economist, little by little, evolves into an apologist and justifier for the ideas of ministers and others further up the hierarchy. What kept him safe, I think, was that remarkable ability, mentioned earlier, to be at once a man of action and a critical self-observer.

In his course with us, Mackintosh never romanticized government. All the usual villains were present in the script: the raving ideologues, the fickle sycophants, the more ward-heeling sorts of politicians, and the stick-in-the-mud and turf-warring bureaucrats of an older school.

He did, however, go so far as to intimate that sometimes the politicians were right and the experts wrong. He told of an afternoon at Bretton Woods when, after a particularly masterful intervention by Keynes, US Treasury Secretary Vinson remarked, in a strong southern accent, 'Well Lord Keynes, it may be as you say, but down where I come from folks just don't think that way'. We dutifully chuckled at this juxtaposition of Cambridge brilliance and Georgia crackerdom, but Mackintosh was at pains to add that possibly Vinson was right. If enough folks (say, in Quebec) really *did* think 'that way', and would not be talked out of it, that was data which the responsible policy adviser ought to take into account. While he admired Keynes enormously, he believed that he was sometimes too clever for the good of his cause, and a much better expositor than persuader (Mackintosh, 1966, p. 14).

I last saw Mackintosh in the summer of 1969, during a sunny noon hour on the Sparks Street Mall in Ottawa. Well into his 70s by then, he was in Ottawa for a meeting of the Bank of Canada Executive Committee, under the Chairmanship of his long-time associate, Governor Rasminsky. He hailed me and promptly launched us into a discussion of the Economic Council's recently released *Interim Report on Competition Policy* (1969), of which I had sent him a copy. I protested that I had never meant him to slog through all of that public service prose; I just thought that, as a former member of the 1950–52 MacQuarrie Committee on competition law reform, he might be interested in some of the Council's ultimate conclusions. No, no, he had read it all, and he was particularly intrigued by the recommendation to put merger and monopoly on a civil law basis. Did I know that the MacQuarrie Committee had been on the verge of recommending the same thing, but had been deterred at the last minute by a seemingly adverse constitutional decision in the Supreme Court on a related matter?

We parted cheerfully. A cynic might well ask how much we had to be cheerful about. From MacQuarrie to Economic Council had been 17 years, and yet another 17 were to elapse before civil merger and monopoly law finally made it into the statute book. As to the Government of Canada *White Paper of 1945*, while successive federal governments felt constrained, until the 1970s, to pay some general regard to its objective of high and stable employment (in which they were much assisted by the Cold War), its undertakings regarding discretionary fiscal policy were never systematically honoured (Gordon, 1966; Wolfe, 1978). The political and bureaucratic rejection of Mackintosh's long-standing ideas (in their origins, pre-Keynesian) about the strategic management of public investment was also a disappointment for him.[9]

Yet we were cheerful. Perhaps we were buoyed by a certain feeling of intergenerational continuity, and by a faith that for all Ottawa's tendency to reject good ideas on various short-term pretexts, they sometimes lived on, under the surfaces like Columbian ground squirrels, to re-emerge eventually in politically more propitious weather.

NOTES

1. I am indebted to David Slater for valuable memory reinforcement and to my Glendon College history colleague, Michiel Horn, for guidance to additional sources.
2. See also Ferguson (1993) and Owram (1986).
3. For what it is worth, in my own quite numerous conversations with Tarshis at Glendon College, I do not recall his making more than very sporadic and passing references to Mackintosh.
4. A good place to start is the text and select bibliography of Bothwell, Drummond and English (1981).
5. I must not make Mackintosh sound too solemn; wit kept breaking through. Once I was unthinking enough to write in an essay, 'United States price control was partly emasculated in 1947'. Back came a pencilled note in the margin, 'Not a question of degree'. My favourite Mackintoshism, however, turned up years later in the course of research into an ancient academic appointment. A letter from Mackintosh in the file said of one potential candidate: 'He is Oxford and Balliol, but has recovered'.
6. For information on Mackintosh's work on the west and on the part of his career spent there, see Ferguson, 1993, pp. 195–209.
7. See Owram, 1986, pp. 166–7 and 268–72.
8. The late Harry Johnson, long a distinguished Canadian member of the Chicago faculty, would perhaps have agreed with Innis on this, if on little else. In conversations I had with Johnson over the years, he seemed to make clear his opinion that economists in governments, if not quite oxymorons, were, with few exceptions, suspect and likely to be self-classified second-raters.
9. See Mackintosh, 1966, p. 20. The standard Ottawa story about this in the 1950s and 1960s was that even in strong boom conditions, vote-hungry politicians would never allow attractive investment projects to be strategically delayed – 'kept on the shelf' – in the interests of

economic stabilization. What was certainly true in the early post-war period was that urban and other growth so exceeded general expectations (bearing out an earlier prediction of C.D. Howe's; see Slater, 1995) that many technically necessary infrastructure supports had to be accelerated rather than delayed.

10. Keynes, Tarshis, real and money wages, and employment[1]

Robert W. Dimand

Lorie Tarshis' careful examination of changes in real and money wages in Britain and the United States (Tarshis, 1938, 1939), together with research by John Dunlop, caused John Maynard Keynes (1939) to draw back from the account of money wages, real wages and employment presented in Chapter 2 of the *General Theory*. Lorie's articles display his firm grounding in empirical data and his deep, sympathetic, but not uncritical grasp of the economics of Keynes, developed in four years of attending Keynes' lectures and Political Economy Club while Keynes was writing the *General Theory* (see Rymes, 1987, 1989 for Tarshis' notes on Keynes' lectures). In Chapter 2, Keynes presented a model of wages and employment that challenged the 'classical' economics of Pigou's *Theory of Unemployment* (1933) on its own ground, accepting the first of what Keynes termed the two classical postulates, but rejecting the second and the classical conclusion that, in theory, money wage cuts could eliminate unemployment. Within two or three years of the *General Theory*, Tarshis and Dunlop published studies of real and money wage movements over the business cycle that cast doubt on the first classical postulate and hence on Keynes' Chapter 2 model. The resulting controversy over real wages and employment continues unabated to this day (as surveyed by Abraham and Haltiwanger, 1995), but its sources are not well remembered (so that the earliest empirical reservations about counter-cyclical real wages mentioned by Abraham and Haltiwanger (1995) were by Ronald Bodkin (1969)).

MR KEYNES AND SOME 'CLASSICS'

Keynes argued that what he termed the 'classical theory of employment' (as presented in Pigou, 1933) was 'based on two fundamental postulates ... I. The wage is equal to the marginal product of labour. II. The utility of the wage when a given volume of labour is employed is equal to the marginal disutility of that amount of employment' (Keynes, 1936, p. 5).

The first postulate, subject to 'qualification ... in accordance with certain principles, if competition and markets are imperfect', holds when competitive firms employ the amount of labour that will maximize their profits (in the more general case where markets need not be perfectly competitive, equating marginal revenue product to marginal factor cost). Similarly, a worker maximizing his or her total utility from income and leisure would supply labour until the marginal disutility of labour equalled the utility of the wage received for the last unit of labour. Leaping the assorted pitfalls of aggregation and assuming that aggregate labour demand and supply curves exist, the first postulate is equivalent to the economy being on the labour demand curve and the second to the economy being on the labour supply curve:

> [T]he volume of employed resources is duly determined, according to the classical theory, by the two postulates. The first gives us the demand schedule for employment, the second gives us the supply schedule; and the amount of employment is fixed at the point where the utility of the marginal product balances the disutility of the marginal employment. (Keynes, 1936, p. 6)

Under the two classical postulates, demand for labour would equal the supply of labour, and there would be no involuntary unemployment.

Keynes (1936, p. 6) allowed for frictional unemployment under the classical postulates, as adjustment to unforeseen changes would not be instantaneous. Any unemployment beyond such frictional unemployment, would, in a classical world, be voluntary, 'due to an open or tacit agreement among workers not to work for less, and that if labour as a whole would agree to a reduction of money-wages more employment would be forthcoming' (Keynes, 1936, p. 8).

Such views were held by leading authorities of the day, more generally than just in *The Theory of Unemployment* (1933) by Professor Pigou, Keynes' colleague at King's College. Pigou (1927b) had drawn on Jacques Rueff's empirical work (1979) to attribute higher unemployment since the war to 'maintenance of wages at too high a level'. Professor Henry Clay of the University of Manchester argued in his Presidential Address to Section F of the British Association for the Advancement of Science at its meeting in South Africa (Clay, 1929) that

> It would appear ... that wage-fixing authorities, acting independently of one another and disregarding the general economic situation, are maintaining wage-rates at a level at which existing industries cannot provide full employment. ... We have interfered with the harsh but effective correctives of wage-demands that restrict employment, namely, the loss of income by unemployment and the expansion of employment where wages are not held up. Either, therefore, we must devise alternative correctives, or we must expect unemployment on a large scale from this cause alone. (Quoted in Beveridge, 1930, pp. 360–61)[2]

T.W. Hutchison (1978) has shown that Pigou did not draw the policy conclusion of wage-cutting as a remedy for unemployment that Keynes thought Pigou's theory implied (cf. Keynes, 1936, p. 20n; 1973, p. 259), but Edwin Cannan, Professor Emeritus at the London School of Economics, did just that in his Presidential Address to the Royal Economic Society (1932), reprinted as the chapter on unemployment in his *Economic Scares* (1933):

> general unemployment is in reality to be explained almost in the same way as particular unemployment. ... General unemployment appears when asking too much is a general phenomenon. ... So-called 'fixed interest' should be allowed to be eaten away by defaults and stoppages without too much attention being given to the injustices involved. Money-wages and salaries should be allowed to be reduced without resistance to the reductions being backed by the state and public opinion. (Cannan, 1932, pp. 366–7, 370)

Pigou (1927b), Clay (1929) and Cannan (1932) all appeared in the *Economic Journal* and would have been read by the journal's editor, Keynes. Pigou (1933) was, as Keynes noted, the only detailed, full-scale presentation of that theory of unemployment, but Keynes encountered shorter accounts in other prominent places such as presidential addresses.

Keynes offered

> two objections to the second postulate of the classical theory ... A fall in real wages due to a rise in prices, with money-wages unaltered, does not, as a rule, cause the supply of available labour on offer at the current wage to fall below the amount actually employed prior to the rise of prices...

and,

> more fundamental ... There may exist no expedient by which labour as a whole can reduce its *real* wage to a given figure by making revised *money* bargains with the entrepreneurs. (Keynes, 1936, p. 13)

given the endogeneity of prices. The economy thus might not be on the supply schedule for labour, given by the second postulate.

However:

> In emphasising our point of departure from the classical system, we must not overlook an important point of agreement. For we shall maintain the first postulate as heretofore, subject only to the same qualifications as in the classical theory ... I am not disputing this vital fact which the classical economists have (rightly) asserted as indefeasible. In a given state of organisation, equipment and technique, the real wage earned by a unit of labour has a unique (inverse) correlation with the volume of employment. (Keynes, 1936, p. 17)

The working-out of the formal implications of Keynes' acceptance of the first classical postulate led Keynes' Chapter 20, 'The Employment Function', to parallel the analysis of Chapters 9 and 10 of Part II of Pigou (1933) (see Brady, 1994). In Chapter 2, 'The Postulates of the Classical Economics', this acceptance led to a view of economic fluctuations according to which, given technology and the capital stock, the economy moved up and down the labour demand schedule, while being in general off the labour supply schedule.

Keynes remarked that

> It would be interesting to see the results of a statistical enquiry into the actual relationship between changes in money-wages and changes in real wages ... in the case of changes in the general level of wages, it will be found, I think, that the change in real wages associated with a change in money-wages, so far from being usually in the same direction, is almost always in the opposite direction. ... This is because, in the short period, falling money-wages and rising real wages are each, for independent reasons, likely to accompany decreasing employment; labour being readier to accept wage-cuts when employment is falling off, yet real wages inevitably rising in the same circumstances on account of the increasing marginal return to a given capital equipment when output is diminished. (Keynes, 1936, pp. 9–10)

– that is, because of the first classical postulate and the rising marginal physical product of labour with decreasing employment and output and a given stock of capital equipment. The statistical analysis that Keynes thought would be interesting was soon forthcoming, notably from Lorie Tarshis and John Dunlop, and the results were not what Keynes had expected.

REAL WAGES IN THE UNITED STATES AND GREAT BRITAIN

Keynes first presented his account of the two classical postulates on 16 October 1933, in his Michaelmas Term lecture series on 'The Monetary Theory of Production'. As shown by surviving lecture notes taken by Lorie Tarshis, Robert Bryce, Marvin Fallgatter and Walter Salant (transcribed in Rymes, 1987 and synthesized in Rymes, 1989), Chapter 2 of the *General Theory* was an expanded version of Keynes' lectures of 16 and 23 October 1933, with the lectures containing the two classical postulates, a definition of involuntary unemployment and the invocation (repeated on page 9 of the *General Theory*) of the United States in 1932 as an example where unemployment could not be plausibly attributed to resistance to money wage cuts or excessive real wage demands, given the sharp drop in money wage rates. Lorie Tarshis thus heard Keynes' earliest public denial of the positive correlation between real and money wages: his notes on Keynes' lectures the previous year reveal no comparable treatment of the labour market.

Having attended Keynes' lectures at Cambridge in four Michaelmas Terms (1932–35) and participated in Keynes' Political Economy Club, Tarshis began that statistical analysis that Keynes had predicted would be so interesting. His first study, on 'Real Wages in the United States and Great Britain' (1938), although its existence was noted by Keynes (1939, p. 394n), received little attention in the ensuing debate. This reflected its isolation on an academic periphery: although Tarshis then taught at Tufts, the paper was presented to the Canadian Political Science Association (then including economics) and published in the *Canadian Journal of Economics and Political Science*, along with a discussion by Robert Bryce, who had also gone from the University of Toronto to Keynes' lectures (1932–34) and the Political Economy Club.

Tarshis (1938) constructed and graphed monthly series for average nominal and real hourly earnings for 89 manufacturing and 14 non-manufacturing industries in the United States from apparently January 1932 to January 1938. Adequate data on earnings and hours of work before 1932 were not available. Tarshis contrasted the series he constructed, showing a rise of nearly 20 per cent in United States real hourly earnings over the sample period, with an existing index of the purchasing power of weekly earnings in Britain, which showed a decline of 4 or 5 per cent. Given Ministry of Labour survey evidence of an increase in overtime, real hourly earnings in Britain would have declined even more than real weekly earnings. Output increased in both countries over the period. Both countries had experienced technical progress raising output per worker, offsetting the higher prices of imported wage-goods. Some of the American increase in real wages could be attributed to the minimum wage provisions of the National Industrial Recovery Act and to the spread of more militant trade unionism associated with the Congress of Industrial Organizations (CIO), but Tarshis felt that this could explain only part of the difference between the two national series.

After allowing for these factors, a striking discrepancy remained:

> changes in the volume of production of American industry probably had no great significance for the level of real wages. It should be noted that the two substantial rises in real wages [late 1933 and 1937] occurred in periods when output was also increasing rapidly. For Great Britain, on the other hand, it would appear that part of the decline in real wages is to be associated with expansion in output. (Tarshis, 1938, p. 372)

> [S]tatistical data suggest that, at least over the range of output ruling in the period studied, diminishing returns to increasing employment did not play any part in the United States (Tarshis, 1938, p. 367).

When most of the firms in the economy are producing close to capacity, it would ... be reasonable to expect real wages to decline with an expansion of output ... But it could hardly be supposed that in either of these countries the volume of production was close to capacity levels for most of the time. But what are the shapes of the marginal cost curves when firms in general are producing on a scale moderately below capacity? (Tarshis, 1938, p. 371)

wrote Tarshis. Looking at data for ten American industries, he concluded that output per person-hour rose, and average labour cost fell, with rising output in almost every case. From these results followed an econometrically infor-mal transition to a very tentative conclusion that marginal costs rose with increasing output in some industries but fell in others, with no overall pattern: 'Free-hand curves were drawn to fit the data as closely as possible and marginal costs were calculated from these rough curves, relating output per man-hour and output' (Tarshis, 1938, p. 371).

CHANGES IN REAL AND MONEY WAGES

John Dunlop (1938, pp. 414, 420), then at Cambridge before spending his career at Harvard in the other Cambridge, found that annual data for Britain from 1860 to 1937 (excluding 1913–19) compiled by G. H. Wood (e.g. 1910) and A. L. Bowley (e.g. 1920) showed that real wage rates and money wage rates tended to increase together (real wage rates rose in 17 of the 25 years of rising money wage rates between 1860 and 1913, fell in five, and were un-changed in three, as well as rising in all six post-war years of rising money wages), but that real wages fell or rose equally often when money wages fell (real wage rates rose in five of 13 years of falling money wages 1860–1913, fell in six and were unchanged in two). He added in a footnote that 'Similar calculations have been made for New Zealand, Australia, Sweden, France, and Germany – without corrections for the **terms** of trade – and these results seem to be confirmed' (Dunlop, 1938, p. 421n), but these calculations were not published. Furthermore, using Dorothy S. Thomas' (1926) dating of British business cycles, British real wages appeared to increase with money wages during the peak years of most booms: both real and money wages rose in each of seven upswings between 1860 and 1913. Even after adjusting for the trend in real wages 1860–1900, real wages rose in four of the five upswings in that period (Dunlop, 1938, pp. 419, 430). Furthermore, Dunlop (1939b, p. 190) showed rising British real wages in every one of eight periods of falling unemployment, 1860–1913 and 1920–29, with only 1933–37 (when real wages declined by only 0.3 per cent) as a counterexample. He also found, contrary to statements by Pigou (1927b), Clay (1929), Gayer and Ohlin (1937a, 1937b), that British 'wage rates in the post-War period were no less responsive to changes in unemployment than in the pre-War days' (Dunlop, 1939b, p. 192; see also Dunlop, 1998 on his contribution and on Keynes' reaction).

In the *Economic Journal* in March 1939, Lorie Tarshis gave a fuller presentation of the data underlying his earlier article and brought the evidence to bear on Keynes' supposition that real and money wages would change in opposite directions. The 1938 article had discussed how the data were compiled, and graphed the course of real and money wages in Britain and the United States. Tarshis (1939, pp. 332–3) provided 75 data points for money hourly earnings in the United States from January 1932 to March 1938, along with a monthly index of real wages per hour (deflating earnings by a combination of the Bureau of Labor Statistics and National Industrial Conference Board cost of living indices) and a 'corrected' index of real wages, adjusted for changes in agricultural prices. Going beyond the free-hand curves discussed the year before, Tarshis (1939, p. 334) presented a scatter diagram of percentage changes in real and money wages, and computed coefficients of association (which would be +1.0 if the changes in the two variables always had the same sign, –1.0 if they always had opposite signs, and 0 if same or opposite signs were equally frequent).

The results were striking: the association between American money wage changes and 'corrected' real wage changes, instead of being negative, was +0.86. Excluding changes smaller than two-tenths of 1 per cent (as changes not significantly different from zero, so the signs would be likely to be due to measurement error) yielded associations of +0.96 between money wage changes and 'corrected' real wage changes, and of +0.94 between money wage changes and uncorrected real wage changes: a strong 'positive association when we should expect, on Mr. Keynes' assumptions, the association to be inverse and negative ... Mr. Keynes' conclusions ... are not borne out statistically for this period' (Tarshis, 1939, pp. 334–5). He attributed this to inflexible prices of wage-goods and to marginal cost curves not sloping upward, also noting Keynes' assumption that money wage rates would only rise once unemployment had fallen quite low (increasing the bargaining power of trade unions). Tarshis' 1939 study of American data obtained stronger results than Dunlop's 1938 examination of British evidence, and applied more formal statistical techniques (coefficients of association and a scatter diagram) to higher-frequency data from a much shorter sample period.

Lorie Tarshis carried out further statistical analysis, directly related to the first classical postulate, after his note had been set up in proof, adding a postscript to report on it (1939, p. 335). He found a coefficient of association of –0.64 between changes in person-hours and changes in 'real hourly wages, uncorrected', and an even stronger association of –0.75 excluding changes smaller than two-tenths of 1 per cent. (Casson (1983, p. 178) errs in referring to the coefficient of association of –0.64 as a correlation coefficient.) This was consistent with the first classical postulate and suggested that the strong position correlation between real and money wage changes reflected inflexible wage-good prices, rather than a failure of marginal cost curves to slope up. However, Tarshis found a surprising shrinkage in the association, to −0.48, when using his corrected index of real wage changes, which he considered a superior measure of the purchasing power of wages.

CRITICAL RESPONSES

Professor J. Henry Richardson of Leeds University responded to Dunlop (1938) and Tarshis (1939) by claiming that 'The traditional conclusion is concerned with the relation between changes in money rates of wages and changes in the cost of living, and not with the relation between changes in money rates of wages and changes in trade and employment' (Richardson 1939, p. 440). Re-examining the British data used by Dunlop, Richardson found that real wage rates and the cost of living usually moved in opposite directions, and that total real earnings varied pro-cyclically. Neither of these results weakened the empirical evidence of Dunlop and Tarshis against Keynes' supposition that money wages and real wages move in opposite directions. The issue of importance to Keynes' Chapter 2 model concerned changes in real wage rates associated with changes in effective demand and employment, not total real earnings or changes unconnected to fluctuations of employment, output and effective demand. As Dunlop (1941, p. 683) remarked of Richardson's 1939 study of total real earnings as a measure of the welfare of the working class, 'These problems are a legitimate field of inquiry, of course, but they are not the problems that were posed by Mr. Keynes nor have they been the focus of subsequent discussions'.

Richard Ruggles (1940), then at Harvard before moving to Yale, denied that Dunlop and Tarshis had succeeded in showing that movements in real wages were caused by movements in money wages, arguing that they could be due instead to movements in the cost of living. He noted that if money wage rates and the cost of living fluctuated randomly and were not correlated with each other, then the probability of real and money wage rates moving in the same direction would be 0.75 (misstated as a coefficient of association of 0.80 (Ruggles, 1940, p. 135)). Dunlop (1941) and Tarshis (1941) pointed out, rather sharply, that neither of them had ever denied the effect of the cost of living on real wages. Further, Ruggles' use of a random relation between money wages and the cost of living as an explanation of a positive association between real and money wages was in no way inconsistent with their empirical refutation of Keynes' supposition of a negative association between real and money wages, which was what was being tested (Tarshis, 1941, p. 694).

'Apparently Mr. Ruggles' "Associations" must be entirely legitimate; they must not have random parents,' remarked Tarshis (1941, p. 692). On the basis of tables of British and Swedish real wage changes arranged by cycle phase, Dunlop held to his own

> contention that the relationship between *real wage rates* and *output* originally suggested by Mr. Keynes is untenable. Rather do real wage rates appear to rise in prosperity (above their long-term movement) and fall in the second phase of the depression, either absolutely or, at least, below their long-time trend. (Dunlop, 1941, p. 691)

Ruggles' most important contribution was not in his original article, but rather in his rejoinder to Dunlop and Tarshis, in which he reported correlation coefficients between money wage rates, the cost of living and real wage rates (but not between real wages and employment, despite the insistence of Dunlop and Tarshis on that as the important issue). Excluding war years and eliminating trend by using link-relatives, Ruggles (1941, p. 699) found positive correlations of 0.24 between English real and money wage rates over a sample of 67 years between 1860 and 1937, and of 0.44 for Swedish real and money wage rates over 62 years between 1860 and 1930 (but dropping to only +0.07 over 46 years between 1876 and 1930, contrary to Keynes' expectation of a negative correlation).

MR KEYNES AND THE NUMBERS

Keynes, having accepted Dunlop's article (1938) and Tarshis' note (1939) for publication in the *Economic Journal*, published his reaction to the findings of the young statistical investigators in the same issue as Lorie Tarshis. Keynes (1939) accepted that real and money wages did not tend to vary in the same direction and expressed surprise that this had not been noticed, since the indices compiled by Wood (e.g. 1910) and by Bowley (e.g. 1920) had long been available. He traced the widespread view about real and money wages, and about real wages and employment, to Alfred Marshall's evidence to the Gold and Silver Commission in 1887 and the Indian Currency Committee in 1899, which Keynes had edited for the Royal Economic Society in Marshall's *Official Papers* (1926) (whose negligible circulation Keynes decried, reminding his readers that members of the Royal Economic Society could still buy it for a trifling five shillings). British real wages had fallen during the recovery of 1880–84 and risen during the depression of 1884–86, shaping the opinion that Marshall offered to the Gold and Silver Commission in 1887 and continued to hold later, but real wages never followed that same cyclical pattern again during any cycle phase in the next 50 years (Keynes, 1939, p. 398).

Keynes (1939, p. 399) noted Pigou (1927a, p. 217) as an exception to the general belief in lower real wages in booms, with Pigou (1933, p. 296) as a return to the Marshallian position.

Keynes related the absence of a counter-cyclical pattern in real wages to the stability of the share of wages in national income, a puzzle which Keynes had recently offered to his research students, with Kalecki (1938) as the only proposed solution. While praising Kalecki's 'brilliant article' and 'highly original technique of analysis into the distributional problem between the factors of production in conditions of imperfect competition, which may prove to be an important piece of pioneer work', Keynes (1939, p. 410) remained exceedingly sceptical of a result in which marginal real costs were constant, while changes in the degree of monopoly were just offset by changes in the prices of materials bought outside the system.

Keynes' article had in parts a defensive tone:

> I complain a little that I in particular should be criticised for conceding a little to the other view by admitting that, when the changes in effective demand to which I myself attach importance have brought about a change in the level of output, the real-supply price of labour would in fact change in the direction assumed by the theory I am opposing – as if I was the first to have entertained the fifty-year-old generalisation that, trend eliminated, increasing output is usually associated with a falling real wage. (Keynes, 1939, pp. 411–12)

He was, however, the first to have used that 50-year-old generalization, the first classical postulate that the economy is on a downward-sloping labour demand curve, to build a model of involuntary unemployment, to derive the aggregate supply function for a given money wage (Kahn (1931) had mentioned, but not formally derived, the supply curve for an output as a whole with a given money wage), and to model how shifts in effective demand change output, employment and the price level.

Keynes insisted that rejection of the counter-cyclical pattern of real wages (and of the first classical postulate) would strengthen and considerably simplify the *General Theory*, 'Particularly in Chapter 2, which is the portion of my book which most needs to be revised' (Keynes, 1939, pp. 400–401). He recalled that, when he and Hubert Henderson wrote their pamphlet *Can Lloyd George Do It?* (1929),

> when I had not developed my own argument in as complete a form as I did subsequently ... I was already arguing ... that the good effect of an expansionist investment policy on employment, the fact of which no one denied, was due to the stimulant which it gave to effective demand. Prof. Pigou, on the other hand, and many other economists explained the observed result by the reduction in real wages covertly effected by the rise in prices which ensued on the increase in effective demand. ... Since I shared at the time the prevailing belief as to the facts,

I was not in a position to make this denial [of Pigou's explanation]. (Keynes, 1939, pp. 400–401)

Despite this, and even though his own table of cycle phases and real wage movements (Keynes, 1939, p. 398) agreed with Dunlop's similar table, Keynes argued that

> we, should, I submit, hesitate somewhat and carry our inquiries further before we discard too much of our former conclusions which, subject to the right qualifications, have *a priori* support and have survived for many years the scrutiny of experience and common sense ... I urge, nevertheless, that we should not be too hasty in our revisions, and that further statistical enquiry is necessary before we have a firm foundation of fact on which to reconstruct our theory of the short period. (Keynes, 1939, pp. 401, 412)

Keynes invoked Tarshis' postscript, which found a negative association between real wages and employment in the United States 1932–38, in warning against hasty jettisoning of the first classical postulate.

Keynes had accepted the first classical postulate because, following Marshall, he thought that the inverse relationship of real wages and employment held as an empirical generalization, and wanted to defeat the 'classical' theory (exemplified by Pigou, 1933) on its grounds, granting it as many of its assumptions as possible yet still showing the possibility of involuntary unemployment and the scope for expansion of effective demand to stimulate the economy. The result was his Chapter 2 model, in which the economy moved along the labour demand schedule while being in general off the labour supply schedule. While Darity and Horn (1983) have argued that Keynes' various definitions of involuntary unemployment are consistent with general clearing of all markets, including the labour market, Keynes in Chapter 2 explicitly identified the second classical postulate (which he rejected) with the economy's being on the labour supply schedule. Acceptance of the first classical postulate, but not the second, provided a clear, succinct account of involuntary unemployment and of how effective demand shifts could alter employment and output.

Keynes claimed in 1939 that recasting Chapter 2 and discarding the first classical postulate (which he hesitated to do) would only strengthen his theory, since an expansion of effective demand could then increase employment without depressing real wages. Lawlor, Darity and Horn (1987) similarly hold that the important action in the *General Theory* takes place outside Chapter 2 and outside the labour market, in the determination of the equilibrium level of output by effective demand, in the influence of fundamental uncertainty on liquidity preference and the marginal efficiency of capital, and in the Chapter 19 ('Changes in Money-Wages') argument that increased wage and price flexibility would be destabilizing.

However, dropping the first classical postulate from Chapter 2 would leave the *General Theory* without an explanation of how a change in equilibrium income, due to a change in aggregate demand, would translate into changes in employment and hence output, rather than just changed prices. Such an explanation can be devised without positing counter-cyclical real wage movements. One can think of the capital utilization rate varying along with employment, so that increased employment does not lower the capital/labour ratio (as it would if capital were considered a fixed factor in the short period). The *General Theory* did not provide such an explanation. Keynes (1939), although he readily abandoned the co-movement of real and money wages, hesitated whether to abandon the first classical postulate, partly on empirical grounds (such as the association noted in the postscript of Tarshis, 1939) and partly because of lack of confidence in possible alternatives (as shown by his scepticism about Kalecki, 1938).

Within three years of its publication, the theory of money wages, real wages and employment presented in Chapter 2 of the *General Theory* was severely shaken by the empirical findings of Lorie Tarshis (1938, 1939, 1941) and John Dunlop (1938, 1939a, 1939b, 1941), although the Chapter 2 model survived into the macroeconomics textbooks of the 1960s and 1970s. Mark Casson (1983, p. 179) regrets that 'It is one of the unfortunate results of the Keynesian revolution that such an obvious relationship [an inverse relation between employment and the real wage] should have been questioned, when the evidence in its favour is so very strong'. Others find the relationship less obvious, and the empirical evidence not so overwhelming, so that Katharine Abraham and John Haltiwanger (1995, p. 1262) conclude in their recent survey article that 'To sum up, correcting for all the measurement problems, estimation problems, and composition problems does not lead to a finding of systematically procyclical or countercyclical real wages'. Lorie Tarshis and John Dunlop did not provide any new certainty to replace the model of Chapter 2 of the *General Theory*. These young economists, first in Cambridge, England, and then in or near Cambridge, Massachusetts, rose to the challenge to statistical investigators raised by Keynes in Chapter 2. They refuted Keynes' hypothesis that real and money wages vary in opposite directions and raised doubts about Keynes' hybrid, half-classical Chapter 2 model.

NOTES

1. Presented to an American Economics Association session, San Francisco, CA, 6 January, 1996. I am grateful to Felice Martinello for a helpful discussion of coefficients of association.
2. Cf. Casson (1983) on Pigou, Clay and Cannan.

11. Keynesian monetary theory and the debt crisis

Sheila C. Dow

INTRODUCTION

In 1984 Lorie Tarshis published *World Economy in Crisis: Unemployment, Inflation and International Debt* through the Canadian Institute for Economic Policy. It was while he was drafting this volume that I first had the privilege of meeting him, having previously known and admired him only from his writing. In *World Economy in Crisis*, Tarshis brought together his lifetime work on macroeconomics to address problems at the international as well as national level – indeed highlighting the interdependence between these levels. In so doing, he provided an insightful analysis of the debt crisis and offered recommendations: for resolving the crisis, for the role of the International Monetary Fund (IMF) and for international banking. These recommendations follow not only from the theoretical analysis which focuses on systemic aspects of the international economic process, but also from a concern to suggest workable solutions which avoid any notion of retribution, and which above all are designed to redress the imbalance of political and economic power for developing countries. It is the purpose here to consider this set of ideas again in the light of what has happened since 1984, and in the light of Keynesian monetary theory. This consideration will draw on developments in international debt and in the institutional framework for international borrowing and lending.

In the next section a brief account is given of the ideas expressed in *World Economy in Crisis*, focusing on the ideas specifically addressed to the problem of soaring international debt. This is followed by an analysis of developments since 1984, and then by a reconsideration of Lorie Tarshis' proposals, both for the institutional arrangements for the international monetary system and for regulation of international financial markets in the light of this experience. It is argued that, while some developments have occurred along the lines Lorie Tarshis suggested, his fundamental critique has still not been addressed. As a result, the problems he identified with the international monetary system and with international banking are still very much in evidence. This fundamental critique is reconsidered in the light of the monetary theory of Keynes and his followers.

WORLD ECONOMY IN CRISIS (1984)

In this volume, Lorie Tarshis addressed simultaneously the problems of soaring inflation, soaring unemployment and soaring debt. In doing so, he brought together in an international context his long-standing ideas on the (interdependent) importance of aggregate demand and aggregate supply. This was combined with Lorie Tarshis' concern with the functioning of the international monetary system and his distributional concerns for developing countries.

Tarshis identified the cause of growing Third World debt as the payments imbalances arising from the 1973 oil price shock and the efforts of international banks to recycle petrodollars from oil exporters to oil importers. He argued that this growth in debt was not inherently problematic, but that it became so because of the efforts in developed countries to control inflation through reducing aggregate demand and thus Third World imports; simultaneously, the high interest rates which were the instrument for reducing aggregate demand increased the debt service burden. Tarshis drew a parallel between this situation and the 1930s, when beggar-thy-neighbour policies designed to cure payments imbalances served to strengthen the world recession and created financial instability to the extent of forcing bank collapses. This parallel should serve as a warning of what might ensue if similar beggar-thy-neighbour policies were to be employed in the 1980s; indeed the greater size and interdependence of the international financial system than in the 1930s might make the term 'crisis' even more applicable in the 1980s.

It was one of the primary aims of the IMF to prevent the recurrence of the experience of the 1930s. The IMF was to promote international financial stability (and particularly exchange stability) by providing liquidity for members experiencing payments imbalance, and making sizable drawing on that liquidity conditional on adherence to a set of policies addressed to curing any non-temporary imbalance. Par value changes were only to occur, by agreement, when other forms of adjustment were inadequate, that is, in cases of fundamental disequilibrium; this adjustable peg system was designed to prevent the recourse to competitive devaluation which had characterized the 1930s. Yet, Tarshis argued, the IMF did not develop in such a way as to meet these expectations. Its capacity to provide liquidity was unduly limited, its influence was asymmetrically focused on deficit countries rather than imposing an equal burden of adjustment on surplus countries, and its policies were unduly influenced by a minority of the membership which wielded power in the global economy. These features served to impose an unduly heavy burden, particularly on deficit countries.

Tarshis' Programme for IMF Reform

Tarshis set out a programme for reform designed to increase the effectiveness of the IMF and to restore exchange stability. This programme was very much in accord with Keynes' original plan for the IMF as a world central bank. The following are the measures that Tarshis proposed:

1. Incentives to encourage surplus countries to reduce their surpluses, which would automatically help to correct deficits. These might include a requirement on surplus countries to deposit 50 per cent, say, of their surpluses with the IMF at a lower-than-market rate of interest, to be lent to deficit countries at interest rates high enough to discourage building up deficits. This would encourage surplus countries to run down their surpluses instead, by lending directly to deficit countries at more favourable interest rates.
2. Increased availability of liquidity from the IMF to deal with exceptional circumstances, via increased quotas; increased Special Drawing Rights (SDR) allocations; and increased IMF borrowing from central banks.
3. Measures to change the role of the IMF from pursuing the interests of a few of the most powerful economies to acting like a world central bank, serving the interests of all its members. This would involve a shift of power to IMF staff from the influence of the governments of the most powerful members.

Tarshis' Programme for International Financial System Reform

Tarshis' analysis of the debt crisis focused not only on the incapacity of the IMF to address it, but also on the functioning of the international financial system whose lending activity had facilitated it. Tarshis drew attention to the absence of regulation in the Eurocurrency market which had served both to attract banks into the market and had allowed the massive expansion of international debt in the 1970s. Just as the opportunities for profit in the 1970s had encouraged the massive expansion of intermediation, so its consequence in increased default risk in the 1980s was encouraging massive disintermediation. The high incidence of inter-bank lending and the apparent lack of a lender-of-last-resort facility in the Eurocurrency market had rendered the market highly vulnerable to the incidence of default.

Accordingly, Tarshis set out proposals for addressing the immediate problem of the debt overhang which was threatening bank solvency and for reforms to make the Eurocurrency market less fragile and less capable of replicating the credit explosion of the 1970s. The following is a summary of his proposals:

1. Efforts should be made to provide liquidity to keep most banks open in spite of bad debts, because of the damaging real consequences for economic activity of significant bank failures. Nevertheless, some bank failures should be allowed to proceed as a demonstration device to encourage prudent bank behaviour.
2. Depositor protection should be provided for non-financial depositors in order to limit the chain reaction of defaults in the system.
3. Government bailing-out operations should be balanced by the acquisition of public equity in the bailed-out banks. The underlying principle would be that banks should not gain unduly from public protection; by the same token banks should not bear the full cost of a situation not all of their own making.
4. Not only non-repayable debt should be forgiven, but also that debt whose repayment would impose an undue burden on the debtor country. This proposal is based on considerations of equity: not only bank shareholders should benefit from rescue packages. It is also based on considerations of avoiding anything (such as import controls by developing countries) which would hinder world economic recovery.
5. The rescue of banks in any country should be conditional on that country agreeing to impose regulation which would prevent the re-emergence of the kind of credit explosion which occurred in the1980s.
6. An international board of bank examiners should be established with the remit to protect creditors and the international financial system in general. The US Securities and Exchange Commission might serve as a model. This board would have the power to call for bank accounts consolidated with respect to international operations and to design rules for bank behaviour as appropriate. In particular, banks would be required to observe rules limiting credit expansion according to some ratios, for example, with respect to capital backing or to the proportion of risk-free assets. Further, banks would be limited in their risk exposure to any one country, corporation or sector.

THE DEBT CRISIS IN THE 1990s

The 1980s saw the eventual introduction of a range of measures designed to avert the realization of the debt crisis, that is, to prevent a widespread debt moratorium and extensive incidence of bank failure. These measures must be judged a success insofar as such a crisis was indeed averted. Further, the rationale for much of these measures echoed to some degree Lorie Tarshis' concern that effective demand should not be unduly dampened, that the distribution of the costs imposed by the debt crisis should not be unfair and that international banking should be supervised.

The Role of the IMF

In the initial phase of the debt crisis, following Mexico's default in 1982, the IMF identified the need for structural adjustment in debtor countries to improve their capacity to service debt. But to allow a gradualist approach to such adjustment (and thus to avoid undue deflation of debtor economies and thus, through trade, creditor economies), the IMF introduced an additional financial facility for borrowers agreeing to structural adjustment packages. However, the scale of this additional facility was very small relative to the amount of outstanding debt. The IMF sought to encourage additional private sector lending, or at least existing debt restructuring, through the banking system. However, the over-riding concern of the banks at the time was to reduce their debt exposure. In the meantime, the banks' risk exposure was being reduced by central bank lender-of-last-resort support designed to avert bank failure (cf. Krugman, 1994).

This approach failed to improve the situation, other than preventing actual bank collapses. This failure stemmed from the persistent expectation that the debt could ultimately be serviced by means of structural adjustment of debtor economies; the problem was seen as one of illiquidity rather than insolvency. The initial problem, created by an incapacity to service debt, was becoming more severe; the debt service ratio (debt service payments relative to exports) increased in aggregate from 19.3 per cent in 1984 to 22.5 per cent in 1986. For Latin American countries the ratio increased from 40.5 per cent in 1984 to 43.9 per cent in 1988; the ratio also increased for African and Asian countries between 1984 and 1986 (see Healey, 1994). While the structural adjustment programmes were purportedly gradualist, they were improving debtors' current account imbalances by reducing imports rather than increasing imports, and this was being achieved by reducing real income in debtor countries. In the meantime, attempts to improve current account imbalances were being hampered by adverse movements in the terms of trade (see Healey, 1994). The restructuring of debt, together with 'new money' had increased the value of total debt from $879 billion in 1984 to $1050 billion in 1986 (see Healey, 1994), but this increase masks the profound reluctance of the private sector banks to increase their exposure. Bank lending to Latin America increased only from $212 billion in 1984 to $222 billion in 1986 (Bank of International Settlements (BIS), 1987). During this period, therefore, the debt problem was resolved only for the banks, which central banks were protecting; the capacity for servicing debt was worsening and debtor countries were experiencing a significant drop in real income (see Palma, 1995).

The Baker Plan

The Baker Plan was announced in 1985 to address this worsening situation, advocating a significant increase in bank lending to debtor countries, with this lending being contingent on IMF conditionality, that is, on agreement to structural adjustment. The philosophy was thus continued that the problem was one of illiquidity during the period of structural adjustment which would eventually resolve the debt-servicing problem. The main innovation was the proposal for the involvement also of the World Bank, reflecting the view that the IMF was straying into development territory where longer-term finance commitments might be more appropriate. But this plan too failed to address the development crisis which was emerging, a crisis which posed the possibility of insolvency rather than illiquidity problems. (See Williamson (1992) for a discussion of this distinction and the need for an international bankruptcy agency to identify insolvency and its causes.) The Plan ultimately failed because there was no adequate incentive to encourage bank lending to the extent Baker had advocated ($20 billion over three years).

In the meantime, the banks were evolving market-based solutions to restructure their portfolios in order to reduce their risk exposure. These instruments represented one aspect of the phase of securitization which the banks were developing more generally to deal with the problems arising from overexpansion of credit in the 1970s and competition from non-bank financial intermediaries (see Gardener, 1988). Securitization of bank assets allows banks to reduce the riskiness of their portfolios and allows the market to allocate the cost of the realization of risk. Thus securitization of Third World debt allowed a discounting of the value of that debt to reflect perceptions of servicing capacity. These instruments allowed an escape for banks from the dual of default or not-default inherent in the loan contract, potentially making the prospect of new lending in the future more attractive to the banks. The distribution of the initial cost associated with discounting of debt between borrowers and lenders depends on the nature of the instrument. (See Healey (1994) for an account of the various instruments employed.)

The Brady Plan

The Brady Plan of 1989 reflected a shift in understanding of the nature of the crisis, with a recognition that not all the debt might be serviceable, that is, that there was an element of insolvency. The solution to the debt crisis thus required an element of debt forgiveness (a solution reinforced by the 1988 Toronto Agreement). The mechanisms for forgiveness were enhanced by the emergence of securitization of debt, with the possibility of borrowers being given some of the direct benefit of the discounting of their debt, as well as the indirect benefits of avoiding default. The Brady Plan encouraged banks to develop a wide range of alternatives for financial support, including elements of debt forgiveness and debt service reduction; the aim was for forgiveness of 30–35 per cent of total debt.

Government involvement was to be a crucial element, with public sector collateralization of conversion bonds to be used to convince banks to reduce their claims on debtors. Brady further encouraged governments to make regulatory changes to facilitate debt forgiveness. Finally, the Plan advocated increased involvement by international agencies. It encouraged the IMF and International Bank for Reconstruction and Development to provide credit to finance buy-backs of debt; in the event the International Development Association has also become involved in finance for this purpose. Further, it encouraged the IMF to use its conditionality provisions to encourage structural adjustment as a means of encouraging increased bank lending, rather than requiring prior agreement on debt restructuring.

The Role of the International Financial System

In the meantime, the BIS (1987) had been addressing the general issue of uncontrolled international credit, notably in the Eurocurrency market. In 1988, guidelines were issued for the imposition of capital adequacy requirements in relation to international credit. The guidelines have been refined to develop weightings appropriate to the risk associated with different types of asset, including off-balance sheet activities; the guidelines are for banks to hold capital (according to precise categories in particular proportions) at a minimum of 8 per cent of the value of risk-weighted assets (cf. Hall, 1989). Banks may then further expand credit only if it is adequately backed by new capital. These guidelines are increasingly being applied also to domestic banking, for example by the European Commission, by the US and by Japan. The intention is to moderate credit expansion except insofar as it is adequately secured by capital backing. The hope is therefore to avoid the massive expansion of credit experienced in the 1970s, of which Third World debt was an important part. At the same time, there has been growing awareness of the need to identify the responsible lenders-of-last-resort in international banking and to develop depositor protection schemes to limit the consequences of individual bank failures.

Cline (1995) paints an optimistic picture of the international banking system in the 1990s. He credits the Brady Plan with resolving the debt crisis, allowing a resumption of new credit to developing countries and a reduction in capital flight. By 1993, 80 per cent of rescheduled debt had been covered by restructuring debt, debt servicing relative to exports had been reduced, and the debt exposure of the nine largest US banks had been quartered (due to increased capital as well as reduced credit-risk exposure). Many of the positive elements contributing to this improvement may be found in Lorie Tarshis' proposals, as outlined above. He had advocated more liquidity provision through international agencies, lender-of-last-resort liquidity to prevent bank failures on any large scale, depositor protection schemes, debt forgiveness and international bank supervision, including the setting of prudent portfolio ratios.

Nevertheless, not all commentators are so sanguine about the resolution of the debt crisis. Palma (1995) and Healey (1994), for example, draw attention to the distribution of the burden of adjustment to the debt crisis, which has been borne primarily by the debtor countries. Both document the massive real resource transfers which have been made by the most heavily indebted countries, in spite of debt forgiveness. The extent of debt forgiveness has been limited by the persistence of an assignment of responsibility for the debt crisis to the debtor countries, in spite of general awareness of the external factors which contributed to their debt. Further, as Cline (1995) acknowledges, the banks were able to shift much of the risk they had undertaken by extending credit to developing countries on to the public sector in developed countries through the lender-of-last-resort facility.

The role of the state has proved crucial, too, in the role evolved for itself by the IMF. Individual banks had neither the knowledge nor the implementation capacity to develop structural adjustment programmes as a condition for further credit; nor was it clearly in the interests of any one bank alone to attempt to make up this lack. In response to market need, the state in the form of the IMF was required to take the macro view. Nevertheless, the nature of the IMF's contribution has been the subject of much criticism. First, inadequate liquidity provision by the IMF has long been a criticism, which the Managing Director, Michel Camdessus, attempted to address at the 50th Annual Meeting (1995), proposing a new allocation of SDR36 billion; allocations had last been increased to SDR21 billion in 1981. However, the political process prevented any new allocations being determined. Second, the structural adjustment programmes have been criticized for their undue emphasis on free market supply-side policies without attention to the damaging consequences for real incomes.

In Light of Tarshis' Programme

The solution to the debt crisis had thus not incorporated the distributional concerns set out in *World Economy in Crisis* (Tarshis, 1984), with the result that the debtor countries had borne an undue burden. Further, no effort has been made to reassess more fundamentally the IMF's structure and role, in particular the focus on adjustment by deficit countries, employing programmes which serve the long-term interests of developed countries more than those of debtor countries.

Further, developments in international bank supervision have not developed adequately in relation to Lorie Tarshis' proposals. The BIS is as close as we have come to an international supervisory agency, but it has no statutory powers and its coverage of countries and off-shore centres is not universal. Further, without statutory power to enforce full disclosure of information, knowledge of the size and composition of the international market is incomplete (cf. Strange, 1986). Finally, no effort has been made to enforce attempts to tighten domestic banking regulation as a condition for international efforts to protect bank assets, as Tarshis had suggested. It is clear from the history of the international financial system that international organizations can enforce their policies only if they have the capacity to provide sufficient inducements or impose sufficient penalties.

While there was a shift towards Tarshis' ideas with the Brady Plan, the shift has not been nearly far enough to absorb his identification of the fundamental problems inherent in the present design of the international financial system. Tarshis' critique stems from a view of the role of the state in the international economy. We consider this critique further in the next section in relation to Keynes' monetary theory and that of his followers.

KEYNES, THE INTERNATIONAL MONETARY SYSTEM AND MONETARY THEORY

Tarshis' proposals for the international monetary system hold much in common with Keynes' plan, considered at Bretton Woods in 1944, for a world central bank, to be called the International Clearing Union. Keynes had envisaged the establishment of a world currency, the *bancor*, which would have averted the identification of the interests of the IMF with the issuers of key national currencies, notably the US dollar. Just as Tarshis saw the SDR as the key to promoting exchange stability, so Keynes had tried to make the IMF a truly international institution.

Second, Keynes had been concerned to ensure that there was equal pressure on surplus countries to adjust along with deficit countries, primarily because of the deflationary effects of adjustment to deficits. Keynes had

envisaged all official transactions going through national government accounts with the world central bank (in the same way as the clearing balances
of commercial banks with national central banks), all recorded in terms of
bancor as the unit of account. Penalties would be imposed on excessive
surplus balances to induce adjustment. The role of the dollar as the reserve
currency under the system which actually emerged from Bretton Woods,
meant that the US had to build up large deficits in order for the supply of
reserves to keep up with demand. But in 1944 it had seemed that the US
would persist as a surplus country, its capital financing the deficits of Europe.
Keynes' plan for penalties on deficits was not therefore regarded as acceptable, and all that remained was the scarce currency clause in the Articles of
Agreement (United Nations [1944]), a clause which has never been invoked.
Implicit in much of the discussion of adjustment to payments imbalance has
been the notion that the responsibility for imbalances lies with deficit countries. The distribution of the burden of adjustment which emerged has thus
reflected a particular moral judgement which has been mirrored in the reluctance to support debt forgiveness in the 1980s and 1990s. Tarshis was at pains
to counter this judgement, arguing that imbalances in capital markets, as in
payments balances, arise simultaneously on two sides of the balance sheet,
and thus simultaneously have two sets of causes.

A Role for the IMF

Having envisaged settlement of international payments going through the
books of the world central banks, Keynes also saw scope for controlling
short-term capital flows. Controls on speculation were also considered by
White, the architect of the US plan, but the proposal was not pursued in the
design of the IMF (see de Cecco, 1979). International payments were starting
from a position of currency inconvertibility, so that the kind of exchange
controls being considered would not have seemed unreasonable at the time.
Nevertheless, the aim of the IMF was to free up international financial markets. With the increasing abandonment of national exchange controls, the tide
has turned against the notion of international exchange controls and towards
liberalization (cf. Akyuz, 1995). Yet there is a continuing concern even further with the strength and potential volatility of international capital (see for
example, Strange, 1994). Proposals are periodically made to control these
flows, for example Tobin's (1978) proposal for a tax on speculation and
Soloman's (1989) proposal for a dual exchange rate system. (See Akyuz and
Cornford (1995) for a discussion of the relative merits of various possibilities.)

Tarshis' approach was to set up the institutional structure which would
allow proposals for regulating international banking to be discussed. He

proposed the setting up of an international bank regulatory agency whose purpose would be to promote stability in international banking. Given the rapidly evolving nature of international finance, surely this is the most sensible suggestion; the institutional structure needs to be established before particular proposals can be considered. It is clear from Akyuz and Cornford's (1995) discussion that controls must have universal application, including, to off-shore centres. What is implied is either that the IMF be transformed into a world central bank with supervisory powers as well as international monetary powers, or, if monetary and supervisory functions were to be separated as in the US model, that a third sister organization be formed.

Finally, Tarshis' proposals for debt forgiveness mirror closely Keynes' stance on German reparations. Again an undue burden was placed on an economy, largely on the grounds of a moral judgement, without attention to capacity to pay or to the consequences for Germany, and the world economy, of the adjustments required to effect the payment.

Keynes' proposals for a world central bank and its operations followed from his monetary theory. For Keynes, money was an intrinsic feature of the economic process in capitalist economies. A successful money, internationally as well as nationally, was one which commanded confidence. In the international context this required the establishment of an international money not tied to any one economy; as experience with Bretton Woods demonstrated, the dollar standard could operate only with a US deficit to ensure a supply of dollars, but this in itself served to erode confidence in the dollar. Keynes was also very much aware of the nature of speculation and its origins in uncertainty; here Keynes was drawing on his theory of probability (see Runde, 1994). Keynes saw speculation as the inevitable outcome of divergent opinions based on (inevitably) inadequate knowledge, and thus as vulnerable to discrete shifts. He was further concerned with the consequences of financial speculation for the real activity it finances. Just as high liquidity preference at the national level, due to an increase in uncertainty, can be deflationary, so at the international level can speculation divert financial resources from real activity. Keynes would no doubt, like Strange (1986), have identified the consequence of the drive for international liquidity in the 1980s in terms of increased deflationary pressure on debtor countries.

A Role for the International Financial System

In the light of the massive growth of international banking, it can be presumed that Keynes would have continued to consider measures for control. Keynes was fully aware of the power of the banking system and its capacity (partially) to determine the volume of credit. It is a common misunderstanding to see Keynes as an exogenous-money man (see Dow, 1997). His general attitude to financial regulation was that it should reduce the efficiency of financial markets, and thus their power over real activity (see Gowland, 1990).

Minsky (1975, 1982) has extended some of Keynes' key ideas on finance in a way which generates a theory of credit creation in the context of the business cycle. In particular, he has extended Keynes' concepts of borrowers' risk and lenders' risk to show how these determine the position and shape of the demand for, and supply of, credit, respectively. The lower the perceived risk, the larger the volume of credit. Yet considering risk again in relation to Keynes' theory of probability, it is not estimable on the basis of frequency distributions; as with most expectations, risk assessment must rely on judgement, convention and 'animal spirits', in addition to whatever knowledge is available. Conventional judgement is particularly important in international capital markets where knowledge of borrowers may not be good; that the banks' knowledge was meagre when embarking on the massive lending programme in the 1970s is now well documented. That their knowledge continued to be inadequate is evidenced by their apparent need to rely on the superior knowledge and experience of the IMF. Yet conventional judgement is subject to discrete change.

It was notable that the relevant evidence suggesting the onset of the debt crisis was taken seriously by the banks only when Mexico defaulted in 1982. There was then a considerable lag before banks made bad debt provision, and before capital markets revised their valuation of bank equity; it was only in 1987 that Citibank took the lead in making provision for bad debts. The importance of the market's capacity for risk assessment is reinforced by securitization. It has been argued (e.g., by Folkerts-Landu, Garber and Weisbrod, 1991) that the banks' unique role derives from their superior knowledge of creditors relative to the rest of the financial system. It is therefore a matter for concern that this superiority may be subverted by market assessment based on inferior knowledge.

With capital adequacy ratios, the risk assessment which ultimately drives credit creation is therefore the risk assessment of the markets. Herein lies the inadequacy of capital adequacy ratios. As Minsky demonstrates, credit expansion and contraction tends to be cyclical. The desire of banks to expand credit thus coincides with optimism in the equity market and thus with the provision of the required additional capital to back the additional credit. There is even a lag before equity markets seem to identify the downturn in the value of banks' portfolios, so that speculative booms may continue to be financed by the equity market even when there is evidence that the boom is no longer sustainable. When banks start to contract credit as perceived risk increases in the downturn, they find the valuation of their capital falling, making the need to contract credit to meet capital adequacy requirements even more acute. Capital adequacy requirements may therefore exacerbate the credit cycle rather than dampen it. The only solution would be a pro-cyclical capital adequacy ratio (see Dow, 1993; St Hill, 1991): a rising ratio in the upturn might dampen credit expansion somewhat, while a falling ratio in the downturn would reduce the impetus for credit contraction.

CONCLUSION

Experience with the international monetary system and international banking in the last decade has reinforced the importance of Lorie Tarshis' arguments for a fundamental change in institutions and practices. The tide has been running in general in favour of market solutions to economic problems. But the debt crisis can be seen as the outcome of the behaviour of an unregulated market operating with inadequate knowledge. The market then had to turn to the state for a solution, in the immediate form of lender-of-last-resort facilities and then in the form of IMF conditionality on which private sector banks to hang their own loans. In the meantime, the content of that conditionality has contributed to the large real transfers from debtor to creditor countries during the period, and has contributed a deflationary bias to an already shaky world economy. Combined with exchange instability, this situation has created increasing uncertainty in international banking, expressed in increased liquidity preference and thus a relative unwillingness to lend.

Just as a domestic economy needs a stable standard of value for the denomination of contracts, so does the international economy. An international institution is necessary to manage that money. Just as the supply of credit domestically is determined primarily by the banking system, even more is that the case internationally. A world central bank is therefore required to influence credit-creation behaviour and to avoid credit explosions, but also to avoid severe contractions which might introduce a deflationary bias (as happens when the pressure to adjust is most strongly felt by deficit countries). The mechanisms for influencing bank behaviour in terms of credit creation overlap with those for ensuring prudent bank behaviour. Much progress has been made by the BIS in regulating international banking, but much more could be done. Capital adequacy ratios are a step in the right direction, but much more comprehensive supervision is required.

Lorie Tarshis was eloquent in arguing for such reforms. He was particularly eloquent in adopting a humane, conciliatory tone which should be emulated. It is to be hoped that further progress may be made in the direction of adopting his approach.

12. A case against muddling through: Lorie Tarshis' proposal and the international debt problem[1]

Franque Grimard

INTRODUCTION

> Soaring prices, soaring unemployment, soaring debt: these are the most obvious symptoms of a crisis that has held most economies in its grip since the late 1960s. While inflation was slowed in 1982–83, unemployment remains dangerously high, and the rising overhang of international debt poses a threat to the financial systems of the developed countries. The costs of the crisis in current and potential losses of income and wealth are almost beyond measure; beyond this is a host of adverse social consequences. (Tarshis, 1984, paperback cover)

This troubled situation is the context that Lorie Tarshis addresses in *World Economy in Crisis: Unemployment, Inflation and International Debt* (1984). The book, written over the 1982–84 period, presents Tarshis' analysis of macroeconomic problems faced by developed countries such as Canada and the US, and their implications for the international economic system. Particular attention is paid to the international situation within which these developed economies operate and to the increasing need for policy-makers to understand that coordination of policies is required. Tarshis lists the international monetary system as a real cause for concern: flexible exchange rates, unregulated Eurodollar markets and high levels of international debt threaten the stability of financial institutions and several developing economies. In this environment, Tarshis (1984) presents a case for effective policies to raise both aggregate demand and aggregate supply of the developed economies. In addition, he argues that some of the Third World debt should be cancelled and proposes a reform of the international monetary system. Tarshis, in subsequent papers (1987–90), pays special attention to the international debt crisis because of its potential to threaten the stability of the banking system in the developed world and the enormous costs encountered by developing economies. His article in *Challenge*, 'Disarming the Debt Bomb' (1987), spells out the main proposal. Tarshis (1988), Tarshis (1989) and Dore and

Tarshis (1990) offer additional insights and greater details on the debt crisis and possible ways to reduce the less developed countries' (LDC) debt burden. In all, Tarshis provides an insightful analysis on the causes of the debt crisis, argues the need for debt reduction (sooner than most observers had) and suggests a plan to resolve the debt crisis.

This chapter reviews Tarshis' contribution to the literature on what has come to be called the 'Third World debt crisis'. It will first offer a brief summary of the crisis to present the main issues, analytical and political, that threatened the stability of the international financial system in the 1980s. It will then discuss Tarshis' plan for dealing with the crisis and draw parallels to proposals by other analysts. The last section concludes with Tarshis' suggestions for the reform of the international monetary system.

THE DEBT CRISIS

Mexico's announcement in August 1982 that it could no longer meet its debt-servicing payments triggered a 'debt crisis'.[2] The integrity of the international financial system was seriously threatened by the high risk of default by several debtor countries and by the perceived consequences for the major banks of the developed countries, whose portfolios consisted of non-performing loans.

A review of the causes of the crisis and the difficulties that have impeded a satisfactory resolution of the problems that plague the actors in this high-finance drama may be helpful.[3] The crisis began with the increase in world oil prices in the early 1970s. Organization of Petroleum Exporting Countries (OPEC) members deposited the substantial windfalls from oil revenues in commercial banks of developed countries, creating excess liquidity in the international financial system. Oil-starved LDCs borrowed from these banks, under the approving supervision of International Financial Institutions (IFIs) and Western aid agencies which saw the recycling of petrodollar funds as a way to reduce the demand for foreign aid and emergency funds in response to the OPEC shock. Throughout the 1970s, the banks, especially the major US ones, increased their lending to developing countries which, after the initial oil shock, enjoyed a relatively high rate of growth. These loans proved to be profitable and, in turn, some banks took a relatively large exposure in lending to developing countries. For instance, at the end of 1982, the equivalent of 288 per cent of the total capital of the nine largest US banks was on loans to LDCs.

Despite the initial profitability of these loans, the situation reversed itself in the 1980s. The benefit of hindsight allows analysts to point to three factors that caused the eruption of the crisis. First, the Volker–Reagan shock that created the world recession of the early 1980s meant a drastic reduction in demand for LDC exports, thereby reducing the foreign exchange earnings needed to service the debt at a time when the second oil shock increased the demand for foreign exchange reserves. Furthermore, the recession caused a decline in the non-oil-producing LDCs' terms of trade and it became more difficult for the LDCs to earn enough foreign exchange to service their debt obligations. Table 12.1 shows the terms of trade of 19 representative debtors for the period 1970 to 1992, with 1980 being the base period. Countries such as Brazil, Morocco, Argentina and the Philippines saw their terms of trade deteriorate after 1980.

The second factor responsible for the crisis was the sharp increase in interest rates starting in 1978. After the inflation of the 1970s, loans to LDCs were mostly short term with variable interest rates. The high real rates of the

Table 12.1   Terms of trade of 19 representative debtor countries

	1970	1975	1980	1985	1990	1992
Algeria	18	75	100	101	63	55
Argentina	135	146	100	86	78	82
Brazil	137	141	100	91	83	88
Mexico	28	32	100	159	143	146
Nigeria	16	53	100	60	43	39
Venezuela	24	61	100	99	65	56
Colombia	59	60	100	101	144	150
Chile	229	123	100	76	94	87
Ecuador	22	60	100	97	68	61
Hungary						
Indonesia	25	70	100	88	93	123
Morocco	85	171	100	103	119	119
Philippines	150	156	100	86	93	101
Turkey						
Zaire	179	98	100	90	86	78
Côte D'Ivoire	83	76	100	85	65	62
Egypt	88	103	100	103	103	71
Pakistan	143	135	100	92	92	82
Peru	146	137	100	85	85	75

Source: Table 7.2, *Handbook of International Trade and Development Statistics 1993,* United Nations (1994).

early 1980s made these new loans more expensive to service and increased the costs of servicing the existing debt obligations. Finally, a third cause of the crisis was the strong dollar, which appreciated against other currencies in real terms by about half, from its low point in 1980 to its high in February 1985. Since bank loans to LDCs were mostly denominated in US dollars, LDCs had to export even more to keep up with their existing obligations.

Tables 12.2 and 12.3 present the ratios of debt-to-GDP and debt-to-exports, respectively for 19 representative debtor countries over the period 1980–93. These ratios were quite high in 1982 and, in particular, the combined effects of the strong dollar, high real interest rates and the world recession caused a severe toll. By early 1982, 32 countries were in arrears on their international loans, and Paul Volker called the potential threat to the international financial system essentially unparalleled in post-war history: if countries could not pay their debt and were forced to default on their loans,

Table 12.2   Debt-to-GDP ratios of 19 representative debtor countries

	1980	1982	1985	1990	1993
Algeria	45.4	83.8	84.2	57.4	48.2
Argentina	48.4	40.1	29.5	46.0	29.6
Brazil	30.4	35.8	48.2	24.9	24.0
Mexico	30.4	52.5	54.9	44.9	35.5
Nigeria	8.9	14.0	21.9	107.3	100.7
Venezuela	49.6	41.3	58.9	70.3	64.3
Colombia	20.9	26.9	42.0	45.4	33.4
Chile	45.3	76.7	143.3	67.9	49.0
Ecuador	53.8	68.2	76.7	122.7	101.9
Hungary	47.4	38.8	64.6	67.2	67.1
Indonesia	27.9	29.4	45.0	66.2	65.9
Morocco	56.2	86.8	146.9	94.3	81.7
Philippines	49.4	62.3	83.4	69.0	63.7
Turkey	34.1	38.2	50.5	194.7	223.4
Zaire	48.2	54.6	135.7	na	na
Côte D'Ivoire	58.3	166.6	120.0	195.9	243.9
Egypt	91.4	122.5	127.6	127.9	104.8
Pakistan	42.4	38.3	43.6	49.7	49.3
Peru	50.8	49.7	83.2	68.2	51.6

Source: *World Debt Tables*, World Bank, various issues.

Table 12.3   Debt-to-export ratios of 19 representative debtor countries

	1980	1982	1985	1990	1993
Algeria	124.9	447.3	493.2	202.2	216.6
Argentina	226.4	118.2	116.8	414.7	446.2
Brazil	303.1	392.8	355.9	320.6	301.8
Mexico	233.3	311.5	326.0	196.7	184.6
Nigeria	32.0	99.5	142.7	241.5	241.7[a]
Venezuela	132.6	159.5	201.0	155.9	216.8
Colombia	117.1	204.3	301.7	181.9	158.3
Chile	192.5	335.9	436.6	183.0	167.6
Ecuador	203.1	291.0	259.5	369.5	396.5
Hungary	101.4	83.4	123.4	186.3	227.9
Indonesia	94.1	124.6	181.9	223.8	219.4
Morocco	223.8	326.9	394.6	280.3	251.3
Philippines	212.0	296.8	331.9	231.7	183.6
Turkey	331.6	195.5	198.3	194.7	223.4
Zaire	200.7	281.9	345.2	444.7	na
Côte D'Ivoire	159.4	317.2	344.1	461.9	596.3
Egypt	179.6	281.5	302.4	315.6	257.1
Pakistan	208.7	201.8	225.4	248.8	261.2
Peru	207.0	293.7	361.1	494.1	466.7

Note: a   1992.

Source: *World Debt Tables*, World Bank, various issues.

several major banks would see their liabilities exceed their assets and be forced to declare bankruptcy. As Tarshis (1984) puts it, the debt burden of the LDCs had direct consequences for industrialized economies:

> It is now widely recognized that the major creditor countries are almost as deeply in trouble over this possibly unrepayable debt. A maxim, possibly attributable to Lord Keynes, has recently been resurrected: 'If you owe £100, you are in trouble; if you owe £100,000,000, your bank is in trouble'. (Tarshis, 1984, p. 7)

Tarshis stressed that the current troubles of the international financial system stemmed from the fact that most large banks were overexposed to bad LDC loans. Of course, there was plenty of blame to spread around. First, several LDCs did not properly invest the funds from loans, increasing their domestic consumption instead.[4] Second, inappropriate economic policies caused capital flight that exacerbated the foreign exchange constraint. Bulow and Rogoff (1990), for instance, present estimates of capital outflows for Latin American citizens that exceed the book value of the countries' government and government-guaranteed foreign bank debt. Banks were not without blame either. In hindsight, they lent too much and without sufficient care, with little experience in assessing the proper risks. Indeed, even small banks joined the band wagon of lending to LDCs in the late 1970s[5] and their inexperience and number made collective debt negotiations very cumbersome.

The crisis was first confronted as if it were a short-term liquidity problem with debt rescheduling as the solution. It was thought that the LDCs were temporarily short of foreign exchange and that they could fulfil their obligations once the recession was over. Consequently, the 1983–84 period was one where debt reschedulings occurred between the debtor countries and the banks under the supervision (and sometimes help) of the International Monetary Fund (IMF), Bank of International Settlements (BIS) and some national governments. Some major elements outside the control of either the banks or the debtor LDCs would eventually determine if the crisis would worsen: namely, the size of government budget deficits in the developed world, the level of real interest rates, the value of the dollar, the decline in terms of trade, the degree of protection against LDC exports, the pace of economic growth in the developing nations, and the level of real interest rates.

By 1985, some conditions had improved. Growth in the developed countries allowed the LDCs to increase their exports and earn additional foreign exchange. Private banks were able to increase their reserves against losses, thereby reducing the risk of a major bank collapse, and real interest rates started to decline from nearly 8 per cent in 1984 to an average of 4 per cent in 1985. Despite these positive points, deep difficulties remained. The flow of bank loans to LDCs had been drastically reduced, and debtor countries were increasingly under pressure to reduce or suspend debt servicing. President Allan Garcia of Peru announced in 1985 that his country would simply stop paying more than 10 per cent of its export revenues in debt servicing. Nigeria followed, limiting its debt payments to 30 per cent of export revenue. Damage to the domestic economies of LDCs caused by the crisis was rapidly emerging. The need to service the debt caused the governments to transfer their spending towards debt repayment even when that meant cutting productive investment and thus hurting development. The fall in aggregate demand brought about by the restrictive measures of the structural adjustment plans also led to a reduction in private investment because of the initial increase in domestic interest rates and taxes, and because of lags in adjusting to the new conditions of reduced government spending and export-orientated measures.

Mere debt rescheduling did not, however, lead to a solution of the crisis. The first large-scale attempt to deal with the crisis in a coordinated way was the Baker Plan.[6] This Plan, in three parts, was launched in October 1985 and recognized for the first time that the crisis was more than a short-term liquidity problem. First, it called on the LDCs to adopt adjustment policies. Second, it asked the banks to increase their lending to the debtor countries. Finally, the World Bank and other regional development banks were asked to increase their lending in return for a greater commitment by the LDCs to domestic economic reform.

By 1988, despite two years of growth in the developed world and structural adjustment in the developing world, the Baker Plan had clearly failed. First, it did not allow for any debt reduction, and second, new loans that would have been needed to ease adjustment were not provided by the commercial banks. In fact, banks actually reduced their loans rather than raising them, to avoid throwing 'good money' after 'bad', non-performing loans. Slowly, the international financial community was coming to the realization which Tarshis (1984) and other observers had come to very early in the crisis: the size of the debt itself was a problem. Terms such as 'debt overhang' and the 'debt Laffer curve' were not only used by academics but also in discussions among international finance officials. Debt reduction was now a goal, for it was realized that some debt papers would never be honoured and that their very existence reduced the probability that the remainder would ever be repaid. The need for debt reduction had already been recognized by the market, where new financial instruments were created to retire existing debt papers, for example debt-for-equity swaps and debt-for-nature swaps. These transactions on the secondary debt market were, nevertheless, limited, and the need for a more concerted effort was required.

The next attempt by the international community to solve the debt crisis was the Brady Plan. In early 1989, US Treasury Secretary, Nicholas Brady unveiled a plan that recognized the need to offer debt relief.[7] In July 1989, Mexico was the first country to reach an agreement under the Brady Plan by which the value of its outstanding debt was reduced. Its current debt paper was basically converted to new bonds with a lower face value but a higher probability of being repaid. The Mexican version of the plan allowed the creditor banks three options: First, a bank could swap old loans for 30–year bonds at a 35 per cent discount on face value, with these new bonds paying the same interest rate as the old loans. Second, it could swap old loans for new bonds paying a fixed interest rate of 6.25 per cent, but with no discount. The third option was to swap old debt for new debt at the old rates and face value, but with a promise to lend up to 25 per cent of their exposure. Under the first two options, creditors that took new bonds would have their interest payments guaranteed for 18 months, with funds made available by the IMF, the World Bank, the United States, Japan and Mexico. Other agreements under the Brady Plan were put into place for countries such as Costa Rica, Nigeria, the Philippines, Venezuela, and recently Brazil.

By 1992, ten years after it had started, the debt situation was no longer a 'crisis'. Ahmed and Summers point out that many middle-income countries (e.g., Mexico, Korea and Chile) had been able to 'put the crisis behind them' (1992, p. 2), thanks to a combination of good domestic policies, debt reduction through the Brady Plan and high growth rates of exports. However, they point out that low-income developing countries, mostly in Sub-Saharan Africa, cannot claim the same. (One could refer specifically, for instance, to the debt-to-GDP and the debt-to-exports ratios of Tables 12.2 and 12.3 for countries such as Côte d'Ivoire (the Ivory Coast), Peru and Zaire.) For these countries, despite their having adopted adjustment policies, the crisis was clearly far from over. Ahmed and Summers (1992) concede that there was a need for considerable debt relief and most, if not all, should be given by official creditors such as the World Bank and IMF. Furthermore, these institutions should increase their lending so that these debtor countries might be able to start reversing the declines in health, nutrition and educational standards that have characterized many of these countries during the 1980s.

Thus, after ten years, the international financial community felt a renewed optimism about a proper resolution of the debt crisis. Some countries had reduced their debt and had adopted several policies to restructure and liberalize their economies. One tangible proof of this optimism was the considerable increase in foreign flows into middle-income LDCs, notably in Latin America, as financial institutions, such as mutual funds and money market funds, discovered these developing markets. 'Emerging market funds' became very fashionable, and considerable amounts of capital were poured into these countries as equity investment. Claessens (1995) estimates that, from 1989 to 1993, total portfolio funds increased more than sevenfold to a level of $55.8 billion in 1993. These funds partly replaced commercial banks' loans and grew in importance. For instance, during the 1980s, foreign inflows of capital to Latin America were less than 1 per cent of the region's GDP. In the 1990s, capital inflows increased to 6 per cent of GDP, thanks partly to equity funds (cf. Naim, 1995).

This optimism came to a crashing halt in December 1994. Once again, Mexico made the news. A year after the ratification of the North American Free Trade Agreement, the Mexican government had to devalue the peso by nearly 40 per cent. This not only caused a major setback for the Mexican economy, but also destabilized currencies and financial markets around the globe. Some Latin American countries felt the after-shock; Chile's stock market, for instance, dropped 13 per cent in the first quarter of 1995, and international investors have been more than wary about Brazil and Argentina.

The devaluation of the Mexican peso was a brutal reality check. Though its origins lie in domestic policies, the peso devaluation was a reminder that the debt problem has not disappeared for these emerging market countries[8]. Given their delicate external debt position, these countries have little margin to manoeuvre when hit by internal or external shocks. They must carry the burden the debt crisis left them. Some have called the 1980s a 'lost decade' for the LDCs: basic human indicators, such as the primary education and infant mortality indicators, shown in Table 12.4, did not improve as much as they had done in previous decades, if not worsen. For instance, Nigeria's infant mortality rate in 1988 was particularly high (103 mortalities per 1000 live births). In Chile, the percentage of the appropriate age group enrolled in

Table 12.4   Some basic human indicators

	Infant mortality rate (per 1000 live births)				Primary education (% of age group enrolled)			
	1965	1970	1988	1993	1965	1970	1987	1992
Algeria	154	139	72	53	68	76	96	99
Argentina	58	52	31	24	101	105	110	107
Brazil	104	95	61	57	108	82	103	106
Mexico	82	72	46	35	92	104	118	113
Nigeria	177	114	103	83	32	37	77	76
Venezuela	65	53	35	23	94	94	107	99
Colombia	86	77	39	36	84	108	114	117
Chile	101	77	20	16	124	107	103	96
Ecuador	112	100	62	49	91	97	117	na
Hungary	39	35	16	15	101	97	97	89
Indonesia	128	118	68	56	72	80	118	115
Morocco	145	128	71	66	57	52	71	69
Philippines	72	71	44	42	113	108	106	109
Turkey	165	144	75	62	101	110	117	112
Zaire	141	na	96	na	70	na	76	na
Côte D'Ivoire	149	135	95	91	60	58	70	69
Egypt	172	158	83	64	75	72	90	101
Pakistan	149	142	107	88	40	40	52	46
Peru	130	116	86	63	99	107	122	119

Source: *World Development Reports*, various issues.

primary education declined between 1965 and 1992. In Morocco and Pakistan, there is a decline in this same primary education percentage between 1988 and 1992.

The situation of LDCs in the early 1990s gave hope that growth could resume in these countries and contribute to the improvement of living standards. Unfortunately, the shadow of the debt crisis still looms over LDCs today. One cannot help but wonder whether a more efficient way of handling the debt crisis could, and should, have been adopted by the international financial community during the 1980s. The following section presents the debt reduction plan which Tarshis proposed early in the crisis. We shall describe it and analyse why a comprehensive debt reduction proposal such as Tarshis' was ultimately not adopted.

THE TARSHIS PROPOSAL

Tarshis (1984) had stressed the need for both debtor and creditor countries to forgive some proportion of the debt. In 1987, Tarshis presented a new plan to deal with the debt crisis. His analysis of the crisis is highly reminiscent of Keynes' approach in *The Economic Consequences of the Peace* (1920). He first points out the inconsistency of the debt problem in the long-run. He claims that the LDCs cannot repay their debt, not because of their inability to repay but because of the lack of readiness of the creditor countries to accept payment. Indeed, if the creditor countries' goal is to be reimbursed over a period of, say, ten years, they must allow their imports of goods and services from the LDCs to exceed their exports to the LDCs by more than $100 billion in each of the ten years, given the interest servicing on the debt, capital flight from developing countries and the principal to be repaid to the creditors.[9] Tarshis (1987) concedes that such a situation, lasting for a year or two, cannot be ruled out. Yet, pointing to Germany's position in the Versailles Treaty, he suggests by analogy that it would be highly unlikely that a developed country would accept a situation in which it is flooded with imports while its possible exports are rejected for an extended period of time. Thus given that the natural solution – a continual recycling of funds from lender to debtor to creditor, with the level of debt rising indefinitely – was not working, Tarshis (1987) saw but one solution left: to have the creditors forgive the debt.

Tarshis believed that this debt forgiveness should be done according to particular principles. First, any proposed solution must be a global solution that relieved the threats to the private sectors of both the LDCs and the developed countries, that is, it must not be a pure crisis management action. Second, the LDCs and the creditor countries must stand to gain from the application of the proposal, which does not imply that the parties involved should not bear any of the costs. In fact, Tarshis points out that any proposal should recognize the costs that the debtors and the creditors have paid already and those that they will have to encounter in the new proposal. The key is for them to recognize that they will be better off under the terms of the proposal. Finally, Tarshis recognizes that the proposal must be incentive-compatible for the parties involved. In particular, what may be individually rational for a bank may not be collectively rational for all banks, and a proposed solution should incite all the creditors to participate.

Tarshis' proposed solution was, as he put it, 'a monetary solution to a monetary problem – too much credit extended by the commercial banks' (Tarshis, 1987). His proposal involves the central bank of a creditor nation buying, at a discount, a portion of the debt certificates held by the commercial banks – say 20 per cent a year – and crediting the deposits of the commercial bank at the central bank. The scheme is analogous to open-market operations. When the US Federal Reserve decides to buy, say, $500 million in US Treasury bills, it owns the Treasury bills and pays the selling banks by adding the amount to the deposits that the banks keep in their bank – the Fed itself. Tarshis argues that the same creative finance can be applied to the bad, or very bad, LDC debt certificates owned by commercial banks. The Fed can buy them from their owners, and if they are bad, the sellers should not expect payment in full. Indeed, he suggests that the Fed might be well advised to pay a small premium over the basic rate. Once the debt paper has been purchased by the Fed, the Fed would, as Tarshis puts it, 'cancel it and send it back to the country of issue, with best wishes.' (Tarshis, 1987). Thus the debtor countries would see part of their debt burden reduced and the banks would have a very questionable asset turned into a sold one, although at a reduced price.

Tarshis was aware that his proposal would encounter several difficulties. First, an obvious fear was that the implementation of the scheme would lead to inflation. Tarshis responded that the authorities could ensure that purchases of debt papers were spread out over a period of say, five years. Another possible step was that the central bank could sterilize the purchases by selling Treasury bills from its own inventory. And if, despite that offset, the monetary base still rose too quickly, the central bank could require, for as long as it was needed, that the commercial banks hold a higher proportion of their deposit liabilities as a reserve. Another problem was that since central bank purchases of debt would be done at a book value in excess of market value, central banks would then contribute lower profits to their respective governments, as each central bank is owned by its government.[10] Therefore, taxpayers would assume some of the loss made by central banks on purchases of LDC debt from the commercial banks.

According to Dore and Tarshis (1990), the Tarshis scheme of 1987 had nevertheless several advantages. First, the proposal is highly incentive-compatible. They argue that the proposal is a stable solution in the sense that a bank has no incentive to follow a non-cooperative strategy. Each bank within a jurisdiction sells the same portion of its debt certificates to the central bank. Thus the relative indebtedness of the banks remains unchanged, as each bank receives the same proportional relief. As the debtor countries have the right to repay part of the loan at face value, the commercial bank would be indifferent between the debtor country's redeeming the debt and the Fed's redeeming it. So, no bank has the possibility of a free ride by not participating. A non-participating bank would simply carry a larger debt, and since all banks would be required to reduce their exposure to the same level as the participating banks, there would be no incentive for not participating. The only other alternative to not participating would be for a bank to increase its capital.

One other scheme proposed at around the same time, was the International Debt Discount Corporation (IDDC), by Kenen (1983, 1990). The idea was to create a new international financial institution that would be financed by developed countries. Its capital would be subscribed by its sponsors and used exclusively to guarantee its own obligations. The IDDC would then issue its own long-term obligations to commercial banks in exchange for their claims on developing countries. As with the Tarshis plan, the IDDC would pay a price lower than the face value for the commercial paper, possibly using the market price on the secondary debt market.[11]

Obviously, neither the IDDC nor the Tarshis Plan was adopted by the international financial community. Instead, the Brady Plan with its piece-meal/menu approach, became the norm. Today, we still live with the consequences of that decision. Why was a more comprehensive plan not adopted?

Analytical Problems Faced by Any Debt Reduction Scheme

The answer to this question lies in the several problems a comprehensive debt reduction plan has to address. First, the nature of the debt contracts between the creditors and the debtors brings in problems of adverse selection and moral hazard. Adverse selection says that any debt reduction scheme is likely to deal with LDC debt that is the least likely to be valuable, and that consequently the costs of cancelling the debt may be higher than initially expected. The moral hazard argument implies that any announced scheme would invite debtor countries to pursue further irresponsible policies, knowing that whatever they borrow would be cancelled. The expectation of an announcement of a debt reduction scheme might lead to a new round of over-borrowing.

The second type of difficulty a debt reduction plan must overcome is the free-rider problem, caused by the fact that there are several banks which are creditors to one country. For Mexico, there were, at one point, close to 600 banks involved in debt rescheduling. During debt reduction negotiations, if one bank believes that the rest will grant debt relief, bilaterally or through some international agreement, it has an incentive to hang back given that the price of the debt paper will increase once some remaining debt has been removed. This problem, similar to the prisoner's dilemma, makes any voluntary reduction of debt very difficult.[12]

Finally, a debt reduction scheme must address the issues related to the financial costs of its execution: how much does it cost; who should pay; are the costs divided fairly? It was first suggested by Kenen that the cost would be relatively small given that most of the debtors suffer from a debt overhang. It was thought that reducing their debt burden would free up resources and allow LDCs to grow faster since most LDCs appear to have curtailed investment to service their debt obligations. As a result, LDCs would then be more capable of servicing their remaining debt obligations. This 'debt Laffer curve' argument applies, however, only if the country is on the downward portion of the curve. Here, the secondary market value of the debt would rise as the debt is forgiven. However, empirical estimates of the relation between the stock of debt and its market value suggested that few debtor countries were in such a position.[13]

Consequently, the costs of debt reduction were then higher than initially expected. It was feared that the creditor governments would end up passing the costs on to their taxpayers. Though the developed economies themselves suffered through a reduction in their exports to debtor countries caused by the debt crisis, it was felt that a bail-out of large banks and some dictatorial developing countries would not be politically feasible.[14] Furthermore, it is not clear that creditor countries' governments could have forced their banks to agree to a settlement which would have decreased their shareholders' return. For instance, Dooley (1995) points out that the Federal Reserve was hostile to imposing write-downs of debt and doubted whether it could be done equitably.

How did the Brady Plan deal with these Problems?

To date, the only debt reduction plan adopted by the international financial community has been the Brady Plan. How did it deal with the problems of free riders, moral hazard, adverse selection and the costs of the scheme? For Mexico, the free-rider problem was solved by ensuring that any banks that tried to free ride would lose everything because the government would essentially refuse to honour the old loans. Creditors either signed up to one of the three options or lost all of their money. This 'voluntary' participation of the creditors was extracted, thanks to the support of Western governments which used moral suasion on the banks. Furthermore, Western governments were not afraid of creating a bad precedent, potentially leading to moral hazard by other countries, because Mexico had earned their support, having undertaken drastic economic reforms with a series of price liberalization and privatization measures. Thus the Brady Plan overcame the serious problems mentioned above and, as a result, private inflows of foreign capital resumed after the Plan went into effect.

The actual debt reduction achieved under the Brady Plan was quite small. Van Wijnbergen (1991) pointed out that Mexico's foreign debt by the end of 1988 was $100.4 billion. With the Brady deal, banks wrote off their claim by $12 billion, while the IFIs' exposure, needed to guarantee the new Brady bonds, was raised by $7 billion. Hence the debt reduction Mexico received, though preferable to nothing, was not large. Furthermore, as Claessens, Diwan and Fernandez-Arias (1992) document, other Brady-Plan countries had only limited debt relief. Other studies also suggest that debtor countries and banks were the gainers, while the IFIs and creditor governments absorbed the losses as the private banks' burden was gradually shifted on to them. For instance, Cohen (1992) and Dooley (1995) note how the creditor banks reduced their exposure, and Ahmed and Summers (1992) implicitly acknowledge the IFIs' role in this when they stress the need for multilateral action on lending to low- and middle-income developing countries.

Although the amount of debt reduction under the Brady Plan was small, it nevertheless restored foreign confidence in some developing countries in the early 1990s. Yet the abrupt withdrawal of the flows from equity investment funds to emerging market economies has shown the precariousness of economic conditions in LDCs, even in those which enjoyed Brady Plan relief.

The impeccable fiscal credentials of Chile were not enough to calm the fears of mutual fund managers who were afraid that the Mexican peso debacle would affect Chile. Early in 1995, international investors suspected that Brazil and Argentina, which had recently enjoyed Brady Plan relief, would be following Mexico.[15]

Why No Adoption of a More Comprehensive Debt Reduction Scheme?

In the light of the above, the question of why a more comprehensive debt reduction scheme, such as the Tarshis Plan or the IDDC, has not been adopted remains. The Tarshis Plan had many advantages. First, as opposed to the IDDC, it was relatively simple and did not create a new bureaucracy to deal with debt papers. Though it would not have been without cost to the taxpayer, the scheme suggested by Tarshis would not have created a visible institution that taxpayers could point to as a direct cost they had to shoulder. Second, as long as commercial banks would be required to sell the same given proportion of their debt paper, and all banks were required to reduce their exposure to the same level as the participating banks, there would be no incentive for not participating because each bank would get the same proportional relief. Consequently, the incentive to hold back in the hope of an increase in the secondary market value of debt is reduced. The problem of adverse selection would have been resolved by the fact that under the Tarshis proposal, the central bank would have *de facto* purchased a diversified basket of debt papers. (This was also what Kenen (1990) suggests the IDDC should do in order to avoid being saddled with the very bad debt papers.)

One lacuna of the Tarshis proposal is that it neglected the problem of moral hazard and precedence. Tarshis was willing to forgive a given percentage of the debt of all countries, whether they were careful or careless borrowers. He did so even if he admitted that, in some countries: 'Too large a share of funds was often frittered away to pay for imports of luxuries and military supplies and to help pay for real estate and bank accounts in such safe havens as Florida and Hawaii and Zurich' (Tarshis, 1989, p. 166). For Tarshis, this was a small cost to pay compared with the benefits that a comprehensive debt reduction scheme would bring. Already in 1987, he would claim:

> The proposals presented here for disarming the debt bomb are radical in only one sense. They cut through a problem bogged down in a welter of law, political science, and ethics. But they do not look at a radical restructuring of the economy. Debts are forgiven because they cannot be paid; because fruitless efforts to service harm the debtors; and because industrialized countries want the debtors as markets. Once it is seen that the losses had already been experienced soon after the funds were borrowed, it will be recognized that 'forgiveness now' costs the creditor much less than stubborn adherence to the letter of an impossible contract; and it benefits the debtor far more. (Tarshis, 1987, p. 217)

This view was not shared by Bulow and Rogoff (1990) who felt that, on equity grounds, a debt bail-out was difficult to justify since the more important debtors were in fact Latin American countries which are middle-income countries. They suggested that spending scarce foreign aid resources on bailing out these countries instead of investing in basic infrastructure, education and health services in poorer countries would not be fair.

At the end of the day, however, it would appear that the major reason a more comprehensive debt reduction scheme has not been adopted by the international financial community was the difficulty in agreeing on a price for purchasing the outstanding debt paper. Indeed, a necessary condition for these schemes to work was to agree, *ex ante*, on a price at which the debt paper would be purchased, presumably much lower than its face value. Without this, the benefits of debt reduction evaporate. Bulow and Rogoff (1988a) show that the debt buy-back itself affects the market value of the secondary market debt. In fact, if a country wants to repurchase a given amount and is known to be willing to do so, then the price at which the transaction will be carried out can only be the *ex post* equilibrium price; otherwise no lender would sell its claim. Bulow and Rogoff cite the March 1988 Bolivian buy-back as an example where the buy-back did not affect the country's debt obligations since the secondary market price rose after the transactions, eliminating the potential gains it could have had in reducing Bolivia's total foreign debt obligations. A buy-back can be beneficial if it is, as Cohen and Verdier (1990) and Cohen (1992) argue, done secretly or anonymously. This secrecy is equivalent to agreeing to an *ex ante* price, and is, in fact, what several Latin American countries did with their foreign debt during the 1930s.[16]

One possible explanation for the difficulty in agreeing to an *ex ante* price lies in the fact that the parties involved in the debt crisis were not only the debtor countries and the banks. The typical view has been to treat the debt negotiations as a two-player game. This is the view adopted in Dore and Tarshis (1990) and by most other researchers. Bulow and Rogoff (1988b) is a notable exception. They present a dynamic bargaining model of the three-way negotiations between creditor banks, debtor countries and creditor country taxpayers.

Indeed, a central player before and after the 1982 announcement by Mexico has been the IFIs and the creditor governments through their central banks and finance ministries. Throughout the crisis, the debt negotiations were different from the neutral view of two players with a selfless agent who helps to internalize some factors that the debtors and banks cannot. Rather, three parties were involved in these negotiations, with the IFIs and the creditor governments having the dual role of lender and guardian of financial stability at the domestic and international level. As such, the IFIs sometimes sided with the creditors (Mexico, 1982 rescheduling), and sometimes with the debtors (Mexico, Brady Plan). Furthermore, creditors and debtors could lobby the IFIs (and their shareholders, the creditor governments) to gain the upper hand in negotiations.

Throughout the debt negotiations, some observers have noted that the banks had been successful in muddling their way through the debt mess. True, they never recovered the full value of the loans and their share prices suffered through the crisis. Yet they avoided a massive write-down of the loans that a comprehensive debt reduction plan would have required. Dooley (1995) argues that the banks expected the creditor governments to bail them out. When they realized that the creditor governments would not do so, they manoeuvred the IFIs into taking an increasing share of the burden, particularly during the Baker Plan. Their lobbying strength appears to originate from the recycling of oil money in the 1970s.

Like Tarshis (1984), Dooley (1995) considers that industrial countries consistently permitted and fostered the banks' intermediating loans to developing countries because of the need to maintain aggregate demand in the oil-consuming world. At that point, the probability of a debt crisis was undoubtedly very low and banks were willing to lend to sovereign countries, given the potential returns. In addition, the banks' attitude towards credit risk was influenced less by the quality of the borrower than by the quality of the collateral. Here, Dooley (1995) points out that the collateral was, first, a debtor government guarantee of loans to the residents of the developing countries and, ultimately, the political commitment of a creditor country to the debtor government. Starting in 1982, when the credits were put at risk by the new economic conditions, the banks called in the collateral, pointing out that they had been asked to recycle the oil money and that the solvency of the banking system was very important to the governments of the industrial countries.

Instead of a rescue package, banks were told by the creditor governments to lend more money to LDCs. Banks, however, perceived this reaction as an *ex post* change in the rules of the game and went on to get from their own governments what they could not collect from their developing country debtors following 1982, by having IFIs substitute their official funds for theirs. The political will needed for a quick resolution of the debt crisis was absent in the minds of Western leaders. Instead they allowed complex negotiations to take place between the banks, the IFIs and the debtor countries. The cost of these negotiations was time, which was particularly expensive for the debtor countries. Dooley (1995) argues that the creditor governments made a major policy error in refusing to provide the expected backstop to the banks. According to him, 'this policy choice transformed an unremarkable financial crisis into a decade-long economic crisis for the debtor countries' (Dooley, 1995, p. 267). Thus the difficulty in achieving an agreement on an *ex ante* price and the enormous costs borne by the debtor countries were the result of prolonged self-interested bargaining between the commercial banks and their own governments, not between the banks and the debtor countries. Unfortunately, these conditions explain why the international financial community could not implement a comprehensive debt reduction plan such as the one suggested by Tarshis (1987) or Kenen (1990).

TARSHIS AND THE FUTURE OF THE INTERNATIONAL MONETARY SYSTEM

This chapter has reviewed Tarshis' contribution to the international debt literature. Tarshis (1984) presents a global view of the links between the industrialized and developing economies and, earlier than most observers, calls for a reduction of the debt burden of developing countries. The chapter has presented

Tarshis' (1987) proposed solution to the international debt crisis of the 1980s and has argued that, although his plan could have worked in principle, its comprehensive and integrated approach towards resolving the crisis was unfortunately a non-starter from the creditor countries' points of view. For many reasons, these countries were, and still are, unwilling to encounter the large short-term cost of cancelling the debt of most debtor countries in return for the longer-term benefits of greater growth in these countries. After spelling out his proposal in his *Challenge* article in 1987, Tarshis tried in his other articles (1988, 1989, 1990) to convince creditor governments of the short-sightedness of their policies and of the need for a comprehensive approach. He did so by recalling Germany's experience after World War I (Tarshis, 1988) and by pointing out that the debtor countries were extremely unlikely to be able to export enough ever to repay the debt, unless the creditor countries were willing to run masive current account deficits for several years (Dore and Tarshis, 1990; Tarshis, 1989). His own view of the Brady Plan was that it was insufficient, both because it did not cancel enough debt for each country and because it was a country-by-country approach.[17] Unfortunately, his voice, as well as those of others, such as Kenen (1990) and Sachs (1989), was not heard by the international financial community.

The consequences of the debt crisis of the 1980s will be felt for a long time. For the low-income debtor countries found mainly in Africa, their debt will eventually be forgiven. Though Ahmed and Summers (1992) recognized the need to cancel their debt obligations, these LDCs are still saddled with obligations to the IFIs and creditor governments. Some action has been taken (for instance, the US government cancelled some of Jordan's debt in the spring of 1995), but some observers have called for a swifter and more comprehensive response from the IFIs. Hardy (1995) and Helleiner (1994), for instance, argue the urgency for multilateral debt relief for severely indebted countries and the need to restore net transfers to low-income Sub-Saharan Africa. However, as Sachs (1994) notes, the IFIs seem obsessed with the problem of moral hazard and, unless a new direction is taken, they will keep using a lengthy, piecemeal approach to debt reduction.

The conditions of the middle-income LDCs are different. Although they could avoid the fate of the severely indebted countries, the debt crisis left them very vulnerable to the new environment of globalization, where the world's economies are now quickly being integrated through trade in goods, services, multinational production and finance.[18] Mexico's peso crisis of 1994 is only one extreme example of how little latitude these countries have when capital flows are shifted rapidly overnight. Other Latin American countries have also suffered from the withdrawal of funds, and adjustments have been difficult to make, with some devaluations and budget restrictions hurting several sectors of their economies.[19]

Therefore, it is not surprising that 50 years after Bretton Woods, in this new world of the globalization of capital flows, several calls have been made to provide a new set of rules for the international monetary system.[20] For instance, in response to capital flows that may temporarily destabilize economies, Tobin's (1978) suggestion of a tax on capital flows has resurfaced. This 'Tobin tax' would be placed on short-term capital flows to reduce their mobility, in effect providing some sand in the wheels of international finance.[21] The practicality of such a tax has, however, been questioned by many observers, and the emphasis has rather been put on reforming the IFIs themselves.[22] Sachs (1994) and Williamson (1995) suggest an increasing role for the IMF, and in particular they stress the need for better surveillance of the IMF and the need for augmenting the pool of funds that the IMF disposes to help stabilize troubled economies. Williamson (1995) proposes that the IMF create a new quick-disbursing facility that could fund a large volume of debt papers and enable a country to offset disequilibrating capital flows in the short and medium term (less than five years). In addition, both Williamson (1995) and Bergsten (1994) call for a less flexible system of exchange rates to facilitate the growth of world trade.

Even though Tarshis' later research put more emphasis on the debt crisis itself, he insisted on several occasions that the international monetary system needed serious reform, and he did so consistently and ahead of most other economic observers. Already in 1984, Tarshis had made similar suggestions to those of Williamson (1995), Bergsten (1994) and Sachs (1994), and went even further. First, as in Williamson (1995), Tarshis (1984) advocates a system of exchange rate bands to ease trade and integration. Second, he proposes increasing the role of the IMF to make it similar to a super-central bank. This new entity would have greater power to increase loans to troubled economies and to augment the liquidity of the whole international system if so needed.

As opposed to Williamson (1995) and Sachs (1994), who suggest a self-regulated system, Tarshis (1984) proposes that this exchange rate system be supervised by the newly empowered IMF. Tarshis' idea here follows that of Keynes' proposal at the Bretton Woods conference.[23] Tarshis (1984) claims that an initial flaw of the IMF is that it not only lacks proper resources but also has only some power over the deficit countries to adjust their balance-of-payments disequilibria. The surplus countries have, in the present system, few incentives to adjust in the short and middle term. Tarshis would give additional powers to the IMF to create incentives for surplus countries to adjust faster to a balance-of-payments equilibrium.

Tarshis (1984) suggests that every surplus country should be required to deposit, say, 50 per cent of its annual surplus in the IMF. The IMF would then be required to provide loans of up to 50 per cent of the amount of their deficits to deficit countries wanting to borrow. Interest would of course be collected from borrowers and paid to depositors. Interest paid on deposits would not be set so high as to press any country to build its surplus still higher. At the same time, the rate charged on IMF loans should not be so low as to persuade deficit countries to increase their deficits. In effect, the IMF would function as a supra-central bank.

Of course, Tarshis' suggestions suffer from the same problem as Keynes' *bancor* proposal: the likely unwillingness of surplus countries to participate in a system in which they may encounter costs. Although Tarshis' suggestions for reforming the international financial system may seem radical, they may in a few years reflect common thinking. With the notable exception of Kenen (1983), who also called for a bail-out plan for the banks, it is obvious that Tarshis' claims for a reduction in the debt burden of LDCs were way ahead of their time and have become accepted by the profession.[24] As national economies become more integrated due to the globalization process, the need for a stronger, supranational central bank may also be recognized. Then, like now, the problem will be to implement a new system in which there are concentrated short-term costs (i.e. the loss of independence of surplus countries) but dispersed and more important long-term gains for everyone due to global trade expansion.

NOTES

1. I thank O. Hamouda, B. Price, S. Rogers and R. Rowley for helpful comments and suggestions. All remaining errors are mine.
2. Given that after more than ten years, the debt burden of some developing countries is still a cause for concern, several observers note that describing the debt problem as a 'crisis', that is, as a 'state of affairs in which a decisive change for better or for worse is imminent' may be stretching the use of the English language. (Cf. Bogdanowicz-Bindert (1989) and Cohen (1992).)
3. For more details on the debt crisis, its origin and the reactions to it, the reader should refer to Tarshis (1984, 1988), Cohen (1992), Sachs (1989) and Dooley (1995). Hogendorn (1992) presents a nice summary of the issues.
4. For more details, cf. the discussion of policy mistakes by the LDCs in Hogendorn (1992).
5. Cf. Kletzer (1984), Guttentag and Herring (1986) and Devlin (1989) for a review of the banks' possible reasons for their excessive lending.
6. For more details on the Baker Plan, see Caskey and Felix (1989).
7. For more details on the Brady Plan, see the articles by Bogdanowicz-Bindert (1989) and Van Wijnbergen (1991).
8. Of course, these countries suffer from more problems than their exposure to foreign debt. See Krugman (1995) and Naim (1995) for a discussion of the problems which Latin American countries face and how one should avoid unrealistic expectations about the results of the structural adjustment policies these countries have undergone.
9. In 1987, most estimates of the total debt of the developing countries were in the $1 trillion range. Tarshis' (1987) example suggests an annual estimate of $100 billion for debt servicing and an annual amount of $40 billion for capital flight, besides the rough amount of $100 billion needed to reimburse the principal.

10. This point has been made by Charles Goodhart (e.g. 1995). Tarshis (1989) argues that the loss was already absorbed by the economy when the crisis erupted. Recognizing it through a lower face value price would only 'officialize' a position that has been recognized for several years.

11. This, however, brings out important incentive problems. First, the mere possibility of the existence of the IDDC should raise the secondary market price of the debt. Second, there is also an incentive for debtor countries to pursue imprudent policies to force down the price of the debt at which the IDDC could buy their debt papers. See Kenen (1990) for more details on the IDDC proposal as well as its difficulties.

12. See Krugman (1989) for an analysis of market-based debt reduction schemes and the problems associated with them.

13. See Claessens (1990) for a discussion of the results.

14. Cf. Bulow and Rogoff (1990) for arguments against a taxpayer bail-out of banks and debtor countries.

15. The article by Naim (1995) discusses how Latin American countries have been affected by the Mexican peso crisis.

16. Cf. Eichengreen and Portes (1989) and Cohen and Verdier (1990) for more details.

17. Personal discussion with him, autumn 1989.

18. For a review of the globalization of equity markets and how it affects the developing countries, cf. Claessens (1995) and Claessens, Dooley and Warner (1995).

19. Cf., for example, the articles by Krugman (1995) and Naim (1995).

20. For a survey of the achievements (and lack of) of Bretton Woods as well as proposals for reform, see Eichengreen and Kenen (1994) and Kenen (1994).

21. Cf. Eichengreen, Tobin and Wyploz (1995) for a discussion of the advantages and disadvantages of such a tax.

22. See Garber and Taylor (1995) for a list of the problems of implementing the 'Tobin tax'.

23. Cf. Moggridge (1977), Volume XXV of *The Collected Writings of John Maynard Keynes*, for a description of the clearing union system and the use of '*bancor*'.

24. Cf. Ahmed and Summers (1992), Cohen (1992), Helleiner (1994) and Dooley (1995).

PART IV

Introductory comments: 'A possible utopia'

Richard M. Goodwin

The modern industrial economies have grown for about two centuries at about 2 per cent. This has meant generally the end of poverty and a real rise in the standards of living of all classes. There is no very strong reason why this remarkable continuous growth should not continue for some time more. But given the satisfactory state of the bulk of the population, it now becomes possible to think about realizable alternatives to this endless accumulation of economic goods.

After much casual thought on the subject, I have arrived at a proposal for a realizable alternative to this, to my mind, unattractive devotion to endless accumulation of economic goods, which are no longer essential and often carry a dubious effect on the life and thought of modern man.

Assuming that technology will continue to improve, as it has in the past for two centuries, why not use the resulting growth in human productivity to alter for the better the quality of life in the modern developed economies?

If this assumption continues to hold in the next half century, then one can ask, could not this accumulation of productivity be used to improve the quality of life rather than the quantity of economic expenditure?

To put a complicated matter in crudely simplistic terms, if one were to keep total aggregate output constant and use the gains of technical productivity to reduce the common work week from 40 hours to roughly 14 hours, then keeping aggregate output constant one could, in half a century, reduce the typical work week to 14 hours. Think of what a magical transformation of the life of all peoples. They could spend much of their lives in doing whatever they like to do, not in what they have to do to earn a living. All commercial advertising should be forbidden and replaced by objective reports on existing goods and services. Think of most people's lives consisting of touring or sport: sailing or fishing, etc ...

13. *Caveat emptor*, investor, depositor?

Charles P. Kindleberger[1]

INTRODUCTION

As one who has not kept up with the subtleties of macroeconomics in which Lorie Tarshis excelled, I was relieved when the editors indicated that one could go beyond government responsibilities in stabilizing the economy, revolutionized by Keynes with Tarshis in attendance, to other problems with government roles. Combining earlier writing on swindling schemes and their role in financial crises (Kindleberger, 1989, Ch. 5) with the few remarks in Lord Skidelsky's second volume on Keynes that dealt with social justice, 'about which he was not passionate' (Skidelsky, 1994, p. 223), I thought it might be useful to worry the problem of whether 'he governs best who governs least', or whether the administration of justice – one of Adam Smith's three public goods – requires some attention to ensuring that the unscrupulous in society do not take advantage of the innocent, the ignorant and perhaps the greedy who lack judgement. The exercise is a limited one, stopping short of treatment of other ethical problems in economics – the distribution of income and wealth, free riders, entitlements of individuals, duties as well as rights, and so on.

It is hard not to believe that the issue is timely as one reads press accounts of Ivan Boesky, Steven Hoffenberg, Charles Keating, Michael Milken, Prudential Investors, et al. In Britain 'hardly a week goes by without some unsuitable product [in life insurance] being foisted on an unsuspecting customer by an overzealous tout' (*The Economist*, 21 January 1994, p. 84). In the United States, 'Revelations in the news media of deceptive sales practices and corporate misconduct involving major insurers, including Metropolitan Life, Prudential Insurance, and New York Life, have brought into question the sales practices of the industry' (*Boston Globe*, 17 February 1994, under the headline 'Exaggerated Salesmanship Hurts Consumers, Companies').

I happen not to be a student of ethics, but as I understand it, there are three broad branches – the utilitarian, natural law and the deontological (Gustafson, 1991). The utilitarian advocates morality because it pays, as implied in the headline just quoted, at least in the long run, if not the short, and for operations with an expectation of repetition. I have no idea what the ethics of natural law may be. The deontological postulates moral behaviour as a duty. I assume that the Kantian Categorical Imperative, that the individual or unit should act only in ways which can be generalized, falls under this class, though it has social utility.

CAVEAT EMPTOR

Caveat emptor (let the buyer beware) is a long-established tradition in law and practice in the Anglo-Saxon world. In rational expectations, consumers are assumed to be intelligent, informed, competent and able to look after their own interests. An even stronger argument can be made for investors, who presumably were intelligent enough to acquire some degree of wealth, or had the luck to be genetically descended from parents who did. Maintenance of justice, apart from prevention or punishment of crime, would in such a world require primarily seeing to it that contracts freely entered into are faithfully carried out. It is assumed that, while there may be some who cannot look after their own interests and some who would take advantage of that inability, the results of such departures from the assumptions of well-functioning markets are readily repaired by charity or government welfare and do not undermine optimistic conclusions as to how the capitalistic system works. In one view, Barro has held that departures from rationality and maximization are random and unpredictable so that they can be neglected (Swedberg, 1990, pp. 74–5). The record suggests otherwise.

Once in his *Lectures on Justice, Police Revenue, and Arms* (1759) and again in *The Theory of Moral Sentiments* ([1759] 1808), Adam Smith brings out the moral chestnut, 'Honesty is the best policy', in both instances slightly qualified. In the *Lectures*, the reasoning runs in terms not of moral duty, but of utility: 'The trader deals so often that he finds honesty is the best policy' (Lerner, 1937, p. xxxiii). This is close to the view of the political scientist, Robert Axelrod (1984), who believes that in two-person, repeat-game theory, tit for tat is the optimal strategy. It finds some support in economic history. Investment in reputation paid off in medieval trade in one detailed account because the short-run benefit from cheating was lower than the long-run profit from faithful trade (Greif, 1989), and a sociologist points out that deals among diamond merchants are conducted with a handshake because of a closely monitored community (Granovetter and Swedberg, 1992, pp. 62–3). Both these cases, however, involved more or less equals, and even then, Granovetter notes (in Granovetter and Swedberg, 1992, pp. 62–3), theft and murder have occurred among diamond dealers. An Italian economist has asserted that investment in reputation is a fragile basis on which to build rational expectations because of the limited ability of economic actors to monitor the behaviour of others (Sacco, 1990). This would seem to be especially true in trade between unequals: seller/buyer, borrower/lender, adult/child, employer/employee.

In *The Theory of Moral Sentiments*, Dr Smith holds that the rule about honesty 'almost always holds true' ([1759] 1808, Vol. 2, p. 142), but the exceptions are not discussed.

Lack of information may impede the efficient operation of markets. In a long list of articles, alone and with collaborators, Joseph Stiglitz has suggested that market failure comes largely from lack of information. George Akerlof, in a widely cited paper (1970), developed the notion of asymmetric information, in which one party to a transaction had information which the other lacked, the classic instance being of 'lemons' in automobiles which never functioned satisfactorily. The defence under rational expectations would run in terms of private markets springing up to provide needed information if there were sufficient demand for it. Such is frequently the case, as credit bureaus, manuals that rate securities and consumer periodicals that grade products for household sale testify. These are sought out by those who know what they do not know, and this does not include everyone. Adverse selection is likely to bring it about that those most in need of information are unaware of that fact.

A highly cynical argument in favour of *laissez-faire*, in contrast to rational expectations, is the public-choice view that governmental personnel are not to be trusted to fulfil the tasks for which they are hired, but are as self-serving and disdainful of duty as those in the private sector, or perhaps more so. The record of governmental corruption in Italy and Japan in the 1990s is especially disturbing, more in Japan where trust has been the basis of society (Dore, 1992). Monitoring by the police and the media caught up slowly with the record of bribes offered for contracts, bribes taken and contracts awarded. Corruption has been endemic in economic history, back in my knowledge to the East India Company (Van Klaveren, 1957, 1958, 1959, 1960), and in the USA to the Credit Mobilier, the Erie Railroad and the Teapot Dome. My interest is less in whether the government can mind its own honesty, or have it minded effectively by others, than in whether private markets need government to patrol the nature of private economic transactions in the market, as well as the fulfilment of contracts.

GOVERNMENT INTERVENTION IN PRIVATE EXCHANGES

Whether theory is justified in arguing against government intervention in private exchanges, either because of rational expectations or the *tu quoque* that it has no higher moral record, economic history shows a revealed preference for such attention. At the most elementary level, government has checked the accuracy of yardsticks and scales for weighing to protect the unsuspecting consumer from the veniality of the retailer. In his chapter on metrology in *American Treasure and the Price Revolution in Spain* (1934), Earl J. Hamilton directs attention mainly to establishing uniform standards of weights and measures himself, the better to make price comparisons. He is, however, also interested in how well towns and villages in Castile adhere to royal standards and in the attempts to combat dishonesty. Public complaint about confusing and ill-kept standards was continuous for centuries (Hamilton, 1934, Ch. vii, esp. pp. 160ff.).

Various classes of promoters and salespeople have in history and literature notoriously taken advantage of unsophisticated consumers and investors, characterized as 'widows and orphans, clergymen, spinsters, retired naval and military officers, magistrates, country gentry, theologians, country misers, authors, grandmothers ...' (Kindleberger, 1989, fn. p. 35). Widows and orphans usually have pride of place among the innocent, and government protection of them goes back to the Code of Hammurabi in Mesopotamia in the 18th century BC. This may be defended by *laissez-faire* economists as a normal exchange transaction in which Hammurabi traded insurance for the wives and children of soldiers against the latters' willingness to fight, which might otherwise not be forthcoming. Closer to the present day, note that there is in Britain an insurance company named Scottish Widows, and recently in France it was asserted that the country has always been protective of 'the widow of Carpentras', not a real historical figure, I gather, but a generic comparable to the 'little old Lady in tennis shoes from Dubuque' (Ploix, 1994, p. 338).

Beyond widows and orphans, in today's world, it is frequently stated, though more than anecdotal evidence would be hard to produce, that certain professions do well financially, but are insufficiently astute investors to safeguard their gains appropriately: doctors, dentists, movie stars, outstanding athletes. These persons, it appears, often retain financial advisers, a few among whom may, on occasion, give poor advice or behave dishonestly, as, of course, others in fiduciary positions may do.

One class of labour which government has felt obliged to protect is sailors, against two kinds of miscreant. On the one hand were crimps, including boarding-house keepers, publicans, brothel operators and in some cases tailors, who extorted the pay of sailors returning from long voyages and/or sold them in a drunken state to ships requiring crews against a payment from the captain, and in most cases the advance note given to the sailor to buy gear for the new voyage (Kindleberger, 1992, pp. 20–21). On the other hand were shipowners who from time to time would recruit sailors, in unseaworthy vessels, often overloaded but insured, with disastrous loss of life. After a series of parliamentary investigations, the British government intervened and required Board of Trade surveys of suspected vessels' loading lines to set limits to freight. Rational expectations gains some support from the fact that Norwegian shipowners had a better record on shipwreck than British, with no government regulation, and early Venetian shipping relied on mutual interest to prevent owners from undermanning, overloading, using defective rigging, and the like. In Britain, however, even the interested insurance companies failed to curb adverse selection by 'a few nefarious shipowners' (Kindleberger, 1992, pp. 35–8).

Minor children, especially orphans, are everywhere deemed to require some government protection of various sorts from various afflictions. It is said that a three-year-old has no clue as to the difference between right and wrong (Etzioni, 1994). Most states in the United States deal with offenders under the age of 18 in special courts where they are given special consideration, although there is a claim that, with drugs, drug money, gang-related incidents and the ease of acquiring lethal weapons, a case can be made for reducing to 16, or in one view to 14, the age when they be treated as adults or when most juveniles can be held accountable for their own actions (Sexton, Graves and Lee, 1993). When, in a person's life, one is deemed competent to take care of property is a matter of varying opinion and legislation. Licences to handle an automobile, a significant piece of property, are issued in most states in the USA at age 16. The voting threshold, based presumably on some measure of judgement, is 18. A person is typically competent to buy alcoholic drinks at 21. Some people of wealth, as I understand it, turn over full control of a bequest left to an heir only at still higher ages: 25, 30 or even 40. Probate courts in Massachusetts do not allow the distribution of funds of a trust being dissolved to minors under 21, with the approval of the court to ensure that the terms of the trust have not been violated. How and when property of wards, in chancery, in Britain or controlled by Orphans' Courts, in Germany, are released I do not know. The significant point is that the property of those deemed not to be fully competent to manage it against misappropriation or unwise allocation is given protection by government.

CHARACTER DIFFERENCES AND VULNERABILITY

Distinctions should of course be made among intelligence, information and judgement on the one hand, and among their opposites, stupidity, ignorance and credulity on the other. Measured on the Wechsler *Adult* Intelligence Scale (emphasis added), IQ (intelligence quotient) follows a normal distribution, with 50 per cent of cases falling within the modal range of 90 to 109, where

100 is the mean, and 25 per cent above and below, consisting of 2.2 per cent above 130 and below 69, 6.7 per cent between 120 and 129 and 70 to 79, and 16.1 per cent between 110 and 119 and between 80 and 89. Whether the cut-off point on sufficient intelligence to handle ordinary consumer transactions is the third standard deviation below the mean (2.2 per cent), or the second and third together, I have no way of knowing. I assume, however, that the intelligence needed for major purposes, for investing significant amounts of money or for determining the quality of the assets of a bank, without deposit insurance, reaches into higher sections towards the central 82 per cent.

Intelligence differs from shrewdness, which, while defined as 'character-ized by or displaying astuteness or sagacity, sharply perceptive, clever and judicious, implying intelligence and wisdom' can, in my judgement, be intui-tive. One ranked low on the IQ scale could have a shrewd sense of being conned by a second-hand automobile dealer or a boiler-room operator in penny stocks. On the other hand, highly intelligent persons on the Wechsler scale seem to have shown themselves credulous.

My interest is more in the innocent and the ignorant than in the greedy. There is a French word, *gogo*, defined in *Petit Larousse*, as a 'credulous capitalist, easy to deceive'. I have seen it used to translate the slang American word 'sucker', which has also made a place in the dictionary, defined in the *Shorter Oxford* as one who is gullible or easily deceived, although the defini-tion did not indicate whether such a person was a capitalist. Capitalists, presumably, should take care of themselves, do more than kick the tyres, including asking questions, and even reading the small print in the advertise-ment and the prospectus.

Some decry 'blaming the victim', but when the victim is credulous or greedy, or covetous of wealth being acquired around him, there may well be merit in blaming him. Before she expressed French sympathy for the widow of Carpentras, Mme Ploix noted that *The Economist* had opposed the British government's making good the losses of the depositors in the BCCI default since they chose that bank deliberately, risking their money for higher returns than those in the market. 'Whether they were irrational (*fou* in the French), greedy or badly informed, the decisions they took were on their own respon-sibility and at their own risk.' She followed this, and the mention of the tradition of protecting widows, by deploring the Japanese banks which took care of the losses only of their wealthy clients (Ploix, 1994, p. 338).

Keynes commented a number of times on ignorance, according to Skidelsky's account. In *A Treatise on Money*, dealing with the 1926 strike of the coal miners and the return of the pound sterling to par, he said that solutions to issues of this sort were above the heads of more or less illiterate voters (Skidelsky, 1994, p. 224). In the 1925 Sidney Ball Lecture on 'The End of *Laissez Faire*', he held that objections to *laissez-faire* might be philosophical or merely practical, in the latter case the prevalence of ignorance over knowledge (Skidelsky, 1994, p. 225): 'Ignorance is the chief political and social evil of the day. It fosters class suspicion, made possible the acquisition of great fortune by insider knowledge ... the nationalization of knowledge is the one case for nationalization that is overwhelmingly right' (Skidelsky, 1994, p. 268, citing Keynes, 1925)

It is not self-evident what nationalization of knowledge is. Omission of 'economic' from the nature of the evil of the day might have been significant had it not been for the reference to great fortunes of the day from insider knowledge. Again in *A Treatise on Money*, in discussing the psychology of investors, Keynes wrote: 'They do not possess even the rudiments of what is required for a valid judgment and are the prey of hopes and fears aroused by transient events and as easily dispelled' (cited in Skidelsky, 1994, p. 336). Some of the ignorance which disturbed the conclusions of classical economic theory was uncertainty, or ignorance of the future (Skidelsky, 1994, p. 539). Despite his genius, sophistication and wide knowledge in many fields, Keynes shared this last brand of ignorance with the rest of the human race as he lost three fortunes, though he made four for himself and one for his college. It is hard to imagine that he would have been taken in by a swindler.

As an economist, I am not competent to judge the work of psychiatrists, psychologists and sociologists on character, both honest and criminal. I am impressed, however, by Eric Fromm's discussion of character as molded by genetics on the one hand and environment in early childhood on the other. Fromm's discussion is limited to the latter. At birth, a child acquires faith in goodness, love and justice, as it is fed, sheltered and comforted when sick or hurt. In many cases, this faith in goodness (or God) is ruined at an early age – four, five or six – sometimes even earlier – by becoming aware of parents lying, fighting, betraying the child's trust in them and in their unceasing benevolence. Some respond by growing independent, others by retreating from self-reliance, frequently moving into worldly aims – money, power, prestige (Fromm, 1964, pp. 28–30). In an earlier study, Fromm distinguished four types of 'unproductive' personality orientations: the receptive, exploitive, hoarding and marketing (Fromm, 1947, pp. 61, 111). The receptive person is trusting and wants to be loved; the exploitive takes what he or she wants by force or cunning, ready to grab and steal, or in intellectual endeavour to plagiarize. He or she is also ridden by envy of others who have more (Fromm, 1947, pp. 62–3). The hoarding and marketing patterns interest me less in the present connection of possible government protection of the innocent from the unscrupulous. Nonetheless, Fromm has some interesting observations. While the exploitive person wants power and wealth, the hoarding orientation is to preserve it and is risk averse. Property in this case is a symbol of self. The marketing orientation calls for education and intelligence, but not reason, and the salesman or shopkeeper who characterizes it is said himself not to be interested in honesty but, echoing Adam Smith and the Maghrib traders cited earlier, interested in what honesty will get him in the market (Fromm, 1947, p. 77). This is belief in ethics for its utilitarian value.

As a psychoanalyst who sees patients with a variety of personality disorders – a skewed sample of humanity – Fromm is presumably not in a position to offer opinions on the proportions of an ordinary population who are receptive, exploitive, hoarding or marketing among the unproductive class, or their size relative to productive persons. Nor does he seem to have an interest in the transition in a family from a buccaneering entrepreneur in one generation to a hoarding descendant interested in trustee-type securities in later generations. Criminologists may have some notions of the relative sizes of the group of exploitive orientation on the one hand, and their possible victims, the group of receptive orientation, on the other, but I have not had an opportunity to open up that foreign field.

CHARACTER DIFFERENCES AND CULPABILITY

It would be helpful if there were measurements of the distribution of honesty, greed and readiness to violate the law, the last separately for violent and for white-collar crime, but psychologists of my acquaintance tell me that they are unaware of any such. One argument against the popular notion of locking up for life those who commit three felonies – 'three strikes and you are out' – is that the propensity for such crime diminishes sharply after age 50. The same may not be true of white-collar crime. In the chapter on swindles in *Manias, Panics and Crashes* (1989), I observed that swindles rose with business booms, as the number of sheep to be fleeced multiplied, and rose again after the bubble burst after asset prices had declined a considerable distance, as speculators, who had lost a great deal of money, tried to dig their way out of trouble by any and all means, including speculation. The caution of consumers and investors seems likely to move with the business cycle, especially with booms and busts in asset markets, in securities to a major degree, but also in real estate and ordinary business ventures, including those starting up in the boom. In an occasional talk on financial crisis, I elicit a nervous laugh in saying that nothing disturbs a person's judgement so much as to see a friend get rich.

Keynes was preoccupied with 'animal spirits', those of investors both in markets for titles to assets and debt, and in markets for productive facilities. These spirits presumably vary within the lifetime of an investor or entrepreneur, with more risk-taking in youth, less in old age. They also varied from generation to generation, as already noted. In the 1920s, Keynes several times observed that Britain was dominated by third-generation men (Skidelsky, 1994, pp. 232, 261):

More is needed than animal spirits. In a *Manchester Guardian Supplement* in 1923, Keynes called for 'clear-eyed public spirit, a substantial amount of which was needed to preserve the balance and complicated organization by which the British lived ... unless men are united by a common aim or moved by objective principles, each one's hand will be raised against the rest and the unregulated pursuit of individual advantage may soon destroy the whole. There has been no common purpose lately between nations or between classes except war ... '. (Skidelsky, 1994, p. 121)

The terms 'clear-eyed public spirit', 'common aim' (or 'common purpose') and 'objective principles' are not self-evident, especially in terms of nations and classes with no mention of individuals. One can infer from the passage, however, that what modern capitalism requires is trust, as has been said by many, notably Kenneth Arrow (1974) and Paolo Sylos Tabini (quoted in Kindleberger, 1993, p. 87). Trust, based on ethical principles, is again an attribute difficult to measure.

One form of knowledge which Keynes does not discuss is that needed by depositors to judge adequately the solvency of banks. Advocates of 'free banking' suggest that any rogue bank that lends too recklessly will be tamed by other banks that demand payment of its banknotes in specie, stop accepting its paper or stop lending it federal funds (Selgin, 1988; for an illustration of the last, cf. Spero, 1980). If such a bank fails under free banking – the absence of bank regulation and of deposit insurance – its ignorant depositors suffer, as most people are unable to judge the worth of a bank's assets and will fail to withdraw their funds in time. Charles Goodhart (1989) observes that bank notes were originally of high denominations, and the poor were left to deal only in coin because of their inability to judge the risk element in bank portfolios. As a prudential matter, the ill-informed and the poor had to be protected (Goodhart, 1989, p. 58). As knowledge of banking spread and so too the utility of paper instead of specie, the denominations of bank notes were progressively reduced, and the ordinary person began to use bank chequing accounts. Even so, deposit insurance was added in the United States after the rash of bank failures in the 1930s. Advocates of free banking argue that the system is self-regulating and that central banks can be abandoned. Goodhart (1989) rejects this notion on the grounds that banks differ from mutual funds. The assets of mutual funds are securities quoted in markets, making their value transparent. Loans of banks, on the other hand, are of uncertain value (Goodhart, 1989, *passim*). One might observe, however, that the *New York Times* ran a series on 7, 8, and 9 August 1994, suggesting that among the rapidly growing number of mutual funds in the last two or three years, some apparently were guilty of conflicts of interest and insider trading in securities that the ordinary investor would find it impossible to monitor.

POSSIBLE NON-GOVERNMENTAL REGULATORY PROTECTION FROM EXPLOITATION

In a *laissez-faire* world it would be adequate if the consumer, the investor and the depositor were wary in protecting their interests, or if sellers and bankers were uniformly competitive and honest in providing full disclosure. Not all consumers, investors and depositors are, or can be made, rational, competent and informed. Those under some age cannot guard their own interests, neither can those at the lower end of the distribution of intelligence or who halted education at a low level. Information is perhaps more readily tackled. Its major source in youth is the family. Where that is unable to provide it to the requisite degree, there is schooling. As noted earlier, it is not clear what Keynes meant by the 'nationalization of knowledge', beyond universal education. Some wariness at an early age is being taught in Boston elementary schools after a series of alleged attempts at the kidnapping of young children. In adolescence and in secondary school, one presumably loses innocence at a rapid rate by exposure to the media on the one hand and, if lucky, to good literature on the other. High school courses in civics, and college and university teaching of history, political science, economics and philosophy may be of use in shopping, investing and dealing with credit.

One who was wary in youth and middle age may become less so, and overly trusting in advanced years. The evidence is primarily anecdotal. Newspapers report cases of a young second wife of a wealthy older man, a housekeeper or a chauffeur in the case of older women, a casual friend or even acquaintance, persuading an old person to write a new will disinheriting relatives and leaving an estate to the newcomer. Suits by the disinherited often seek to prove 'undue influence' and the falsity of the statement of the testator that she or he was 'of sound mind'. There is little that education or government can do in such cases, beyond adjudication of the matter in court.

If wariness in the face of exploitative conduct cannot be taught, what of honesty and fair dealing? The view that a three-year-old cannot tell the difference between right and wrong has been noted, as well as the psychiatrist's opinion that personality is strongly influenced by experience in the few years immediately following. Ethics and its teaching in the United States have been called a growth industry, with a new profession of ethicist having developed in the past 30 years (Gustafson, 1991). An experiment exploring personality traits is afforded by the 'ultimate game' in game theory, in which one person (A) is given a sum of money to divide with another (B), under a rule of the game that if B accepts what A awards, both keep the sums they have, whereas if B rejects the award, neither gets any money. In a rational world, A awards B the smallest finite amount, because B either accepts it or gets nothing. In practice, however, in repeated experiments with small amounts of money such as $10, A awards nearly half the sum to B, on the basis of some notion of 'fairness'. (Other outcomes might occur, the experimenters hypothesize, if sums as large as $100 or $1000 or $10,000 were involved.)

Fairness probably differs from honesty, if there is truth in the cliché concerning honour among thieves. Presumably principles of fairness and honesty are expounded, if not in the family at an early age, in kindergarten and the early elementary grades, as well as in more advanced years. A former commissioner of the Securities and Exchange Commission gave $10 million to the Harvard Business School for the research and teaching of ethics, but the courses are elective, the professors do not include the stars of the faculty, and registration for the classes is reported to be low, as students are preoccupied with learning technical business courses. James Gustafson reports 'one would be hard put to it to provide solid evidence that an undergraduate course in ethics makes student behavior more moral', and that 'the limited success of the growth industry of ethics to date, or in the future, may be rooted in the deeper tendency of individuals, communities and institutions to pursue their own desired and immediate self interest – a tendency not readily reformed by ethics teaching alone' (Gustafson, 1991).

Without a solid understanding of the matter, I gather that the teaching required must come in the early formative years and in the family. If, as seems evident in the United States today, well-functioning families are not universal in a time of divorce, desertion, units where both parents work and children are warehoused in day-care establishments, little can be done by government policy, at least in the short run, in shoring up support for spreading trust in economic life. I am afraid I have no view as to whether help can be found in programmes like Head Start, a project funded by the United States federal government to provide instruction and daytime activities to pre-school-age children of disadvantaged homes and neighbourhoods.

There is always the possibility of postgraduate education when the person enters the real world of work. Professions typically set standards for the conduct of their membership, sometimes enforced by licence, after passage of examination and attestation to the individual's good character. To some degree, such standards are a cartel device to limit numbers and raise income levels. If one ignores the latter possibility, one may call attention to a new code for lawyers laid down by the Committee on Ethics and Professional Responsibility, which expounds 'elementary ethical notions', presumably acquired in childhood, such as that a lawyer should not charge two clients for the same time if, for example, she or he worked on one case while travelling by airplane to deal with another. The Committee Report urged a high level of conduct because violations hurt the public opinion of lawyers and may inhibit laymen from using the legal system. Amitai Etzioni (1994) decries this utilitarian or consequentialist notion of ethics, as contrasted with moral behaviour that would obtain in a world of trust. Other professions – medical doctors, accountants, financial advisers, even real-estate dealers and the like – produce codes. Monitoring behaviour to see that it conforms to the standards of the side, however, seems difficult to carry out through peer surveillance and is generally left to the police and/or courts.

One device to protect investors against the abuse of insider information is the appointment of outsider directors, who are not executives of the company. In one view, while insider trading in securities markets troubles most people, 'it probably contributes to the efficient dissemination of information' (Hochman, 1994, p. 18). There should be legal, efficient and fair ways to this end. A difficulty with the device is that outsiders are typically insiders in other companies, with insiders' points of view, appointed by insiders of the company in question and beholden to them. Such boards can lose their 'contestability', as the watcher and the watched share the goals of company profits and higher share prices ('Survey', *The Economist*, 29 January 1994). German practice is to have two boards: one for management, which includes a company's executives, and a supervisory board which does not, though it typically includes the company's bankers. The supervisory board of Metallgesellschaft, which went bankrupt after losing more than $1 billion trading oil futures in New York, claimed that the management board never informed it of its trading in oil futures. One wonders whether the supervisory board would have been equally disturbed if the speculation had gained substantial profits instead of losses. All too recently, the *New York Times* recorded large profits from trading in options on the stock of the Grumann (airplane) company beginning 1 March 1994, when the announcement of its takeover by the Martin Marietta company was not made until 7 March. A profit of $218,700 was made by an unknown player on an investment of $12,500 to buy options on 25,000 shares on the Chicago Board Options Exchange (8 March 1994, p. D-1).

The New York Stock Exchange monitors for insider trading within its precincts by computer study of activity in shares which rise or fall precipitously before the announcement of news affecting the company's profitability. At a meeting at the Exchange some years ago, I was told that in some cases, people with insider information would place orders abroad using public telephones, in an effort to escape this surveillance. Small orders to buy or sell which could be handled on the foreign bourse would not attract attention. When an order was large, however, the Zurich market, let us say, might find it necessary to lay off part or all of an order in another foreign market. Brokers in London, it was said, had become wary of large orders in American shares coming from other European markets, and found it useful to 'mislay' the order for a few days, to see if there were breaking news.

Those hurt by misleading sales pitches may recover their losses in whole or, more usually, in part, through bringing suits in courts, in some instances in concert with others in class-action suits. Independent suits are expensive, unless a lawyer is employed on a contingent-fee basis, paid nothing unless he wins the case, in which instance he may earn as much as a third or half of the award. As trust leaks out of American capitalism, lawyers multiply, advertise their readiness to help people who have been injured in any way by suing in the courts, and sit on both sides of business deals – ordinary contracts, but especially mergers and acquisitions, takeovers both hostile and friendly, bank-ruptcies, incorporations, initial public offerings (of previously privately owned stock), etc., etc. Legal advertising speaks primarily to people's rights, rather than duties, and ascribes any injury to the wrong-doing of another, rather than to the randomness of events. Lawyers abhor limits to malpractice suits and no-fault accident insurance. Asians, especially the Japanese, are more stoical in these matters, and have and use fewer lawyers in relation to population size. Ronald Dore writes that the Japanese especially dislike low-trust relations, and dislike poker in which bluffing plays a large role (Dore, 1992, p. 170).

Use of the courts can be overdone. 'Strict liability' frequently penalizes the producer of a product when the injury occurs through the carelessness of the user. A philosopher, Albert Borgmann, is reported as stating that rampant individualism in the United States has led to a movement to dismiss personal responsibility and take on the role of the victim (Staples, 1994). On the other hand, the other party understandably seeks to blame the victim, even in cases of those inexperienced because of youth, old age or low intelligence, where it may not be warranted. Often it is appropriate, to be sure, as in the BCCI case referred to above, quoting Mme Ploix. There is no general rule, and as in much of life, circumstances alter cases.

POSSIBLE GOVERNMENTAL REGULATORY PROTECTION FROM EXPLOITATION

If a society contains unscrupulous members ready to exploit the incompetent, and maintenance of high standards cannot be handled privately by profes-sional and industrial groups, the maintenance of justice falls to government. The control of monopolies and suppression and punishment of outright fraud I leave to the anti-trust division of the Department of Justice and the Attorney General at the national level, and public prosecutors at the state and local level. More is called for, however, as the existence of the Bureau of Stand-ards, Pure Food and Drug Administration, Federal Trade Commission, Secu-rities and Exchange Commission, Federal Deposit Insurance Corporation, Comptroller of the Currency, Federal Reserve System, state insurance com-missions, etc., etc. demonstrate. A problem with these agencies is that they are sometimes captured by the industry they are supposed to regulate, although this can be nothing more than an attempt of regulator and regulated to work out a means of operating. That such is usually the case seems unduly optimistic. One issue on the current agenda in Washington is whether the four agencies that supervise banking should be consolidated into one, so that the responsibility is unambiguously fixed. The proposal to this end, resisted by the Federal Reserve System, may be a response to the view that competition among the regulating agencies has evolved into a competition in deregulation (Kane, 1987).

In addition, regulation may be porous rather than watertight. Deposit insurance initially covered deposits of $5000, a number gradually raised with inflation to $10,000, $20,000 and then to $40,000. I am told (hearsay, but from a reputable source) that the joint committee of the Congress to reconcile bills calling for a further increase, one from the House specifying $50,000, the other, $60,000, compromised on $100,000. The market then developed 'deposit brokers' who would take deposits in the millions and divide them among many banks, $99,000 or some such number in each; weak banks offered high rates of interest to gain such deposits, many of them later failing. Meanwhile wealthy, competent depositors earned high rates of interest, fully insured, from banks which, without insurance or much lower limits, they would have avoided.

CONCLUSION

I conclude somewhat pessimistically that there is no easy general rule, whether leaving the individual to guard his or her interests in purchasing, investing and banking, wary of the danger of malfeasance, or closely regulating industry, finance and banking. Business-to-business dealings between firms of broadly comparable size can doubtless be left to the market, and in many (most?) cases this is true of business dealings between firms and individuals. But some business-to-individual exchanges and some individual-to-individual ones may involve the unscrupulous and the naive. Improving the quality of the family, schools, policing the activity of markets, and improving the efficiency of courts of law all are needed, but the likelihood of substantial and rapid improvement is slight. In a bromide which includes the word 'price' but is not economic, the price of liberty is eternal vigilance.

NOTE

1. Thanks are due to Mrs Jane King, a psychologist, who provided guidance in a field in which my knowledge is grossly deficient, and to Peter L. Bernstein.

14. On Keynes and Ramsey on probability

Ian Parker

[If the results of new economic research] are to go into the common stock of knowledge and belief as a substantial contribution they will have to conform to those canons of knowledge and belief that rule the road for the time being.

Veblen, [1925] 1934, pp. 3–5, 9

... [N]either wants nor expectations fulfil the conditions of measurability.

Georgescu-Roegen, 1966, p. 120

... [I]n writing economics one is not writing either a mathematical proof or a legal document. One is trying to arouse and appeal to the reader's intuitions: and, if he has worked himself into a state when he has none, one is helpless.

J.M. Keynes to R.B. Bryce, 1935, in Patinkin and Leith, 1977, p. 128

INTRODUCTION

This chapter differs somewhat from most of the contributions to this volume honouring the memory of Lorie Tarshis as a careful and not uncritical student of Keynes (Tarshis, 1939); at times a (non-reductionistic) propagandist for Keynes' ideas; a creative and original economist in his own right; a gentle, self-effacing and generous colleague; and a 'tough-as-nails' combatant in the arena of ideas, when he believed that another was misguided, misinformed or theoretically off-base.[1] The principal difference between this chapter and most of the others is that it focuses on an aspect of Keynes' work that did not survive the transatlantic passage in the first wave of diffusion of Keynes' ideas in North America: his theory of probability, expectations and uncertainty.

Since the early 1980s, and particularly in the last decade, increasing attention has been paid to Keynes' views in this area: indeed, it has become a minor growth industry within that penumbral sub-field that straddles economic theory and economic methodology. Yet to this day, the centre of gravity of that work is much closer to Great Britain and Europe (with a few important contributions from elsewhere) than to North America.

There are a number of potential partial explanations for the limited degree of transmission of Keynes' approach to probability, expectations and uncertainty to North America. At an abstract level, Veblen's classic argument, in *Imperial Germany and the Industrial Revolution* (1915), that many of the subtleties of a technical innovation are lost or suppressed in the process of technological diffusion, may be considered as applying as well to the means of mental (and not merely material) production. Veblen was aware of 'The Merits of Borrowing', but he was not unaware of the potential attendant costs. Simplification may entail increases in productivity, but these productivity increases may be purchased at the cost of certain losses in capacity.

A second partial explanation is related to an 1890 comment by Friedrich Engels to Joseph Bloch, in which Engels attempted to explain what he viewed as the overemphasis on economic factors by the younger generation of 'Marxists' (Engels' quotation marks), and placed part of the blame on himself and Marx: 'We had to emphasize the main principle *vis a vis* our adversaries, who denied it, and we had not always the time, the place or the opportunity to allow the other elements involved in the interaction to come into their rights' (Engels, in Tucker, 1978, p. 762).

It would be unfair to accuse Keynes himself of such a neglect of the fundamental role played by uncertainty and expectations in the *General Theory*. Bertil Ohlin was still struck, 40 years after the fact, that

> when [Keynes] came to Stockholm in the autumn of 1936 and gave a lecture to our little Political Economy Club he – to our surprise – emphasised the analysis of [the *uncertainty of the future* and the importance of opinions about the future as a basis for action by businessmen and consumers] as more of an innovation than any other aspect of the *General Theory*. (Ohlin, in Patinkin and Leith, 1977, p. 160)

Similarly, in his 1937 response in the *Quarterly Journal of Economics* to four critiques of the *General Theory*, Keynes' first substantive argument centred on the pivotal role of uncertainty in his theory (*CW*, 1973, Vol. XIV, pp. 109–32).

Yet it cannot be said that this aspect of the *General Theory* really weathered the passage across the Atlantic well. For that matter, it appears to have receded into the background in most British economic debates as well, at least in any systematic sense. The 'Engels effect' appears to account, at least in part, for this recession: the *General Theory* needs to be taken as a whole if it is to be fully appreciated, and yet it offers such an embarrassment of riches *and* of difficulties that from a rhetorical and forensic standpoint it is very difficult to communicate *in toto*. In this context, there are strong economic pressures to focus on the most obvious, least contentious or vulnerable, and most easily communicated aspects of a theory, if one wishes to accelerate its diffusion and acceptance. One of the most difficult and potentially contentious elements to grasp in the *General Theory* is Keynes' theory of expectations and uncertainty, and hence in terms of the economics of rhetoric, it was one of the components of the *General Theory* that was most vulnerable to reductionism or elimination in the debates that followed its publication.

A third factor that partially explains the relative neglect in North America (and elsewhere) of Keynes' understanding of probability, uncertainty and expectations as integral to the argument of the *General Theory* was the rapid emergence of interpretations and glosses of Keynes, notably J.R. Hicks' 1937 IS–LM framework and later Alvin Hansen's (1953) *Guide*, in which Keynes' concept of uncertainty and its economic role was moved to the back burner or effectively eliminated. Lorie Tarshis, particularly in his focus on, and treatment of, Keynes' aggregate supply function, was one of the least culpable of falling into this expositional trap. Hicks' work during the 1930s, culminating in Parts III and IV of *Value and Capital* (1939), does give significant attention to expectations and risk, albeit not on Keynes' lines; yet 'Mr. Keynes and the Classics' (1937) as an expository article severely limited its references to Keynes' views on probability and uncertainty. While in the second edition of *Value and Capital* ([1939] 1946, p. 337), Hicks criticized Samuelson for 'pure concentration on mechanism', rather than on 'expectations and so on', Hicks' own IS–LM construction is vulnerable (if not, perhaps, to the same extent) to the same strictures that he directed against Samuelson's work.

Yet from the standpoint of pedagogical economy, the Hicks–Hansen framework was much more 'teachable', to most undergraduates and even to average graduate students, than was the *General Theory* itself. At the same time, Hicks, Metzler, Samuelson and others had taught economics students the joys of the mathematical games that could be played with multiplier–accelerator interactions, the properties of $n \times n$ matrices, stability analysis, and the like. Keynes' own macroeconomic theory, with its focus on expectations and uncertainty, was displaced not only by the *external* competition from calculus-based and later analysis-based mathematical general equilibrium economic theory, but also by the *internal* competition from more accessible and mathematically determinate versions of Keynes' own theory, versions from which Keynes' own preoccupation with expectations and uncertainty had effectively been excised.

A fourth factor that contributed to the continued neglect of Keynes' view of probability and expectations as a basis for macroeconomic theory was the incorporation and hegemony of various versions of '"Bayesian" cardinal subjective-probability theory' in the core of the contemporary mainstream analysis of what came to be known, somewhat loosely, as 'decision-making under risk or uncertainty'. This strand of thought, which traces its modern origins to the writings of Ramsey (1931), von Neumann and Morgenstern ([1944] 1953), Savage ([1954] 1972) and others, was incorporated into the Arrow–Debreu extension of certainty-based mathematical general equilibrium theory to situations involving what Arrow himself has vacillated between describing as situations of 'risk' and situations of 'uncertainty'.

A crucial feature of all of the above-mentioned approaches to risk or uncertainty is that they presuppose that a *cardinal* measure of the probability of the occurrence of each of certain, somehow well-defined, states of the world actually exists, even if it is only subjectively in the mind of the beholder. One significant mathematical advantage of adopting this presupposition is that (under further assumptions) it is possible, as von Neumann and Morgenstern demonstrated ([1944] 1953), to generate *quasi*-cardinal *'utility'* measures, invariant up to a linear transformation, for the ranking of choice alternatives in terms of their expected 'utility'.

From this standpoint, there were mathematical drawbacks to the theory of probability in Keynes' *Treatise on Probability* ([1921] 1973, *CW*, Vol. VIII), which also included cases in which *at best ordinally comparable* degrees of belief in the probability of an hypothesis existed, and cases in which probabilities were *strictly incomparable* in quantitative terms (either cardinal or ordinal). The notion of an at best *partially* ordered probability-field (or even, for that matter, a *completely* pre-ordered *ordinal* probability-field) creates radical, mathematically intractable problems, using standard current methods, for the economic theory of decision-making under uncertainty. This 'limitation' of Keynes' *'general* theory of probability' – that in some respects it directly contradicted *and* also required a different analytical method from what became the mainstream theoretical economic and other approaches to decision-making under uncertainty – led to its being disparaged on these grounds alone, apart from any inherent merits or limits of Keynes' approach in and of itself (some of which are examined below).[2]

Keynes' own approach and framework of analysis in the *Treatise on Probability*, based as they were on the immediate influence of G.E. Moore (1903), and Whitehead and Russell (1910) (leaving aside Keynes' reasonably exhaustive forays into the historical literature on probability), constituted a fifth obstacle to the diffusion of his ideas on probability, uncertainty and expectations. These aspects of Keynes' approach will be addressed further below.

At this point, however, we can note that Moore's *Principia Ethica* (1903), to which Keynes acknowledged his indebtedness ([1921] 1973, p. xxiv; *CW*, 1972, Vol. X, p. 435ff.; Moggridge, 1992, pp. 99–100, 131–6, *et passim*; Skidelsky, 1983, pp. 133–55),[3] adopted what has been described as an 'ethical intuitionist' stance. There are epistemological affinities between G.E. Moore's ethical intuitionism and L.E.J. Brouwer's mathematical intuitionism: Moore's central thesis, as Foot (1967, p. 2, emphasis added) put it, 'was that goodness is a simple non-natural property discovered by intuition', and that 'judgments [regarding 'goodness'] were *objective*, and ... were made by intuition'. This use of the term 'objective' is imbedded in the *Treatise on Probability* (Keynes, [1921]

1973, p. 4 *et passim*)[4] and in the *General Theory* itself (as in Chapters 5, 8, 9, 11 and 12), perhaps most transparently in the case of Chapters 8 and 9, where a number of the factors Keynes describes as 'objective' would be treated by many as at least partly 'subjective', just as some of his 'subjective' factors could be viewed as having an 'objective' component. Keynes' specialized use of the term 'objective' (and its correlative, 'subjective') likely led to a degree of confusion (and a corresponding neglect) regarding the implications of the distinctions he was drawing for his theory of economic behaviour under the influence of time and uncertainty.

The influence of Russell himself and the work that led up to Whitehead and Russell's *Principia Mathematica*, of which Volume I first appeared in 1910, similarly likely deepened, but also limited, the accessibility of the *Treatise on Probability* and the approach to probability and expectations in the *General Theory* insofar as it depended on the *Treatise*. *Principia Mathematica* was undeniably a *tour de force*: stemming in part from the example of the axiomatizations of arithmetic by Peano (See 1973) and particularly Frege (1934), it was a compendious essay in the subsumption of mathematics as a sub-branch of logic. It came to be viewed as one of the principal texts in support of the *logical* view of the foundations of mathematics, as distinct from the *formalist* view associated with Hilbert and the *intuitionist* view associated with Brouwer.

This view has been held notwithstanding the failure within *Principia Mathematica* itself to develop a logical axiomatization of calculus (a project which, in relation to Abraham Robinson's (1966) subsequent development of 'non-standard analysis', would seem attainable with the use of Boolean ultra-filters); what some, including Tarski ([1941] 1965, p. 230), viewed as its failure 'to come up to the strict requirements of present-day methodology'); the radical negative implications of Gödel's (1931) 'undecidability' theorem for the project of completely axiomatizing mathematics; and the ramifications of Wittgenstein's (1953, 1956) implicit and occasionally explicit criticisms of the *Principia* in his post-*Tractatus* works, centred on notions such as 'use', 'activity' and 'games' (in a general, not a von Neumann–Morgenstern, sense). Russell himself, in a later reflection, indicated that the work on *Principia Mathematica* had been mentally 'back-breaking' labour, and that he was uncertain in retrospect whether the game had been worth the candle. Russell, in his reflection, did not specify precisely whether it was the limits of *Principia Mathematica* in its finished version (as sketched above), or the time which the project consumed when Russell believed himself to have been at the peak of his creative powers, or the enervating and constricting effects of the demands of the project on his intellectual capacities, or some combination of the above, that was the principal source of his reservations.

Regardless, it was the Whitehead and Russell of the *Principia Mathematica* whom Keynes confronted when he produced his thesis on probability, which was published in 1921 as the *Treatise on Probability*, after an extended hiatus of over a decade, during which time Keynes was able to work on it only intermittently, as his attention was diverted by many other activities and projects. Keynes ([1921] 1973, *CW*, Vol. VIII, pp. 19–20, 20n) provided a reasonably subtle and essentially rhetorical and pragmatic rationalization for his non-adoption of the *Principia Mathematica* notation in the *Treatise*, and had he not diverged from this notation, many of the results in the *Treatise* that entailed the use of calculus methods would not have been open to him. Yet that Keynes felt it necessary, even in 1921, to 'appease the gods' in this fashion, suggests one or more of the following: that Keynes wished to acknowledge the intellectual guidance of Whitehead and Russell without being constrained by the mathematical limitations of *Principia Mathematica*; that he regarded the *Treatise* as a debased addendum to the *Principia*, insofar as it did not attain the degree of logical rigour of the *Principia*; that Keynes was more interested in communication than in notation; and/or that Keynes believed by 1908, and with even greater weight after a decade and a half of work on induction and probability, that extending the Whitehead–Russell logical-mathematical approach to mathematics directly to the logic of *partial* belief was in principle impossible. Of these four hypotheses, I would regard only the second proposition as 'improbable' (in the sense that the probability of its converse exceeds its own probability), based on the existing body of knowledge with which I am familiar and which I recall at the time of writing this sentence.

Practically speaking, what do this set of judgements and the preceding arguments have to do with the diffusion of Keynes' economic approach to probability, expectations and uncertainty? In the first place, the immediately preceding set of judgements should have come across, in their present form, as *obiter dicta*. If I were challenged on any one of them, because I was being either too bold or too cautious, I would then likely marshall a subset of the arguments on which I had based my own probability-judgements that I viewed as likely to be most convincing, in rhetorical and dialectical terms, in order to communicate the bases of, and lend credence to, my judgements. From the standpoint of a critical reader, these arguments (if they provided 'new' evidence to the reader) would increase the weight of the argument for that reader, and should also alter its probability (either upwards or downwards) in the reader's mind. In contrast, if I were confronted by the reader with (to my mind) new and convincing evidence that directly contradicted my previous probability-judgements, these new arguments could alter my degree of belief in the 'probability' of the propositions I have advanced above.[5]

This image of the way in which probability-judgements, interpreted in terms of degrees of rational partial belief, are reached involves processes that have an economic dimension, but that are not readily incorporated into the currently dominant approaches to behaviour under uncertainty. Moreover, Keynes' framework, to the extent that it was in part an embodiment of an ongoing dialogue with Moore and Russell, was couched at points in terms which to those 'outside the loop' and unfamiliar with the implicit assumptions and lexicon of that arena of discourse, often appeared esoteric, difficult and obscure: the *Treatise on Probability*, regardless of one's training and background, is not Keynes' most accessible work.

When these difficulties are compounded by occasionally idiosyncratic notational conventions, unspecified, inadequately defined and/or inadequately grounded terms, and outright errors, one senses at points that one is in the presence of a highly gifted, profound and illuminating amateur, but an amateur nonetheless. This is not to my mind the appropriate reading of the *Treatise*, in that it involves a significant undervaluation of the potential worth of the work as a critical and constructive guide, but the above limits of Keynes' exposition provide the unsympathetic reader of the *Treatise* with an excuse for not taking its argument with the seriousness it deserves. If one were to choose not to read the *Treatise* sympathetically, Keynes himself has provided much of the ammunition that the sceptic would require for such a decision.

If the *Treatise* is neglected, then *a fortiori* the significant elements of continuity between the *Treatise* and Keynes' later economic writings will tend to be neglected, with deleterious consequences for the interpretation of Keynes' approach to economics. It is this consequence that furnishes a major justification for the argument of this chapter.

OUTLINE OF THE ARGUMENT

The primary focus of the chapter is on Keynes' theory of probability and expectations, as presented in his A *Treatise on Probability* ([1921] 1973, *CW*, Vol. VIII). In his 'Editorial Foreword' to the 1973 edition of the *Treatise* and elsewhere, R.B. Braithwaite produced a rather questionable 'critique' of Keynes' analysis of probability which has been adopted by others. In the 'Foreword', Braithwaite (Keynes [1921] 1973, *CW*, Vol. VIII, p. xxi) implied that Frank P. Ramsey's 1926 treatment of probability (and prior and subsequent discussions) had evoked from Keynes a major concession and revision of his views, as registered in Keynes' 1931 review of Ramsey's posthumously published *The Foundations of Mathematics*.

In this context, following a brief sketch of some of the major features of the *Treatise on Probability* itself, the chapter has several objectives. First, it is intended to indicate some of the shortcomings in Braithwaite's and related appraisals of the *Treatise on Probability*. Second, it suggests some reasons for supposing that what Braithwaite views as Keynes' partial 'capitulation' to Ramsey's approach is rather more semantic than substantive, and that in its substantive aspects, any 'capitulation' by Keynes to Ramsey is at most decidedly marginal in character.

Third, the chapter applies principles drawn from the *Treatise on Probability* to Ramsey's (1931, pp. 138–211, 256–9) framework for probability analysis, in order to suggest that on the criteria set out in the *Treatise on Probability*, Ramsey's own account of probability is seriously limited. Insofar as Ramsey's analysis bears a close family resemblance to other subsequent cardinally based, subjective-probability theories of probability, such as that in Leonard Savage's *The Foundation of Statistics* ([1954] 1972), which underlie the conceptual apparatus of most modern mainstream theoretical economic analyses of decision-making and behaviour under uncertainty, this third objective has wider ramifications.

The final objective of the chapter is to suggest the relevance and implications of the *Treatise on Probability* for the future development of economics. In one sense, as has already been suggested, for economically intelligible reasons the Ramsey–Savage 'subjective-probability' view has effectively displaced Keynes' 'logical-probability' approach in current mainstream economic theory. Yet other developments, such as the rapid historical expansion of what has come to be known as the 'information economy', Herbert Simon's (1957; see also 1982) development of the concept of 'bounded rationality' and the steady growth of 'experimental economics', particularly insofar as it focuses on decision-making with imperfect information under conditions of uncertainty, all tend to underline the limits and call into question the adequacy of the prevailing Ramsey–Savage approach to uncertainty, as it has been incorporated into mainstream theory. Moreover, they open a sphere of enquiry in which Keynes' approach (notwithstanding its relative intractability in principle with regard to 'straightforward' cardinal probability measures in contexts of uncertainty) can potentially assume greater importance.

One of the core elements of the chapter, a brief version of a Keynesian critique of Ramsey's view of probability, first saw light in my Yale doctoral thesis in economics (Parker, 1977). It was written before I had had the opportunity of 'picking the brains' of Lorie Tarshis and other colleagues at Scarborough College in the University of Toronto hired by Tarshis, such as Don Moggridge and Susan Howson, whose fundamental Keynes-related studies need no comment. Without directly or in any way implicating Lorie Tarshis himself (or Sue Howson or Don Moggridge) in the conclusions of this chapter, however, it is fair to say that its conclusions would have been more tentative had Tarshis not provided both his own wisdom on Keynes and that of Howson and Moggridge as an environment for the study of Keynes.

THE ARGUMENT

Keynes' *Treatise on Probability* (hereinafter, simply the *Treatise*, since his *Treatise on Money* will not be treated in the chapter), was published in 1921, although, with the principal exception of significant additions in Part V on 'The Foundations of Statistical Inference', much of it had already appeared in his second, successful, fellowship dissertation, completed in 1908. Its central objective is to establish a view of probability as concerned with the logic of rational partial belief: 'The theory of probability is logical, therefore, because it is concerned with the degree of belief which it is *rational* to entertain in given conditions, and not merely with the actual beliefs of particular individuals, which may or may not be rational' (Keynes, [1921] 1973, *CW*, Vol. VIII, p. 5).

The object of the book 'has been to emphasise the existence of a *logical relation between two sets of propositions* in cases where it is not possible to argue demonstratively from one to the other' (Keynes, [1921] 1973, *CW*, Vol. VIII, p. 9).

As noted above, the influence of Moore and Russell on the approach of the *Treatise* was significant, even when it was not explicit. Russell's influence is most directly apparent in the first two parts of the *Treatise*, particularly in Part II: 'Fundamental Theorems'. Moore's influence, which is most apparent in Part I and in Chapter 26, 'The Application of Probability to Conduct', was more diffuse and indirect, although at least as profound, particularly in Keynes' emphasis on probability as intuited and objective, and in his reluctance to define probability (Carabelli, 1988, and 1991, pp. 120–21; Keynes, [1921] 1973, *CW*, Vol. VIII, pp. 3–9; Shionoya, 1991, pp. 6–29). Keynes does *not* say that a definition is in principle unattainable, but he does say 'I do not know how the element of logical doubt is to be defined, or how its substance is to be stated, in terms of the other indefinables of formal logic', and effectively treats it in the *Treatise* as an indefinable. Chapter 26 has been read by some as an effort by Keynes to 'extend' Moore's ethical thought, yet while the focus of the chapter may stem from Keynes' struggle to come to terms with Moore's views, the chapter contains some serious criticism of Moore (Keynes, [1921] 1973, *CW*, Vol. VIII, pp. 341–3), and its major emphasis is on a critique of utilitarian ethical theory, conducted on technical lines quite different from Moore's and centred on the non-cardinality of utility and particularly of probability.

The *Treatise* is a compendium of a wide range of issues in the logic of partial belief, or probability broadly defined, from the epistemological bases of probability; to the development of a framework for the logical analysis of probability; to the assessment of the circumstances under which probabilities may be cardinal, ordinal or incomparable; to the axiomatic bases and 'fundamental theorems' of probable inference; to the theory of induction (in which Keynes emphasizes the fundamental role of 'analogy', rather than the mere multiplication of instances, or 'pure induction'); to the philosophical relations of probability and chance and probability and ethics; to the foundations of statistical inference. Corresponding to this range of subject matter is a range of rhetorical styles, from the philosophical to the technical-philosophical to the 'common-sensical' to the mathematical (the latter particularly in Parts II and V), which tend to reflect the style of the considerable literature Keynes had read on each of the subjects he treated.

The *Treatise* contains much original constructive thought, as well as providing a framework in terms of which the ramifications of Keynes' concepts of probability can be seen in their interrelationships. Yet, without underestimating the value of the constructive work, it may be that, to his own mind at least, some of Keynes' most important contributions in the *Treatise* lay in the sphere of criticism.

About the value of his constructive proposals Keynes was often tentative (as Keynes, [1921] 1973, *CW*, Vol. VIII, pp. 10, 13–14, 17, 77, 99, 125). About his justification for his approach to induction, after explicating his 'hypothesis of the limitation of independent variety' and explaining its *logical* necessity, he asked rhetorically, 'What right have we to make it?' and answered,

> 1 do not believe that any conclusive or perfectly satisfactory answer to this question can be given, so long as our knowledge of the subject of epistemology is in so disordered and undeveloped a condition as it is in at present. No proper answer has yet been given to the inquiry – of what sorts of thing are we *capable* of direct knowledge? (Keynes, [1921] 1973, *CW*, Vol. VIII, p. 291)

At the conclusion of the *Treatise*, Keynes remarked:

> In writing a book of this kind the author must, if he is to put his point of view clearly, pretend sometimes to a little more conviction than he feels ... It is a heavy task to write on these problems; and the reader will perhaps excuse me if I have sometimes pressed on a little faster than the difficulties were overcome, and with decidedly more confidence than I have always felt. (Keynes, [1921] 1973, *CW*, Vol. VIII, p. 467)

Yet if he had doubts about some of the constructive work of the *Treatise*, the critical component was much more pointed and sure-handed: it was harder to say what could be said than to say what could *not* be said. Keynes' view of probability as a *logical* relation ($a/h=P$, where 'the hypothesis h invests the conclusion a with probability [or degree of belief which it is rational to entertain] P' has the value 'that it contains explicit reference to the data [h] to which the probability relates the conclusion' (Keynes, [1921]

1973, *CW*, Vol. VIII, p. 43). This starting-point permits the classification of probability-relations as cardinally comparable, ordinally comparable or incomparable, as represented by Keynes ([1921] 1973, *CW*, Vol. VIII, p. 42) in an heuristic taxonomic diagram. By his emphasis on knowledge (and ignorance) in the determination of probability-judgements, Keynes had provided himself with an Archimedean point from which to criticize the notion that probabilities were necessarily cardinal (and hence invariably commensurable) in nature.

His critique (in Chapters 4, 5 and 15) of the 'principle of non-sufficient reason' and of the contradictions to which its misuse could give rise, synthesized and systematized a number of earlier objections to the principle, and clarified the restrictive nature of the circumstances in which it could be applied. His theory of analogy and induction, if it was not airtight in its constructive aspect, at a minimum provided a sufficiently secure foundation for his critical analysis of statistical correlation in Part V: 'The Foundations of Statistical Inference'.

Keynes himself did not regard the *Treatise* as 'the last word' on the subject, if his own words are to be believed. Rather, given the predominance for centuries of the 'algebraic exercises' of probability being viewed as a branch of mathematics rather than of logic, he viewed his effort in the contrary direction as a pioneering one, subject to the limits of the pioneer: 'There is much here, therefore, which is novel, and, being novel, unsifted, inaccurate, or deficient' (Keynes, [1921] 1973, *CW*, Vol. VIII, p. 25). Yet the *Treatise* provided additional scope and additional degrees of freedom for the treatment of probability, by allowing for classes of situations in which noncardinal probability-judgements arose; by linking probability-judgments to knowledge and the 'weight' of evidence (Keynes, [1921] 1973, *CW*, Vol. VIII, pp. 77–85; O'Donnell, 1991, pp. 69–88) within a framework that gives insight into the role of the process of *production* of probability-judgements under uncertainty; by its illustrations, drawn from spheres such as commerce, insurance and law (Keynes, [1921] 1973, *CW*, Vol. VIII, pp. 23–30, 198–204) of ways in which decision-making under uncertainty could be (and had been) accomplished in the absence of cardinal probabilities; and by his argument (Keynes, [1921] 1973, *CW*, Vol. VIII, pp. 23, 32, 83–4) that in some situations involving conflicting evidence, 'it will be rational to allow caprice to determine us and to waste no time on the debate', (this argument, although it is expressed somewhat quixotically, may properly be regarded as an 'economic' one, related to the cost of production of probability-judgements).[6]

In his critical introduction to the *Treatise* (in Keynes, [1921] 1973, *CW*, Vol. VIII, pp. xv–xxii, recapitulated in M. Keynes, 1975, pp. 237–42), R.B. Braithwaite identified some of what he viewed as its limitations. He correctly observed (in Keynes, [1921] 1973, *CW*, Vol. VIII, pp. xvi–xvii) that by later standards the axiomatic development of the theorems in Part II of the *Treatise* was formally deficient, although he failed to mention the subsequent work of B.O. Koopman (summarized in Carnap, 1962, pp.150–53), which establishes a firm axiomatic basis for Keynes' classes of probability-relation, including those which are strictly incomparable. Braithwaite's own interested (and utilitarian?) bias regarding Keynes' view that some probabilities are strictly incomparable was that it 'leads to intolerable difficulties without any compensating advantages'. His suggestion (in Keynes, [1921] 1973, *CW*, Vol. VIII, p. xvii) that 'empirical' scientific statements (such as that regarding the half-life of a radium atom) 'present insuperable obstacles to being incorporated into a logical theory of probability' seems radically to misread Keynes' approach and attitude to such phenomena, as embodied, for example, in the culminating paragraph of the *Treatise* (Keynes, [1921] 1973, *CW*, Vol. VIII, pp. 467–8).

Braithwaite's own preference (in Keynes, [1921] 1973, *CW*, Vol. VIII, pp. xix–xxi) lay with the approach that has come to be known as 'Bayesian' subjective-probability, particularly as manifested in Frank Ramsey's (1926) 'Truth and Probability' (which was first published in the posthumous 1931 collection of Ramsey's essays edited by Braithwaite). He provided a truncated and rearranged version of Keynes' own 1931 comments on Ramsey's treatment of probability ([1931] 1972, *CW*, Vol. X, pp. 338–9) to suggest that Keynes may have been sufficiently persuaded by Ramsey's critique of the *Treatise* and constructive theory to jettison or modify some of his own, although Braithwaite acknowledged that Ramsey's theory did not provide the 'justification for inductive inference' that was one of Keynes' objectives in the *Treatise* (in Keynes, [1921] 1973, *CW*, Vol. VIII, p. xxii).[7] Yet it would appear that Braithwaite's (and others') interpretation of the *context* of Keynes' 'concession', 'So far I yield to Ramsey – I think he is right' ([1931] 1972, *CW*, X, p. 9), involves an overestimate of the extent of the concession Keynes actually made. Keynes clearly accepted Ramsey's argument that 'the calculus of probabilities simply amounts to a set of rules for ensuring that the system of degrees of belief which we hold shall be a *consistent* system' and that humans have developed certain 'useful mental habits' that provide 'the basis of our degrees of belief', at the level of 'human logic' as distinct from 'formal logic'. Yet Keynes goes on to say that '*in attempting to distinguish 'rational' degrees of belief from belief in general* [Ramsey] *was not yet, I think, quite successful. It is not getting to the bottom of the principle of induction merely to say that it is a useful mental habit*' (Keynes [1931] 1972, *CW*, Vol. X, pp. 338–9; emphasis added).

Significantly, in his critical introduction to the *Treatise*, Braithwaite did *not* quote the italicized passage which was Keynes' *sole* specific and explicit criticism of the probability theory of his recently deceased colleague.

From Keynes' highly compressed response to Ramsey, it is not possible to determine with certainty whether Keynes' 'yielding' to Ramsey involved Keynes' retraction of his view that probability is concerned with 'objective relations between propositions', or merely an acceptance of Ramsey's 'consistency' argument; *nor* is it possible to determine what precisely Keynes viewed as the shortcomings in Ramsey's theory. Keynes was not explicit on either point.[8] Carabelli (1988), O'Donnell (1989) and Lawson (1985) have all made compelling arguments, from different standpoints, supporting the view that Keynes' later writings on economics and statistics do not involve any fundamental shift in Keynes' approach to probability from that of the *Treatise*.

In the remainder of the chapter, I propose to take a somewhat different tack and to examine an example from Ramsey's 'Truth and Probability' in light of considerations drawn from Keynes' *Treatise*. Ramsey's example is as follows:

I suggest that we introduce as a law of psychology that [an individual's] behaviour is governed by what is called the mathematical expectation; that is to say that, if *p* is a proposition about which he is doubtful, any goods or bads for whose realization *p* is in his view a necessary and sufficient condition enter into his calculations multiplied by the same fraction, which is called the 'degree of his belief in *p*'. We thus define degree of belief in a way which presupposes the use of the mathematical expectation.

We can put this in a different way. Suppose his degree of belief in *p* is *m/n*; then his action is such as he would choose it to be if he had to repeat it exactly *n* times, in *m* of which *p* was true, and in the others false. [Here it may be necessary to suppose that in each of the *n* times he had no memory of the previous ones.]

This can also be taken as a definition of the degree of belief, and can easily be seen to be equivalent to the previous definition. Let us give an instance of the sort of case which might occur. I am at a cross-roads and do not know the way; but I rather think one of the two ways is right. I propose therefore to go that way but keep my eyes open for someone to ask; if now I see someone half a mile away over the fields, whether I turn aside to ask him will depend on the relative inconvenience of going out of my way to cross the fields or of continuing on the wrong road if it is the wrong road. But it will also depend on how confident I am that I am right: and clearly the more confident I am of this the less distance I should be willing to go from the road to check my opinion. I propose therefore to use the distance I would be prepared to go to ask, as a measure of the confidence of my opinion; and what I have said above explains how this is to be done. We can set it out as follows: suppose the disadvantage of going *x* yards to ask is $f(x)$, the advantage of arriving at the right destination is *r*, that of arriving at the wrong one *w*. Then if I should just be willing to go a distance *d* to ask, the degree of my belief that I am on the right road is given by

$$p = 1 - f(d)/(r - w).$$

For such an action is one it would just pay me to take, if I had to act in the same way n times, in np of which I was on the right way but in the others not.

For the total good resulting from not asking each time

$$= npr + n(1 - p)w$$

$$= nw + np(r - w),$$

that resulting from asking at distance x each time

$$= nr - nf(x).$$

[I now always go right.]

This is greater than the preceding expression, provided

$$f(x) < (r - w)(1 - p),$$

∴ the critical distance, d, is connected with p, the degree of belief, by the relation

$$f(d) = (r - w)(1 - p)$$

or

$$p = 1 - f(d)/(r-w)$$

as asserted above. (Ramsey, [1926] 1931, pp. 174–5)

Let us ignore certain minor difficulties in Ramsey's account, all of which could be modified: the frequentist element; the 'repeatable-events' expression (with its confinement to rational numbers and its – in this context – necessary assumption of periodic selective amnesia); and, in his specific road and field example, the requirements that $r > w$ and that $f(x)$ is a strictly monotonically increasing function of x. Has Ramsey adequately characterized the decision-situation? In the first place, we can note that neither d nor, *a fortiori*, $f(d)$ is necessarily observable, since if d is less than 880 yards, Ramsey will not cross the field, and if d is greater than 880 yards, he will stop after reaching the individual. This issue, of course, does not pose a difficulty for Ramsey himself, although it would for an observer trying to interpret Ramsey's behaviour.

Yet Ramsey *does* significantly underspecify his decision-situation. He implicitly presupposes that he can judge precisely how far away the individual is – that the individual will *remain* where he is when Ramsey starts across the field, rather than, say, moving further away as Ramsey approaches him; that the individual knows the right road; that he is prepared to tell Ramsey the truth, rather than 'having a little fun' with this Cambridge fellow; and that Ramsey will understand what he says. All of these hypotheses are implicitly treated as certainties in Ramsey's account; yet from the standpoint of the *Treatise*, they would need to be assessed, in their interrelations and in terms of one's degree of rational belief in each of the hypotheses, in order to determine one's degree of rational belief in the proposition that crossing the field would yield the correct information, *at which point* (using Ramsey's mathematical expectation or some other criterion) one could decide whether or not to cross the field. In short, Keynes' problem is not precisely Ramsey's problem, and hence it would be surprising if Ramsey's 'solution' fully satisfied Keynes' requirements.

Keynes' respect for Ramsey's intellect manifested itself in many forms, and there may have been an element of the autobiographical in his reference to 'the simplicity of [Ramsey's] feelings and reactions, half-alarming sometimes and occasionally almost cruel in their directness and literalness' (Keynes, [1931] 1972, *CW*, Vol. X, pp. 335–40; Moggridge, 1992, pp. 210, 364–6; Newman, 1987, p. 188). Nonetheless, while Ramsey ([1926] 1931, pp. 158–66) advanced some solid criticisms of the argument of the *Treatise* (as well as some others that missed the mark), they were not such as to undermine Keynes' overall approach.[9] Moreover, the subjective approach to probability, in Ramsey's and in later hands, is vulnerable to the sorts of criticism that have been raised above, particularly insofar as the concept of 'degrees of belief' is theoretically divorced from the grounds of evidence and the processes of argument and judgement in terms of which *rational* partial belief is produced.

It is this concern that has motivated the present chapter. It is a truism that we live in uncertain times, but occasionally a truism can be true. Perhaps paradoxically, the present has also with justice been described as an 'age of information'. Yet the paradox is more apparent than real, once we allow for the possibility that changes in systems of information and communication are themselves major agents of structural political-economic change (Parker, 1994, pp. 37–60). In this context, the need to integrate more sophisticated understandings of the production and distribution of knowledge more closely into our theories of probability, expectations, economic behaviour under risk and uncertainty, and statistical inference becomes acute.

In the *General Theory* Keynes introduced probability, expectations and uncertainty into his economic theory in an essential way. In his writings on statistics, in his reviews, his controversy with Pearson and his debate with Tinbergen (Keynes, *CW*, 1983, Vol. XI; 1973, Vol. XIV), he made important contributions to statistical methodology. Underlying his contributions in both areas is the approach and framework of the *Treatise on Probability*.[10] It is to my mind a safe bet – or, more properly, my degree of rational partial belief in the proposition is greater than in its converse – that the potential critical and constructive contribution of the *Treatise* is still far from having been fully tapped.

NOTES

1. It is probably not inappropriate to mention Tarshis' prowess on the squash courts in this context. Even in his late 60s, he was still humbling the best of his junior colleagues on the courts, through a combination of experience, tenacity, subtlety, deftness and strategy; characteristics that could equally be assigned to his economic work. One of his proudest memories was that he had once won a single point against the then world softball squash champion in a workout, although with his characteristic honesty and self-deprecating humour, Tarshis would then go on to say that he barely saw the ball on the next point, which Khan offered to play 'for the world championship', and hence did not become world champion.

2. Cf. Georgescu-Roegen (1966, pp. 184–274) for a critical perspective on some of Keynes' critics. The point made here is reinforced by George Stigler's 'Introduction' to the reissue of Frank Knight's *Risk, Uncertainty and Profit* (1921), in which Stigler suggests that Knight's distinction between risk and uncertainty can be subsumed simply within a Bayesian subjective-probability framework. On my reading, however, Knight's approach to uncertainty (*mutatis mutandis*) was much closer to that of Keynes on probability than to the 'standard' Bayesian approach, and Stigler's 'creative' offer of a reduced-form Frank Knight belongs in the 'bait-and-switch' category of idea-marketing strategies.

3. On the dating of Keynes' Apostles paper, 'Ethics in Relation to Conduct', in which Keynes develops some notions that foreshadow the *Treatise on Probability*, Moggridge (1992, pp. 131–6) demonstrates quite convincingly that Skidelsky's (1983, p. 152) suggested date of 23 January 1904 is probably incorrect, and that its composition more likely belongs to late 1906 or early 1907. The misquotation of Keynes' title in the heading of Moggridge's Appendix I (1992, p. 131) does not affect Moggridge's substantive evidence. Although Skidelsky's apparent misdating results in a rather seriously misleading view of the chronological development of Keynes' views on probability, his overall discussion of Moore and Keynes contains some useful material, if it is read with the above *caveat* in mind.

4. It should be noted that in Chapter 24 of the *Treatise* (Keynes, [1921] 1973, pp. 311–23), Keynes *does* refer to his theory as one of 'subjective' probability, *'for the purposes of this chapter'* ([1921] 1973, p. 311, emphasis added), in order to distinguish it from the traditional doctrine of 'objective chance' and of 'randomness' associated, for instance, with the likelihood of getting a six on a toss of a die. Yet by 'subjective', Keynes here means 'a sort of probability which depends on knowledge and ignorance, and is relative, in some manner, to the mind of the subject' ([1921] 1973, p. 311) – what Keynes refers to elsewhere in the *Treatise* as 'objective', as Moggridge (1992, pp. 158–60) accurately observes.

5. Two points should be made here. First, the passage in the text has intentionally been couched in ordinal terms, using the relation 'more probable than': indeed, while I do not intend to be deliberately obstructionist or obscurantist, I am not at all clear what would be gained by (or what meaning could be attached to) my assigning *cardinal* 'betting-quotients' to the 'truth' of each of the propositions, leaving aside the consumption of significant scarce resources, including time, on the part of all involved in the (actual or putative) bets in order to establish the criteria for determining how one would 'win' (or 'lose' – or 'draw'?) each bet. The betting coefficients are not independent of the betting-situation. 'The numerical determinations of science are schematically patterned upon a constitution of the world which is already made before them' (Merleau-Ponty, 1967, p. xxvii).

    Second, the expenditure of resources necessary to convert my initial ordinal probability-judgements into bases for cardinal betting coefficients would alter the nature of both the situation and the judgements. My (artificial and externally induced) adoption of cardinal measures of my degree of belief would involve the introduction of a spurious sort of Procrustean 'precision' relative to my initial ordinal judgements: they would *not* be the probability-relations at which I had *originally* arrived relative to the evidence available to me. Moreover, they would be affected by my attitudes towards risk-bearing and uncertainty; by the fixed costs of constructing the betting-situation(s); and by the potential for 'gamesmanship', in the Stephen Potter and Wittgenstein as well as the von Neumann–Morgenstern senses, inherent in the concurrent determination of the cardinal betting coefficients and the structure of the betting-situation(s) or game(s). In short, the production process for transmuting ordinal apples into cardinal oranges involves difficulties that are at least as problematic as those of the medieval and early modern alchemists who sought to transform lead into gold.

Here, given the radical disjunction between ordinal and cardinal probability-judgements as outlined above, it is possible to suggest, as an aside, that Lakatos' brilliant *Proofs and Refutations* (1977) warrants detailed attention not only to the direct and indirect epistemological relationships between Lakatos and Plato, Wittgenstein and Polya (as well as Braithwaite and Popper, for obvious reasons), but also to the implicit role of *hubris* and defensive re-definition (or 'creative restatement') in Lakatos' vision or model of the process of production of mathematical-scientific advance. At a more speculative level, just as Harrod's particular 'dynamization' of elements of Keynes' *General Theory* caused Keynes serious difficulties (Keynes, 1973, *CW*, Vol. XIV, pp. 295–350), one could conjecture that Keynes might, at least initially, have resisted aspects of Lakatos' approach, although at one level Lakatos' study may be regarded as a dialectical or 'dynamized' version of aspects of Keynes' *Treatise on Probability* in relation to the temporal-*heuristic* element in the development of mathematical proofs (cf. Polya, 1945).

This judgement, of course, presupposes certain limits on Keynes' concept of the economics of the *structure* of time, notwithstanding his acute sensitivity to the implications of the temporal dimension of economic activity and of the resultant sorts of uncertainty for economic behaviour. It also reflects the relatively static and unspecified view of the formation and re-formation of probability-judgements or expectations in the *Treatise*, insofar as the *Treatise* provides virtually no explicit guidance as to the methods of appropriating (or even the appropriate notation for analysing the effects of) new sets of propositions, some elements among which may strengthen the original probability-judgement, some elements among which may tend to weaken or lower one's degree of belief in the original probability-judgement. Particularly if the new set of propositions is not strictly 'additive' nor purely 'subtractive', so that some of the new propositions reinforce the original conclusion while others negate (or call into question) the original conclusion, Keynes provides little guidance in the *Treatise* as to how (actually or potentially) *contradictory* sets of new propositions are to be treated or modelled, except implicitly in terms of his view that such added sets of propositions will generally increase the 'weight' (as outlined in Keynes, [1921] 1973, *CW*, Vol. VIII, pp. 77–85) of the probability-judgements to which they are relevant, but may either increase, decrease or leave unchanged the degree of rational belief in the original probability-judgement.

6. See note 5 above.
7. A much less cautious version of Braithwaite's argument is found in B.W. Bateman (in Bateman and Davis 1991, pp. 55–68).
8. In his valuable and well-documented discussion of Keynes' 1931 response to Ramsey's critique, O'Donnell (1989, pp. 138–48) makes a strong case for the essential continuity of Keynes' views on probability between the *Treatise* and Keynes' later writings. Yet apart from a reference to 'Keynes's concession to Ramsey, *whatever its nature*' (emphasis added), O'Donnell does not take full account of the syntactic ambiguities in Keynes' response (identified above in the chapter), and hence his reference to '*literal* interpretations of the review' concedes more than is entailed by Keynes' words themselves, *if they are taken literally.*
9. Perhaps Ramsey's (1931, pp. 163–5) most damaging criticism of the *Treatise* stems from his identification of what appears to be a genuine contradiction in the *Treatise*, in which Keynes appears to want to have his cake and eat it too. On the one hand, Keynes is concerned with 'the degree of belief which it is *rational* to entertain in given conditions, and not merely with the actual beliefs of particular individuals, which may or may not be rational' (Keynes, [1921] 1973, *CW*, Vol. VIII, p. 4). On the other hand, Keynes elsewhere holds that probability is 'relative to the principles of *human reason*' (Keynes, [1921] 1973,

CW, Vol. VIII, pp. 18, 35, 269–78) and himself provides examples of the irrationality of human behaviour, as in his 'Dutch Book' empirical example from the 1912 US Presidential election.

Another vulnerable aspect of the *Treatise*, not touched on directly by Ramsey but about which Keynes himself expressed concerns that would be shared by others, relates to his 'primitive' concept of 'direct knowledge', which Keynes recognized is an epistemological minefield. Moreover, in what is not intended as an exhaustive enumeration, there is a 'black-box' element to Keynes' 'fundamental equation', $a/h = P$, insofar as the process of *production* of the degree of rational partial belief P in argument a relative to h is not specified. As an heuristic framework the equation is extremely useful, but it is not a tool-kit, nor an operational basis for 'decision-making under uncertainty', and on an off-day it would be possible to suppose that the box is empty. (Cf. also note 5 above.)

10. On these matters, see Bateman and Davis (1991), Burks (1977), Georgescu-Roegen (1966, 1971), Godambe and Sprott (1971), Hamouda and Rowley (1996), Hamouda and Smithin (1988, Vol. II, pp. 3–31), Lawson and Pesaran (1985), Mini (1974) and Raiffa (1970, pp. 268–78).

15. Keynesian economics and the meaning of uncertainty

Charles R. McCann, Jr and Mark Perlman[1]

INTRODUCTION

In his 1979 'The Aggregate Supply Function in Keynes's *General Theory*', Lorie Tarshis quoted Keynes (in a letter to Dennis Robertson) as denying that he had been willing to 'throw over all my fundamental economic principles when I come and study fluctuations' (Tarshis, 1979, p. 392). Tarshis then raised the concern that, if Keynes were alive, he would lead the condemnation of contemporary economics (and contemporary economists) for doing just that, that is, for being too ready to 'throw over' fundamental principles.

While Tarshis was basing his assessment of Keynes' concern with 'fundamental economic principles' on the theoretical models of economic fluctuations, there is a more basic sense in which this rigidity applies, one which Tarshis did not consider. This more basic sense applies not to the specifics of fluctuations or considerations of demand and supply, but rather goes to the heart of economic decision-making: this sense is in the manner of our treatment of uncertainty and expectations. Keynes might as well have been signifying his unwillingness to 'throw over' his principles respecting the epistemic nature of uncertainty, as he moved from the *Treatise on Probability* of 1921 to the *General Theory of Employment, Interest and Money* of 1936. This is the focus of the current chapter.

We will begin in the next section with identifying key structures which certain of the Keynesian and post-Keynesian interpreters of Keynes have suggested are important to an understanding of the modal Keynesian model. We then move to a review of what Keynes himself wished to demonstrate, in light of the epistemological stance of the *Treatise on Probability* (1921). The point here is to show that Keynes, in moving in the *General Theory* (1936) from the emphasis in the *Treatise*, on uncertainty as reflective of the subjective apprehensions of the individual, to the model behaviour of the aggregate or collective as the centre of the economic problem, is perceived (incorrectly) as having disavowed the position taken in his earlier work, despite the fact that he incorporated in the famous Chapter 12 the essence of his earlier epistemology. By the time of the 1937 *QJE* article, 'The General Theory of Employment', he was again, however, arguing directly from his earlier position, clarifying his stance to an audience which perhaps misinterpreted (to be generous) the earlier message, and in so doing, restating the subjectivist basis of that position, in contrast to the apparent objectivist, aggregative stance of the *General Theory (sans* Chapter 12). We conclude the third section by asserting that the real difference between Keynes' works is not fundamental but rather due to the mistaken belief on the part of his readers that the collective can be asserted to behave as does the individual, a position of which Keynes may not have been aware, since the addition of an epistemological chapter served to state clearly his earlier proviso. In a fourth section we consider the problem as one of an appropriate choice in rhetoric, not as a change in belief. A fifth section concludes the chapter.

KEYNESIAN AND POST-KEYNESIAN INTERPRETATIONS OF KEYNES' MESSAGE

It is by no means an easy task to identify a modal Keynesian or post-Keynesian intellectual strain. We shall, however, attempt to identify some aspects of the two readings of Keynes which should serve to clarify certain aspects of our present topic.

Axel Leijonhufvud, in his 1968 *On Keynesian Economics and the Economics of Keynes*, made the following observation of those advocating a new Keynesian programme: 'In the mythology of the New Economics, the *General Theory* made a clear break with Keynes' own previous major contributions, while his later efforts show a regrettable tendency to "relapse" into modes of thought that the *General Theory* – i.e., the income-expenditure version of it – had made outmoded' (Leijonhufvud, 1968, p. 18).

In other words, the New Economics held that Keynes had somehow 'got it right' in the *General Theory* (at least in those parts consistent with the new paradigm), while his attempts to place the central theme of the *General Theory* within the context of his earlier philosophical convictions were little more than the ruminations of a senescent scholar.

In his own appraisal of Keynes' work, Leijonhufvud set himself the very limited objective of attempting to show '*that Keynes' theory is quite distinct from the "Keynesian" income-expenditure theory*' (1968, p. 8; emphasis in original). His own belief was that Keynes' contributions to theory were

> part of a great over-all effort to *extend* the use of the (largely received) tools of general value theory beyond the area represented by problems of general equilib-

rium and into the area of macro-disequilibrium. His contribution, in other words, has been viewed as an attempt to carry on from the points where an older generation left off, *not* as an attempt to sweep the boards clean of traditional theory. (Leijonhufvud, 1968, p. 333; emphasis in original)

Keynes was on this interpretation to be classed as a neoclassical economist whose success lay in his extension of classical theory to account for the phenomenon of non-clearing markets. Leijonhufvud's proposal to facilitate the restoration of Keynes in the economists' pantheon was to employ the Walrasian model as a covering hypothesis; Keynes' concerns could then be postulated to be mere coordination problems.

A contrary view was held by Alan Coddington, who maintained that Keynes explicitly 'attacked a body of theory that he designated "classical"'. So important was Keynes' attack that 'his work was recognised as posing a threat to some quite deeply entrenched aspects of the methods of economic analysis practised at the time' (Coddington, 1983, p. 92). It was in this connection that Coddington introduced the 'Keynesian dichotomy', separating the determination of output from the determination of price; these he characterized respectively as the hydraulic and mark-up principles (Coddington, 1983, pp. 11–12).

Coddington in effect relegated Keynes' economics to the determinism of the formal model stipulated in the *General Theory,* ignoring the import of uncertainty and expectations. Coddington indeed went so far as to suggest that Keynes' interest in uncertainty was but a 'passing one', and that to take seriously his subjectivism would be an exercise in nihilism (Coddington, 1983, p. 62). It was from this belief that Coddington classed Keynesians into the fundamentalist and hydraulic camps, the former committed to the 'nihilistic' Keynes, the latter to the 'textbook' Keynes.[2]

Post-Keynesians – Coddington's nihilists – reject the mechanical explanations of the textbook (Hicksian) model of the *General Theory* (the IS–LM approach) and desire instead a return to the 'true' message of the book. In his 1980 'Post-Keynesian Economics: A Promise that Bounced?', Tarshis identified 'two decidedly important features' of the *General Theory* 'which had been almost obscured by the neoclassical synthesis', a synthesis which created post-Keynesianism as an antithesis. These features were 'that economic processes occur in *historical* rather than in *logical* time; and that practically all decisions at firm, household, and government levels must be made in the face of serious uncertainty' (Tarshis, 1980, p. 10). It is the 'feature' of uncertainty which for our purposes here is the more interesting of the two.

In their desire to endogenize uncertainty, modern post-Keynesians have sought (and continue to seek) to incorporate (or at least discuss) uncertainty and expectations within a 'Keynesian' framework. Here we must differentiate within post-Keynesianism between the post Keynesians (unhyphenated) and the New Keynesians.[3] The difference is not fundamental, but it is in a way enlightening to the nuances of the debate. Post Keynesians, represented for the purposes of the present discussion by Paul Davidson (1991), take the position that 'true' uncertainty obtains from the fact that decisions are made in a non-ergodic environment (where an ergodic environment is one based on uniformity, that is, in which the 'averages calculated from past observations cannot be persistently different from the time average of future outcomes' (Davidson, 1991, p. 132)). Thus neither objective nor subjective probability analysis will be of use in cases of 'true' uncertainty. Institutional arrangements then assume great importance in reducing uncertainty (i.e, in generating ergodicity).

New Keynesians, represented by Rod Cross (e.g. 1993), handle the same problem by introducing the concept of *hysteresis*. A reference to the phenomenon of the persistence of a force after that force has been removed, the concept originated in the empirical physical observation that, as a magnetic charge is applied to, then removed from, certain metals, they fail to return to their initial state, that is, they retain the charge. This is applied to the social realm, in other words, past history has an influence on the present and the future.[4] Hysteretic processes are non-stationary (non-ergodic) and irreversible.[5] The important point to be noted is that, under hysteresis, 'the behaviour of the system cannot, *ex hypothesi*, be explained by reference to state variables alone: instead the past history of the system has to be invoked, as well as state variables, in order to explain the behaviour of the system' (Cross and Allan, 1988, p. 26).

Applied to economic choice, this suggests that preferences change endogenously, 'the preferences of individuals changing in response to their experience of the objects of their preferences' (Cross and Allan, 1988, p. 34).

Whichever version of post-Keynesianism one accepts, it is clear that the fact of central import is the postulation of a non-stationary environment. It is in this that we see the centre of the difficulty with this position. The crux of the problem is in those variants of post-Keynesianism wherein uncertainty is considered as being of the same scalar nature as probability. Probability – in respect of the frequency interpretation so beloved by post-Keynesian writers – requires a scale, with zero set equal to impossibility and unity set equal to ontological certitude. Uncertainty, however, can exist even under the condition of ontological certitude, while certainty can obtain even in the face of obvious impossibility. Should there be any doubt on this score, try to convince a conspiracy theorist of the errors in his apprehension of the details!

KEYNES ON UNCERTAINTY: A FUNDAMENTAL INCONSISTENCY?

All of these interpretations have attempted to reconcile aspects of Keynes' works to construct a single, underlying theme. Some use Keynes' later works as the appropriate model and fit the early works into this scheme; some begin with the early works and follow an evolutionary line of thought through the later ideas.

There does, however, appear to be a unifying theme in Keynes, one which has little to do with economics in its received scientific guise. This theme is philosophical, one based on the logic of probability which Keynes saw as important in all fields. Statements of Keynes' epistemological position are found in his *Treatise on Probability*, Chapter 12 of the *General Theory*, and the 1937 reprise of the *General Theory*, 'The General Theory of Employment'. These three works spell out in convincing detail the basis of individual behaviour and the handling of unpredictable events. This is commonly taken to be the study of behaviour under uncertainty, but we contend it is errone-ously so, for the reason that one does not *behave* under uncertainty, but rather *is* uncertain as to the coming of events. We consider now each of Keynes' noted three works in its turn.

The significance of the *Treatise* on *Probability* (1921) lies in its emphasis on subjective apprehensions of the individual to external environmental stimuli. Uncertainty in this regard reflects a misapprehension on the part of the individual of the 'signals' in the 'environment', this misapprehension being promoted by insufficient information or by an inability to digest adequately the available information. But this is not the only way in which uncertainty can arise. Uncertainty can also be regarded as manifested in the *manner* in which we perceive events. For example, one may be hard-pressed to convince an ardent believer in the paranormal that certain events are the result of a worldly cause, since he may truly believe (i.e. be certain) that the cause is other-worldly.

A coincident concern for Keynes is that of rationality, documented in Rod O'Donnell's (1989) analysis of his published and unpublished writings. In the *Treatise on Probability* (1921), Keynes was clearly outside the Benthamite framework in which a correspondence between self-interest and action is discernible even to an outside observer. He was not satisfied with the object-ive weighing of known benefits and costs, utilities and dis-utilities. The position of Keynes on this matter appears in fact to have been not inconsist-ent with that of Vilfredo Pareto (1935) with his distinction between logical and non-logical behaviours: an action which appears on the outside to be contrary to the interests of an actor may in fact have a rational basis. When Keynes stated that one of his desires in the *Treatise on Probability* was 'to explain how a degree of belief *could* be rational, and thus not merely a matter of the believer's psychological make-up but one which all rational men under similar circumstances would share' (1921, p. xxi; emphasis added), he was stating the very essence of Pareto's theory.

Keynes' account of rationality holds that non-logical behaviour is not inherently irrational (hence, Coddington's (1983) notion that Keynes in the *General Theory* was specifying *irrational* behaviour on the part of investors, simply cannot be sustained). Self-interest is fundamentally subjective. On this interpretation, we see Keynes attempting in the *Treatise* to detail the *process* underlying action – by which we mean the logic involved in decision-making – and not to provide an *explanation* of those actions, nor by extension to *judge* the *rationality* of action. He was, in short, not attempting to identify *rational* behaviour so much as he was desirous of explaining *logical* behaviour. (We see in this some identity with the later positions of Frank Ramsey (e.g. 1926) and Leonard Savage (e.g. 1972).)

In the *General Theory* (1936), the focus shifted from a concern with the bases of individual decision-making in a confusing and chaotic (read 'unpredictable') environment, to a concern with the identifiable disruptive 'macroeconomic' problems of inflation and unemployment; that is, we see a movement from a concern with the non-measurable and the incommensurable to a concern with the seriable and the stable. To achieve the simplicity required for a model of macroeconomic fluctuations, some (albeit minor) damage had to be done to Keynes' philosophical beliefs. The most severe involved his employment of aggregate measures as his principal variables. To further his analysis, Keynes had to *assume* the existence of a collective. The collective, once postulated, could be taken as representative of the modal individual, and so be endowed with the traits of the individual, including 'constrained' rationality.[6]

While the main philosophical argument of the *General Theory* centred on the fundamental notion of uncertainty and the manner in which expectations are engendered in dealing with an unpredictable environment, the manner in which Keynes handled the problem was to treat it as essentially external to the model; as J.R. Hicks opined, expectations and uncertainty in the *General Theory* were treated as pathological, irrational elements of human behaviour, not as 'elements that are moulded in the course of the process that is being analyzed' (Hicks, 1969, p. 313). But this is not too far removed from the statement of the *Treatise on Probability* regarding the inductive method, a method important to nearly 'all empirical science' (Keynes, 1921, p. 241). In the *General Theory,* Keynes was compelled by the nature of the world he had created to base expectations on *conventions* – extrapolations into the (immediate) future of current and past experiences – but with the understanding (again from the *Treatise on Probability)* that these conventions could be modified with reference to a better understanding of their constitution; thus the conventions themselves had a degree of malleability. As Rod O'Donnell noted: '[t]he upshot is that Keynes's expectations are not uniquely tied to past data, but are given a potential degree of freedom' (O'Donnell, 1989, p. 251). So long as Keynes held to the aggregate model of economic behaviour, it was only reasonable to treat expectations in this manner and to regard unpredictable events as mere random disturbances to the conventions; the deterministic model of the classical economists gained thereby a flavour of stochasticism, but the model remained nonetheless a viable explanation of the economic process.

The problem, of course, with this form of analysis is that, despite the fact that we now have a well-defined aggregate as the basis of our economic argument, it cannot be true that our study is any more concerned with *knowledge* and rational *behaviour*. We have explicitly removed the object from the individual to the community and so have divorced our analysis from the epistemic to marry it with the ontologic; that is, we have moved from the bases of behaviour to the existential nature of an artificial statistical construct. The construct, however, may be treated *as though* it exhibited a rationality of its own, despite the fact that the behaviour exhibited is the behaviour of the *group*, not the *individual*. Keynes in the *General Theory* was thus faced with an interesting dilemma, one which he himself only imperfectly apprehended: can the collective act independently from the individuals comprising it, and what does this in fact mean? Put another way, does the collective have a motivation beyond the individual motivations of its constituents, or is it simply an artificial construct from which motivation has been eliminated?

In the *QJE* article (1937), Keynes attempted to address the issue. Here he stated explicitly that one of his 'simple basic ideas' – and for our purposes the only one we need consider – was that the classical model relied too heavily (at least implicitly) on frequentistic probability as a method of computing risk; this he regarded as misguided. It is simply not true that 'facts and expectations' are 'given in a definite and calculable form', but rather the converse is true, *viz.*, that 'we have, as a rule, only the vaguest idea of any but the most direct consequences of our acts' (Keynes, 1937, pp. 212–13). Since human conduct in most activities is concerned with the remote consequences of action, wealth being in Keynes' estimation the most significant, it follows that a theory predicated on a rule which neglects the fundamental uncertainty coincident to those remote consequences of action is a poor one at best.

While the need to incorporate the concept of fundamental uncertainty is (or should be) a paramount concern of economists, still

> the necessity for action and for decision compels us as practical men to do our best to overlook this awkward fact and to behave exactly as we should if we had

behind us a good Benthamite calculation of a series of prospective advantages and disadvantages, multiplied by its appropriate probability, waiting to be summed. (Keynes, 1937, p. 214)

To pursue this practical remedy required for Keynes the consideration of three techniques, each of which he had employed in varying degrees in the *General Theory*: (1) we can 'ignore the prospect of future changes about the actual character of which we know nothing', (2) we can accept the '*existing* state of opinion' as correct, 'unless and until something new and relevant comes into the picture'; and (3) we can fall back on '*conventional* judgment' (Keynes, 1937, p. 214; emphasis in original). From a consideration of these 'techniques' we can then produce a model 'subject to sudden and violent changes' (external shocks or even 'animal spirits') within which '[n]ew fears and hopes will, without warning, take charge of human conduct'. This suggests, however, that 'the vague panic fears and equally vague and unreasoned hopes are not really lulled, and lie but a little way below the surface' (Keynes, 1937, pp. 214–15). Thus we can in such a model justify, for example, the holding of money balances as a 'barometer of the degree of our distrust of our own calculations and conventions concerning the future' (Keynes, 1937, p. 216).

Thus we see the difference (slight as it may be) between the *Treatise on Probability* and the *General Theory*, viz. that Keynes in the *Treatise* held to a subjectivist (individualist) philosophy, maintaining that uncertainty as an epistemic concern was fundamentally subjective and qualitative, and so not incorporatable into formal economic models, while Keynes in the *General Theory* and later restatement invoked 'conventions' as just such a means of handling it within the confines of the social collective (ostensibly for purposes of the model, but of course the political implications are obvious). These conventions were, however, nothing more complicated than average behaviour, as the economist aggregated the individuals into a collective to which could be applied the calculus of probability and statistical reasoning; while *individual* choice is not amenable to the probability calculus, *social* choice affords the requisite series. Thus we see Keynes writing of the psychological propensities to save, to hoard and to consume, statistical artefacts reflecting the 'behaviour' of the fictional modal individual *qua* macroeconomic 'agent'.

To understand better the problem as we have posed it, it may be useful to provide an example of what we conclude are misperceptions regarding Keynes' employment of probability as he shifted emphasis from the problems treated in the *Treatise on Probability* to the problems treated in the *General Theory*. In this regard, consider the statement of Bradley Bateman:

Whereas the youthful Keynes would have had 'reliable, rational' people willingly contemplating the good that would result from their actions and the degree to which they could believe this good would occur, the mature Keynes was left with people pursuing a plethora of ends (good, bad, and otherwise) and employing subjective degrees of belief regarding the likelihood of their outcomes. (Bateman, 1991, p. 63)

The basis for such a statement proceeds from a misunderstanding of Keynes' position *vis-à-vis* probability, which leads directly to a misapprehension of the key elements of both the *Treatise* and the *General Theory*. Specifically, the statement relies on a conflation of the probability *relation* with the probability *value*. With respect to the probability *relation*, Keynes in the *Treatise on Probability* maintained indeed that it was objective and logical, not 'subject to human caprice' (Keynes, 1921, p. 4). With respect to the probability *value* or *judgement*, on the other hand, Keynes held in the *Treatise* that such judgements were subjective and epistemic (i.e. they do not have numerically definite values, but correspond instead to beliefs); epistemic probability valuation was in fact the key to his theory – he even went so far as to state explicitly that the subjective nature of belief was paramount to his interpretation of probability in respect of uncertainty: 'The method of this treatise has been to regard subjective probability as fundamental and to treat all other relevant conceptions as derivative from this' (Keynes, 1921, p. 312).[7]

We see this notion resurface in the *General Theory*, especially as restated in the 1937 paper. Here, despite his legitimization of the use of aggregates, Keynes nonetheless maintained the centrality of the incalculable elements of human decision, even to the point of denigrating the very method of handling uncertainty made viable by reference to the aforementioned statistical series.[8] In Chapter 12 of the *General Theory*, 'The State of Long-Term Expectation', while stressing that 'the state of long-term expectation is often steady, and, even when it is not, the other factors exert their compensating effects' (Keynes, 1936, p. 162), Keynes considered explicitly that the preponderance of our 'positive activities' was not amenable to mathematical expectation, 'whether moral or hedonistic or economic' (Keynes, 1936, p. 161). Frequencies are not sufficient to incorporate belief, and are generally, in any event, not to be had, the very point he made in the *Treatise* on *Probability*. It is for this very reason that Keynes invoked 'animal spirits' as a shorthand for these incommensurable 'positive activities', behaviours the existence of which we must acknowledge, all the while being cognizant of the fact that we can do little with them in a formal aggregative economic model:

Most, probably, of our decisions to do something positive, the full consequences of which will be drawn out over many days to come, can only be taken as a result of animal spirits – of a spontaneous urge to action rather than inaction, and not as the outcome of a weighted average of quantitative benefits multiplied by quantitative probabilities. (Keynes, 1936, p. 161)

Keynes was then taken to assert in the *General Theory* the real shortcoming of employing the probability calculus in instances involving economic choice. It is obvious

> that human decisions affecting the future, whether personal or political or economic, cannot depend on strict mathematical expectation, since the basis for making such calculations does not exist; and that it is our innate urge to activity which makes the wheels go round, our rational selves choosing between the alternatives as best we are able, calculating where we can, but often falling back for our motive on whim or sentiment or chance. (Keynes, 1936, pp. 162–3)

Thus could Keynes in the *General Theory* combine the factors of individual rationality, epistemics and the fallback position of mathematical expectation into a single economic framework, propounding an aggregative model, all the while whispering the *caveat* of 'scholar beware!'.

The import of the above is obvious. While Keynes did in fact employ mathematical expectation in the *General Theory* (in the sense of aggregates), he did so as part of a change in *design,* not as the result of a change of *conviction* as to the nature of probability or because of a conversion to the expected utility model. The framework employed in the *General Theory* allowed the use of a procedure designed specifically to handle aggregates, a procedure which has no function when dealing with the uncertainty underlying individual choice. When dealing with the individual and the processes respecting personal decision-making, Keynes was clearly of the view – a view he maintained consistently – that judgements are subjective and that therefore any general interpretation of probability must be defined with respect to epistemics and not confined to ontological description. There is no basis under such an interpretation upon which to define a suitable statistical series which could serve as a basis for mathematical expectation, for the frequency interpretation of probability is too restrictive.

When on the other hand we deal with the economy as a whole, and so need to reflect on the social basis of organization, the situation is markedly different. Here one can readily construct statistical series and so can legitimately employ the frequency theory and the technique of mathematical expectation; the constructs here are ontological. Keynes then did not need to *abandon* (nor did he do so) his early philosophical motivation for probability, when moving from the *Treatise on Probability* to the *General Theory.* The subjective necessarianism of the *Treatise* was predicated on *individual* behaviour, while the *General Theory* relied instead on seriable aggregates, on 'psychological propensities' derived from statistical series, not on motivation or volition.[9]

The underlying epistemic base remains nonetheless, and is expounded for those desirous of understanding the nature of changes in the fundamental magnitudes.

THE KEYNES PROBLEM AS A STUDY IN RHETORIC

Interpretive (post-) Keynesians have in general attempted to reconcile the views of the Keynes of the *General Theory* and the Keynes of the *QJE* article (and to a lesser extent the *Treatise on Probability*) by including digressions on uncertainty and rationality. While some of these interpretations do in fact confront the statements of Keynes as to the importance of understanding uncertainty in economic life, others – principally Keynesians as a distinct group – pay mere mention to the problem and then continue to ignore its import. Coddington, for example, went so far as to maintain 'that one can make far more sense of Keynes's position as a whole by treating Chapter 12 as a manifestation of animal spirits rather than as a carefully considered piece of analysis' (Coddington, 1983, p. 88).[10]

While it is understood today that the treatment of these concerns can be handled in a technical sense within a model predicated on household behaviour – that is, we can construct a *macroeconomic* model explaining inflation and unemployment on the basis of *microeconomic* foundations – for Keynes the concern was more with employing the appropriate rhetoric. His principal concern for the format of the *General Theory* was in making an argument to a sufficient degree of generality which would allow his central message to be transmitted to the broadest audience. In other words, Keynes was not desirous of presenting to academic economists a systematic model dealing with fluctuations and their consequent effects on employment and prices (despite his statement in the Preface that the book was addressed to fellow economists (Keynes, 1936)), but rather was concerned with persuading government ministers and other like types of the viability of state intervention in reducing the volatility of investment. If nothing else, Keynes the master rhetorician knew his audience and so knew how (meaning, just what it took) to persuade. For the policy-maker, a simple, *ad hoc*, model from which one could identify gross changes was sufficient to the task. For the professional philosopher, by contrast, what was needed in his philosophical disquisitions of the *Treatise on Probability* was a formal presentation of the distinction between uncertainty and unpredictability, and the manner in which probability could be applied to human decisions in the face of the unknown and the unknowable.

Given the time and the environment in which the *General Theory* was written, the need to persuade a non-academic, political audience to accept his policy prescriptions is evident. One reason Patinkin (1990) gave for the many different (and divergent) opinions of the 'meaning' of the *General Theory* was the fact that the book had *political implications* and was thus designed to present and promote a *political* message. Keynes himself had a political agenda which framed the argument (Patinkin, 1990, pp. 233–4). Thus the *General Theory* is both a political and an economic tract – likely intended to be powerful in both arenas. Moreover, the political themes one finds in the book cross ideological boundaries. We find Murray Milgate (1982) attributing to Keynes a Marxian analytic, while Allan Meltzer (1988) attempted a reappraisal of Keynes as a monetary conservative who preferred rules to discretion (and also paved the way for the new neoclassical economics of rational expectations), points also made by Patinkin (1990).

The rhetoric employed fit the audience to be persuaded: to convince the policy-maker of the cogency of his message and the validity of his policy recommendations, Keynes was compelled to reduce his model to its barest essentials. The aggregate consumption function and the investment function became central concepts, but of course the academic economist and the moral philosopher – in whose camps Keynes felt equally at ease – would understand that behind each was an implicit model of *individual* behaviour.

In the *QJE* article, Keynes himself expressed best his intention for the *General Theory:*

> I am more attached to the comparatively simple fundamental ideas which underlie my theory than to the particular forms in which I have embodied them, and I have no desire that the latter should be crystallized at the present stage of the debate. If the simple basic ideas can become familiar and acceptable, time and experience and the collaboration of a number of minds will discover the best way of expressing them. (Keynes, 1937, pp. 211–12)

CONCLUSION

Problems abound with interpreting Keynes' *General Theory*, both on its own merits and in its relation to his earlier works. Interpretations can be on the one hand doctrinaire or, on the other, hermeneutic. The real problem, however, with attempting any textual exegesis of Keynes' work is that the *General Theory* seems a study in cognitive dissonance: in the work Keynes appears to have held two incompatible philosophical positions, as he attempted to construct an aggregate economic model (a model predicated on the communitarianism afforded by reference to the collective) on the basis of an individualist philosophy.

Yet, as we have seen, the tension is at best superficial. Keynes' works – from the *Treatise on Probability* through to the *QJE* article – promote a central theme of individual choice in the face of genuine (epistemic) uncertainty, brought about by: (1) a chaotic or otherwise unpredictable environment, (2) informational limitations, (3) a misunderstood notion of rationality, and even (4) the lack of a logical approach to reason. This is the essential element of Keynesian economics, the economics actually practised by Keynes.

NOTES

1. The authors wish to thank Jochen Runde for comments on an earlier version.
2. Coddington admitted he was not in the least concerned 'with what Keynes actually said, nor with what he really meant when he said it, nor even what, according to various guardians of the purity of his thought, he was really trying to say and is only now succeeding in saying through them' (Coddington, 1983, p. 1).
3. Earlier, James Crotty (1980) had identified two wings of post-Keynesianism: neo-Keynesians, including Joan Robinson, Nicholas Kaldor and Luigi Pasinetti, a group whose issue was growth; and post-Keynesians, including Paul Davidson, Hyman Minsky, G.L.S. Shackle and (here too) Joan Robinson, a group whose issue was uncertainty and finance (Crotty, 1980, p. 20). Thus we see that, within the span of a decade, the terms had been given new identities.
4. Cross and Allan attributed to Joseph A. Schumpeter, in his 1934 *The Theory of Economic Development*, the notion of hysteresis as an explanation of dynamic economic systems. This influence was felt through the work of Nicholas Georgescu-Roegen (1971) in his employment of the physical concept of entropy to economics. (Cf. Cross and Allan, 1988, pp. 31–2.)
5. Davidson (1993) held otherwise.
6. O'Donnell maintained, 'it is a premiss of the *GT* that agents behave rationally, or, more precisely, that they behave as rationally as their circumstances permit' (O'Donnell, 1989, p. 248).
7. This explains the position of, among others, O'Donnell (1989), that Keynes did not capitulate to Frank Ramsey's (1926) critique. He did not need to. Keynes had always held that the *relation* of probability was objective, while the *degree of belief* one held in a proposition was subjective and not numerically definite, the point Ramsey stressed in his review. Keynes never held the *relation* itself to be subjective, even in response to Ramsey; he agreed with Ramsey only on the question of belief.
8. Don Patinkin seems to have accepted the conclusion of the importance of belief, while making the case that it simply did not matter to the conclusions or the basic tenets of the *General Theory*: 'Thus even after taking account of the major influence of "the state of confidence" on expectations, Keynes still speaks of a determinate investment demand schedule in the short-run context which is the concern of the central message of the *General Theory*' (Patinkin, 1990, p. 218).
9. No less a Keynesian and Keynes scholar than Patinkin confused Keynes' presentation of uncertainty with that of Frank H. Knight, and by so doing minimized the contribution in this area of the *General Theory*. Patinkin contended that 'the nonprobabilistic nature of economic uncertainty can hardly be considered to be a contribution of the *General Theory* ...' (Patinkin, 1990, p. 219). The problem with such a conclusion is that it is predicated on a misunderstanding of some basic concepts. Knight's was an *ontological* theory of uncertainty, not an *epistemic* one; Keynes' theory by contrast was entirely epistemic. Patinkin seems to have neglected Keynes' work in the *Treatise on Probability* (it does not appear as a reference in the writings we have had the privilege to peruse, that is, 1965, 1990, 1993a, 1993b), which, had he consulted it, would have enlightened him as to this important distinction between Keynes and Knight.
10. Cf. Jochen Runde (1991) for a cogent refutation of the position of Coddington with respect to the question of uncertainty.

Bibliography

Abraham, Katherine G. and John C. Haltiwanger (1995), 'Real wages and the business cycle', *Journal of Economic Literature*, 33 (September), 1215–64.

Ahmed, M. and L. Summers (1992), 'A tenth anniversary report on the debt crisis', *Finance and Development*, 29 (3, September), 2–5.

Akerlof, George A. (1970), 'The market for "lemons": quality uncertainty and the market mechanism', *Quarterly Journal of Economics*, 84 (5, August), 488–500.

Akyuz, Y. (1995), 'Taming international finance', in J. Michie and J. Grieve Smith (eds), *Managing the Global Economy*, Oxford: Oxford University Press, pp. 55–90.

Akyuz, Y. and A. Cornford (1995), 'International capital movements: some proposals for reform', in J. Michie and J. Grieve Smith (eds), *Managing the Global Economy*, Oxford: Oxford University Press, pp. 172–96.

[anonymous] (1960), *Keynes at Harvard: Economic Deception as a Political Credo, A Veritas Study*; identified as authored by Dobbs, Zygmund and Olin Glenn Saxon (rev. and enlarged ed. 1962), West Sayville, New York: Probe Research Inc. Publishers.

Arrow, Kenneth (1974), *Essays in the Theory of Risk-Bearing*, Amsterdam: North-Holland Pub. Co. and New York: American Elsevier Pub. Co.

Asso, Pier Francesco (1990), *The Economist behind the Model: The Keynesian Revolution in Historical Perspective. A Study of Some Unpublished Evidence of How Keynes Went to America*, Quaderni di Richerche, 18, Rome: Ente per Gli Studi Monetari, Bancari e Finanziari Luigi Einaudi.

Axelrod, Robert (1984), *The Evolution of Cooperation*, New York: Basic Books.

Bank for International Settlements (1987), *International Banking and Financial Market Developments*, April, Basel: BIS.

Barber, William J. (1987), 'The career of Alvin H. Hansen in the 1920s and 1930s: a study in intellectual transformation', *HOPE*, 19 (7), 191–206.

Bateman, Bradley W. (1991), 'The rules of the road: Keynes's theoretical rationale for public policy', in Bradley W. Bateman and John B. Davis (eds), *Keynes and Philosophy: Essays on the Origin of Keynes's Thought*, Aldershot/Brookfield, VT: Edward Elgar, pp. 55–68.

Bateman, Bradley W. and John B. Davis (eds) (1991), *Keynes and Philosophy: Essays on the Origin of Keynes's Thought*, Aldershot/Brookfield, VT: Edward Elgar.

Benham, Frederic (1941), *Economics, A General Textbook*, New York/Chicago: Pitman Publishing Co.

Bensusan-Butt, David M. ([1967] 1980), 'Keynes's General Theory: then and now', in D.M. Bensusan-Butt (ed.), *On Economic Knowledge, A Sceptical Legacy*, Canberra: Australian National University, pp. 1–10.

Bergsten, C.F. (1994), 'Managing the world economy of the future', in P.B. Kenen (ed.), *Managing the World Economy, Fifty Years after Bretton Woods* Washington, DC: Institute for International Economics.

Beveridge, William (1930), *Unemployment, a Problem of Industry (1909 and 1930)*, London: Longmans.

Bodkin, Ronald G. (1969), 'Real wages and cyclical variations in employment: a re-examination of the evidence', *Canadian Journal of Economics*, 2 (August), 353–74.

Bogdanowicz-Bindert, C.A. (1989), 'The Brady Plan: the US reconsiders its LDC debt strategy', paper presented at the conference on 'Global Disequilibrium' at McGill University, Montreal, Quebec, May.

Bothwell, R., I. Drummond and J. English (1981), *Canada since 1945 – Power, Politics and Provincialism*, Toronto: University of Toronto Press.

Bowen, Howard R. (1953), 'Graduate education in economics', *American Economic Review*, Supplement 43 (4), i–xvi, 1–223.

Bowley, A.L. (1920), *The Change in the Distribution of the National Income, 1880–1913*, Oxford: The Clarendon Press.

Brady, Michael E. (1994), 'Keynes, Pigou, and the supply side of the *General Theory*', *History of Economics Review*, 21 (Winter), 34–46.

Braithwaite, R.B. (1969), *Theory of Games as a Tool for the Moral Philosopher*, Cambridge: Cambridge University Press.

Brown, A.J. (1988), 'A worm's eye view of the Keynesian revolution', in J. Hillard (ed.), *J.M. Keynes in Retrospect: The Legacy of the Keynesian Revolution*, Aldershot: Edward Elgar, pp. 18–44.

Brown, Douglass V., Edward Chamberlin, Seymour E. Harris, Wassily Leontief, Edward S. Mason, Joseph A. Schumpeter and Overton H. Taylor (1934), *The Economics of the Recovery Program*, New York: Whittlesey House, McGraw-Hill.

Brown, W.A. (1940), *The International Gold Standard Reinterpreted*, New York: National Bureau of Economic Research, CAMS Press.

Bryce, Robert B. ([1935] 1977), 'An introduction to a monetary theory of employment', in Don Patinkin and J. Clark Leith (eds), *Keynes, Cambridge and 'The General Theory'*, Toronto: University of Toronto Press, pp. 127–45.

Bryce, Robert B. (1938), 'Discussion of Lorie Tarshis, "Real wages in the United States and Great Britain"', *Canadian Journal of Economics and Political Science*, 4 (August), 375–6.

Buckley, Willam F., Jr (1951), *God and Man at Yale: The Superstitions of Academic Freedom*, Chicago: Henry Regnery.

Bulow, J. and K. Rogoff (1988a), 'The buyback boondoggle', *Brookings Papers on Economic Activity*, 2, 675–98.

Bulow, J. and K. Rogoff (1988b), 'Multilateral sovereign debt reschedulings', *International Monetary Fund Staff Papers*, 35 (December), 644–57.

Bulow, J. and K. Rogoff (1990), 'Cleaning up Third World debt without getting taken to the cleaners', *Journal of Economic Perspectives*, 4 (1), 31–42.

Burks, Arthur W. (1977), *Chance, Cause, Reason: An Inquiry into the Nature of Scientific Evidence*, Chicago: University of Chicago Press.

Burns, Arthur F. (1946), 'Introduction' in 'Economic Research and the Keynesian Thinking of our Time', *Twenty-Sixth Annual Report of the National Bureau of Economic Research*, New York, NY: The Bureau, pp. 3–29.

Cairncross, Alec (1953), *Home and Foreign Investment, 1870–1913*, Cambridge: CUP; rpt 1967, New York: Kelley.

Cairncross, Alec and Nita Watts (1989), *The Economic Section, 1938–1961: A Study in Economic Advising*, London: Routledge.

Camdessus, Michel (1995), "Presentation of the 50th Annual Report", "Introductory Note" and "Concluding Remarks", *Summary Proceeding of the Annual Meeting of the Board of Governors, 10–12 October*, Washington, DC: International Monetary Fund Publication Services; (on-line version), *www.imf.org.news.managing director's speeches*.

Camdessus, Michel (1996), *Facing the Globalized World Economy: The IMF Experience: Four Addresses*, Washington, DC: International Monetary Fund Publication Services.

Cannan, Edwin (1932), 'The demand for labour', *Economic Journal*, 42 (September), 357–70.

Cannan, Edwin (1933), *Economic Scares*, London: P.S. King & Son.

Carabelli, A.M. (1988), *On Keynes' Method*, London: Macmillan.

Carabelli, A.M. (1991), 'The methodology of the critique of the classical theory: Keynes on organic interdependency', in Bradley W. Bateman and John B. Davis (eds), *Keynes and Philosophy: Essays on the Origin of Keynes's Thought*, Aldershot/Brookfield, VT: Edward Elgar, pp. 104–25.

Carnap, R. (1962), *Logical Foundations of Probability*, Chicago: University of Chicago Press.

Caskey, J. and D. Felix (1989), *The Baker Plan: Eight More Years?*, Working Paper No. 127, St Louis, MO: Washington University.

Casson, Mark (1983), *Economics of Unemployment: An Historical Perspective*, Oxford: Martin Robertson and Cambridge, MA: MIT Press.

Chester, Norman (1986), *Economics, Politics and Social Studies in Oxford, 1900–85*, London: Macmillan.

Chisholm, R.M. and Robert J. Swartz (eds) (1973), *Empirical Knowledge*, Englewood Cliffs, NJ: Prentice-Hall.

Claessens, C. (1990), 'The debt Laffer curve: some estimates', *World Development*, 18, 1671–7.

Claessens, C., I. Diwan and E. Fernandez-Arias (1992), *Recent Experience with Commercial Debt Reduction*, Working Paper No. 995. Washington, DC: World Bank.

Claessens, S. (1995), 'The emergence of equity investment in developing countries: overview', *The World Bank Economic Review*, 9 (1), 1–18.

Claessens, S., M. Dooley and A. Warner (1995), 'Portfolio capital flows: hot or cold?', *The World Bank Economic Review*, 9 (1), 132–53.

Clark, Colin (1937), *National Income and Outlay*, London: Macmillan.

Clay, Henry (1929), 'The public regulation of wages in Great Britain', *Economic Journal*, 39 (September), 323–43.

Cline, W.R. (1995), *International Debt Reexamined*, Washington, DC: Institute for International Economics.

Coddington, Alan (1983), *Keynesian Economics: The Search for First Principles*, London: George Allen & Unwin.

Cohen, Daniel (1992), 'The Debt Crisis: A Postmortem', *National Bureau of Economic Research Macroeconomic Annual, 1992*. Cambridge, MA: The MIT Press.

Cohen, Daniel and Thierry Verdier (1990), 'Secret Buy-Backs of LDC Debt', CEPR Working Paper No. 462.; (1995) '"Secret" buy-backs of LDC debt', *Journal of International Economics, Supplement*, 39 (3–4), 317ff.

Colander, David C. and Harry Landreth (1996), *The Coming of Keynesianism to America*, Brookfield, VT: Edward Elgar.

Collins, Robert M. (1981), *The Business Response to Keynes, 1929–1964*, New York: Columbia University Press.

Cottrell, A.E. and M.S. Lawlor (eds) (1995), *New Perspectives on Keynes*, Durham, NC: Duke University Press.

Cross, Rod (1993), 'Hysteresis and post-Keynesian economics', *Journal of Post-Keynesian Economics*, 15 (3, Spring), 305–8.

Cross, Rod and Andrew Allan (1988), 'On the history of hysteresis', in Rod Cross (ed.), *Unemployment, Hysteresis, and the Natural Rate Hypothesis*, Oxford: Basil Blackwell, pp. 26–38.

Crotty, James R. (1980), 'Post-Keynesian economic theory: an overview and evaluation', *The American Economic Review Papers and Proceedings*, 70 (2, May), 20–25.

Darity, William A., Jr and Bobbie L. Horn (1983), 'Involuntary unemployment reconsidered', *Southern Economic Journal*, 49 (January), 717–33.

Davidson, Paul (1991), 'Is probability theory relevant for uncertainty? A post Keynesian perspective', *Journal of Economic Perspectives*, 5 (1, Winter), 129–43.

de Cecco, M. (1979), 'Origins of the post-war payments system', *Cambridge Journal of Economics*, 3 (March), 49–61.

Dennison, Henry S., Lincoln Filene, Ralph E. Flanders and Morris Evans Leeds (1938), *Toward Full Employment*, New York: McGraw-Hill Book Company, Inc. and London: Whittlesey House.

Devlin, R. (1989), *Debt and Crisis in Latin America: The Supply Side of the Story*, Princeton, NJ: Princeton University Press.

Dooley, M. (1995), 'A retrospective on the debt crisis', in P.B. Kenen (ed.), *Understanding Interdependence: The Macroeconomics of the Open Economy*, Princeton, NJ: Princeton University Press.

Dore, M.H.I. and L. Tarshis (1990), 'The LDC debt and the commercial banks: a proposed solution', *Journal of Post Keynesian Economics*, 12 (Spring), 452–65.

Dore, Ronald (1992), 'Goodwill and the spirit of market capitalism', in Mark Granovetter and Richard Swedberg (eds), *The Sociology of Economic Life*, Boulder, CO: Westview Press, pp. 159–79.

Dow, S.C. (1993), *Money and the Economic Process*, Aldershot: Edward Elgar.

Dow, S.C. (1997), 'Keynes and Endogenous Money', in G.C. Harcourt and P.A. Riach (eds), *The Second Edition of Keynes's General Theory*, London: Routledge, Vol. 2, pp. 61–78.

Dunlop, John T. (1938), 'The movement of real and money wage rates', *Economic Journal*, 48 (3, September), 413–34.

Dunlop, John T. (1939a), 'Cyclical variations in wage structure', *Review of Economic Statistics*, 21 (February), 30–39.

Dunlop, John T. (1939b), 'Trends in the "rigidity' of English wage rates', *Review of Economic Studies*, 6 (June), 189–99.

Dunlop, John T. (1941), 'Real and money wage rates: a reply', *Quarterly Journal of Economics*, 55 (August), 683–91.

Dunlop, John T. (1998), 'Retrospectives: real money wage rates', *Journal of Economic Perspectives*, 12 (Spring), 223–34.

Durbin, Elizabeth (1985), *New Jerusalems: The Labour Party and the Economics of Democratic Socialism*, London: Routledge.

Economic Council of Canada (1969), *Interim Report on Competition Policy*, Ottawa: Supply and Services.

Eichengreen, B. and P.B. Kenen (1994), 'Managing the world economy under the Bretton Woods system: an overview', in P.B. Kenen (ed.), *Managing the World Economy, Fifty Years after Bretton Woods*, Washington, DC: Institute for International Economics.

Eichengreen, B. and R. Portes (1989), 'After the deluge: default, negotiation, and readjustment during the interwar years', in B. Eichengreen and P. Lindert (eds), *The International Debt Crisis in Historical Perspective*, Cambridge, MA: MIT Press.

Eichengreen, B., J. Tobin and C. Wyploz (1995), 'Two cases for sand in the wheels of international finance', *Economic Journal*, 105, 162–72.

Ely, Richard T. (1893, 1908, 1918, 1926, 1931, 1938), *Outlines of Economics*, New York: The Macmillan Company.

Ely, Richard T. and George Ray Wicker (1904; rev. 1919), *Elementary Principles of Economics: Together with a Short Sketch of Economic History*, New York/London: The Macmillan Company.

Etzioni, Amitai (1994), 'What's Wrong?', *New York Times*, 14 February, A, 17:2.

Fairchild, Fred Rogers, Edgar Stevenson Furniss and Norman Sydney Buck (1924, rept. 1926; rev. ed. c. 1930, 1931; 3rd ed. 1936, 1939, 1948), *Elementary Economics*, New York: The Macmillan Company, 2 vols.

Fellner, W. and Bernard F. Haley (eds) (1946), *Readings in the Theory of Income Distribution*, Philadelphia/Toronto: Blakiston.

Ferguson, B. (1993), *Remaking Liberalism – The Intellectual Legacy of Adam Shortt, O.D. Skelton, W.C. Clark and W.A. Machintosh 1890–1925*, Montreal: McGill-Queen's University Press.

Feuer, Lewis S. (2nd ed. 1982), *Einstein and the Generations of Science*, New Brunswick, NJ: Transaction Books.

Fisher, Irving (1911; re-ed. 1912; 3rd ed. 1918, 1921, 1928), *Elementary Principles of Economics*, New York: The Macmillan Company.

Folkerts-Landau, D., P.M. Garber and S.R. Weisbrod (1991), 'Supervision and regulation of financial markets in a new financial environment', in C. Wihlborg, M. Fratianni and T.D. Willett (eds), *Financial Regulation and Monetary Arrangements after 1992*, Amsterdam: North-Holland, pp. 43–57.

Foot, P. (ed.) (1967), *Theories of Ethics*, Oxford: Oxford University Press.

Frege, Cottlob (1934), *Die Grundlagen der Arithmetik, eine Logischmathematishe Untersuchung über den Begriff der Zahl*, Breslav: Verlage M. & H. Marcus.

Fromm, Eric (1947), *Man for Himself*, New York: Holt, Rinehart & Winston.

Fromm, Eric (1964), *The Heart of Man*, New York: Harper & Row.

Furniss, Edgar S. (1947), 'Introduction', in Lorie Tarshis, *The Elements of Economics: An Introduction to the Theory of Price and Employment*, Boston: Houghton Mifflin Co., pp. i–xii.

Galbraith, John Kenneth (1965), 'How Keynes came to America', *New York Times Book Review*, 16 May, VIII, p. 1.

Galbraith, John Kenneth (1971), *A Contemporary Guide to Economics, Peace and Laughter*, A.D. Williams (ed.), Boston: Houghton Mifflin Company.

Garber, P. and M. Taylor (1995), 'Sand in the wheels of foreign exchange markets: a sceptical note', *Economic Journal*, 105 (January), 173–80.

Gardener, E.P.M. (1988), 'Innovation and new structural frontiers in banking', in P. Arestis (ed.), *Contemporary Issues in Money and Banking*, London: Macmillan, pp. 7–29.

Garver, Frederic B. and Alvin H. Hansen (1926; rev. ed. 1928), *Principles of Economics*, Minneapolis: Perine Book Co.; (rev. ed. 1938), Boston: Ginn.

Georgescu-Roegen, Nicholas (1966), *Analytical Economics*, Cambridge, MA: Harvard University Press.

Georgescu-Roegen, Nicholas (1971), *The Entropy Law and the Economic Process*, Cambridge, MA: Harvard University Press.

Gideonse, Harry, 'Review of R. Gilbert et al. (1938), *An Economic Program for American Democracy*', *Political Science Quarterly*, vol. 54 (1939), pp. 266–8.

Gilbert, R.V., G.H. Hildebrand, Jr, Arthur Stuart, M.Y. Sweezy, P.M. Sweezy, L. Tarshis and J. Wilson, E. Despres, W.S. Salant and A.R. Sweezy (1938), *An Economic Program for American Democracy*, New York: Vanguard Press.

Ginzberg, Eli, 'Review of R. Gilbert et al. (1938), *An Economic Program for American Democracy*', *Saturday Review*, March 11, 1939, p. 18.

Godambe, V.P. and D.A. Sprott (eds) (1971), *Foundations of Statistical Inference*, Toronto: Holt, Rinehart & Winston.

Gödel, Kurt (1931), 'Überformal mentscheidbare Sätze der *Principia mathematica und vertwandter System I*', *Monatshefte für Mathematik und Physik*, 38, 173–98

Good, I.J. (1965), *The Estimation of Probabilities*, Cambridge, MA: MIT Press.

Good, I.J. (1971), 'The probabilistic explication of information, evidence, surprise, causality, explanation and utility', in V.P. Godambe and D.A. Sprott (eds), *Foundations of Statistical Inference*, Toronto: Holt, Rinehart & Winston, pp. 108–27.

Goodhart, Charles (1989), *The Evolution of Central Banks*, Cambridge, MA: MIT Press.

Goodhart, Charles (1995), *The Central Bank and the Financial System*, Cambridge, MA: MIT Press.

Gordon, H.S. (1966), 'Twenty year perspective: some reflections on the Keynesian revolution in Canada', Canadian Trade Committee in S.F. Kaliski (ed.), *Canadian Economic Policy since the War*, Montreal: Private Planning Association of Canada, pp. 23–46.

Government of Canada (1945), *White Paper on Employment and Income*,

Ottawa: King's Printer; (extracts rpt 1966) 'Appendix' in S.F. Kaliski (ed.), *Canadian Economic Policy since the War*, Montreal: Private Planning Association of Canada, pp. 135–54.

Gowland, D. (1990), *The Regulation of Financial Markets in the 1990s*, Aldershot: Edward Elgar.

Granatstein, J. (1982), *The Ottawa Men – The Civil Service Mandarins 1935–1957*, Toronto: Oxford University Press.

Granovetter, Mark and Richard Swedberg (eds) (1992), *The Sociology of Economic Life*, Boulder, CO: Westview Press.

Greif, Avner (1989), 'Reputations and coalitions in medieval trade: evidence on the Magribi traders', *Journal of Economic History*, 49 (4, December), 857–82.

Guillebaud, C.W. (1948), 'Review of Lorie Tarshis (1948), *The Elements of Economics: An Introduction to the Theory of Price and Employment*', *Economic Journal*, vol. 58 (1948), pp. 557–9.

Gustafson, James M. (1991), 'Ethics: an American growth industry', *The Key Reporter*, 56 (3), 1–5.

Guttentag, J.M. and R.J. Herring (1986), *Disaster Myopia in International Banking*, Essays in International Finance No. 164 (September), Princeton, NJ: Princeton University, International Finance Section, Department of Economics.

Haberler, G. (1946), *Prosperity and Depression: A Theoretical Analysis of Cyclical Movements*, Lake Success: United Nations.

Haberler, G. (1976), 'Alvin H. Hansen: some reminiscences', *Quarterly Journal of Economics*, 90 (1), 9–13.

Hall, M.J.B. (1989), *Handbook of Banking Regulation and Supervision*, New York: Woodhead-Faulkner.

Hamilton, Earl J. (1934), *American Treasure and the Price Revolution in Spain, 1501–1650*, Cambridge, MA: Harvard University Press.

Hamouda, O. and R. Rowley (1996), *Probability in Economics*, New York: Routledge.

Hamouda, O. and J.N. Smithin (eds) (1988), *Keynes and Public Policy After Fifty Years*, New York: New York University Press, 2 vols.

Hamouda, O., R. Rowley and B. Wolf (eds) (1989), *The Future of the International Monetary System*, Aldershot: Edward Elgar.

Hansen, Alvin H. (1953), *A Guide to Keynes*, New York: McGraw Hill.

Hansen, Alvin H. (1941), *Fiscal Policy and Business Cycles*, New York: Norton.

Hardy, C. (1995), '*The Case for Multilateral Debt Relief for Severely Indebted Countries*' (mimeo), Washington, DC: International Development Training Institute.

Harrod, R.F. (1936), *The Trade Cycle*, Oxford: The Clarendon Press.

Harrod, R.F. (1937), 'Mr. Keynes and traditional theory', *Econometrica*, 5 (1), 74–86.

Hawtrey, R.G. (1937), *Capital and Employment*, London: Longmans Green.

Healey, N.M. (1994), 'The international debt crisis: the end of the beginning, not yet the beginning of the end', *Banca Nazionale del Lavoro Quarterly Review*, 47 (March).

Helleiner, G.K. (1994), *External Debt and External Finance for Sub-Saharan Africa: The Continuing Problem*, (mimeo), Toronto, ON: University of Toronto.

Hicks, J.R. (1936), 'Mr Keynes's Theory of Employment', *Economic Journal*, 46 (June), 238–53; (rpt 1982), in *Money, Interest and Wages, Collected Essays on Economic Theory*, Vol. II, Oxford: Basil Blackwell, pp. 84–99.

Hicks, J.R. (1937), 'Mr. Keynes and the classics: a suggested interpretation', *Econometrica*, 5 (2, April), 147–59.

Hicks, J.R. (1939), *Value and Capital*, Oxford: Clarendon Press; (2nd ed., 1946) London: Oxford University Press.

Hicks, J.R. (1969), 'Automatists, Hawtreyans, and Keynesians', *Journal of Money, Credit, and Banking*, 1 (3, August), 307–17.

Hirschman, Albert O. (1989), 'How the Keynesian revolution was exported from the United States and other comments', in Peter A. Hall (ed.), *The Political Power of Economic Ideas: Keynesianism across Nations*, Princeton, NJ: Princeton University Press, pp. 347–59.

Hochman, Harold M. (1994), 'Economics and distributive ethics', Inaugural Lecture of 3 February, Easton, PA: Lafayette College, unpublished.

Hogendorn, J. (1992), *Economic Development*, New York: Harper Collins.

Homer, ([1611] 1969), *The Iliads of Homer*, George Chapman (trans.), English Experience Series, no. 115, New York: Da Capo.

Huber, J. Richard (1948), 'Review of Lorie Tarshis (1948), *The Elements of Economics: An Introduction to the Theory of Price and Employment*', *Annals of the American Academy of Political and Social Science*, 255, 206.

Hutchison, T.W. (1978), 'Demythologizing the Keynesian revolution: Pigou, wage-cuts and the *General Theory*', in T.W. Hutchison (ed.), *On Revolutions and Progress in Economic Knowledge*, Cambridge: Cambridge University Press, pp. 175–99.

Innis, H.A. (1950), *Empire and Communications*, Oxford: The Clarendon Press and Toronto: Oxford University Press.

Kahn, Richard F. (1931), 'The relation of home investment to unemployment', *Economic Journal*, 41 (2, June), 173–98.

Kaldor, N. (1937), 'Professor Pigou on money wages in relation to unemployment', *Economic Journal*, 47 (4), 745–53.

Kalecki, Michal (1938), 'The distribution of the national income', *Econometrica*, 6; (rev. 1939), in M. Kalecki, *Essays in the Theory of Economic Fluctuations*, London: George Allen and Unwin, pp. 13–41; (rpt 1946), in W. Fellner and Bernard F. Haley (eds), *Readings in the Theory of Income Distribution*, Philadelphia/ Toronto: Blakiston, pp. 197–217.

Kalecki, Michal (1939), *Essays in the Theory of Economic Fluctuations*, London: George Allen & Unwin.

Kaliski, S.F. (ed.) (1966), *Canadian Economic Policy since the War*, Montreal: Private Planning Association of Canada.

Kane, Edward J. (1987), 'Comparative financial regulation: an international perspective', in R. Portes and A. Swoboda (eds), *Threats to International Financial Stability*, Cambridge: Cambridge University Press, pp. 111–45.

Kenen, P.B. (1983), 'Third World debt, sharing the burden: a bailout plan for the banks', *The New York Times*, 6 March, III, 3:1.

Kenen, P.B. (1990), 'Organizing debt relief: the need for a new institution', *Journal of Economic Perspectives*, 4 (1), 7–18.

Kenen, P.B. (ed.) (1994), *Managing the World Economy, Fifty Years after Bretton Woods*, Washington, DC: Institute for International Economics.

Keynes, John Maynard (1920), *The Economic Consequences of the Peace*, New York: Harcourt, Brace & Howe.

Keynes, John Maynard (1921; rpt 1973), 'Treatise on Probability', in *Collected Writings of John Maynard Keynes*, Vol. VIII, London/Basingstoke: Macmillan and New York: Cambridge University Press for the Royal Economic Society.

Keynes, John Maynard (1925), [*The Economic Consequences of Mr. Churchill* first appeared as] 'Unemployment and monetary policy', *Evening Standard* (22, 23, and 24 July); (rpt 1971), in *Collected Writings of John Maynard Keynes*, Vol. IX, *Essays in Persuasion*, London: Macmillan and New York: Cambridge University Press for the Royal Economic Society, pp. 207–230.

Keynes, John Maynard (1925), 'The end of *laissez faire*', Sidney Ball Lecture, at Oxford, November 1924, London: Hogarth Press (July); (rpt 1971), in *Collected Writings of John Maynard Keynes*, Vol. IX, *Essays in Persuasion*, London: Macmillan and New York: Cambridge University Press for the Royal Economic Society, pp. 272–94.

Keynes, John Maynard (1930), *A Treatise on Money*, London: Macmillan and New York: Harcourt Brace, 2 vols.

Keynes, John Maynard (1931; rpt 1972), 'Review of Frank P. Ramsey, *The Foundations of Mathematics*'; in *Collected Writings of John Maynard Keynes*, Vol. X, London/Basingstoke: Macmillan and New York: Cambridge University Press for the Royal Economic Society, pp. 335–40.

Keynes, John Maynard (1931–2), Letters to Dennis Robertson; (rpt 1973), in D.E. Moggridge (ed.), *The General Theory and After, Collected Writings of*

John Maynard Keynes, Vol. XIII, Part I, London/Basingstoke: Macmillan and New York: Cambridge University Press for the Royal Economic Society, pp. 201–336 passim.

Keynes, John Maynard (1933), Letter to the Editor, *New York Times,* 31 December, (rpt 1973) in D.E. Moggridge (ed.), *Collected Writings of John Maynard Keynes,* Vol. XXI, London/Basingstoke: Macmillan and New York: Cambridge University Press for the Royal Economic Society, pp. 289–97.

Keynes, John Maynard (1935), Letter from John Maynard Keynes to George Bernard Shaw; (rpt 1973) in D.E. Moggridge (ed.) *Collected Writings of John Maynard Keynes,* Vol. XXVIII, London/Basingstoke: Macmillan and New York: Cambridge University Press for the Royal Economic Society, p. 42; (rpt 1992) in Robert Skidelsky, *John Maynard Keynes: The Economist as Savior 1920–1937,* London: Macmillan, pp. 520–21; and D.E. Moggridge, *Maynard Keynes: An Economist's Biography,* London/New York: Routledge, pp. 469–70.

Keynes, John Maynard (1936), *The General Theory of Employment, Interest and Money,* London: Macmillan for the Royal Economic Society; (rpt 1964) New York: Harcourt Brace, Jovanovich; (rpt 1973) in *Collected Writings of John Maynard Keynes,* Vol. VII, London/Basingstoke: Macmillan and New York: Cambridge University Press for the Royal Economic Society.

Keynes, John Maynard (1937), 'The General Theory of Employment', *The Quarterly Journal of Economics,* 51 (February), 209–23; (rpt 1973) in D.E. Moggridge. (ed), *Collected Writings of John Maynard Keynes,* Vol. XIV, London/Basingstoke: Macmillan / New York: Cambridge University Press for the Royal Economic Society, pp. 109–32.

Keynes, John Maynard (1937a), 'Alternative theories of the rate of interest', *Economic Journal* 47 (2), 241–52.

Keynes, John Maynard (1939), 'Relative movements of real wages and output', *Economic Journal,* 49 (March), 34–51; (rpt 1973) as "Appendix 3" in *Collected Writings of John Maynard Keynes,* Vol. VII London/Basingstoke: Macmillan / New York: Cambridge University Press for the Royal Economic Society, pp. 394–412.

Keynes, John Maynard (1940), *How to Pay for the War. A Radical Plan for the Chancellor of the Exchequer,* New York: Harcourt, Brace and London: Macmillan.

Keynes, John Maynard (1971–1989), Donald E. Moggridge and E.A.G. Robinson/Elizabeth Johnson (eds), *The Collected Writings of John Maynard Keynes* [*CW*] London: Macmillan for the Royal Economic Society, 30 vols.

Keynes, John Maynard ([1929] 1972), 'Mr Churchill on Peace' in *Collected Writings of John Maynard Keynes,* Vol. X, London/Basingstoke: Macmillan and New York: Cambridge University Press for the Royal Economic Society, pp. 52–7.

Keynes, John Maynard and H.D. Henderson (1929), *Can Lloyd George Do It?: An Examination of the Liberal Pledge*, London: The Nation and Athenaeum.

Keynes, Milo (ed.) (1975), *Essays on John Maynard Keynes*, Cambridge: Cambridge University Press.

Kindleberger, Charles P. (1989), *Manias, Panics and Crashes*, New York: Basic Books.

Kindleberger, Charles P. (1991), *The Life of an Economist: An Autobiography*, Oxford: Basil Blackwell.

Kindleberger, Charles P. (1992), *Mariners and Markets*, New York: Harvester/Wheatsheaf.

Kindleberger, Charles P. (1993), 'Social intangibles relevant to economic processes', in S. Biasco et al. (eds), *Markets and Institutions in Economic Development*, New York: St Martin's Press, pp. 87–101.

Klein, Lawrence R. (1947), *The Keynesian Revolution*, New York: Macmillan.

Kletzer, K. (1984), 'Asymmetries of information and LDC borrowing with sovereign risk', *Economic Journal*, 94, 287–307.

Knight, F.H. (1921), *Risk, Uncertainty, and Profit*, Chicago: University of Chicago Press.

Kregel, J.A. (ed.) (1988), *Memoirs of Eminent Economists*, London: Macmillan.

Krugman, P. (1989), 'Market-based debt-reduction schemes', in J. Frenkel, M. Dooley and P. Wickham (eds), *Analytical Issues in Debt*, Washington, DC: International Monetary Fund, pp. 258–78.

Krugman, P. (1994), 'LDC debt policy', in M. Feldstein (ed.), *American Economic Policy in the 1980s*, Chicago: University of Chicago Press, pp. 691–722.

Krugman, P. (1995), 'Dutch tulips and emerging markets', *Foreign Affairs*, 74 (4, July–August), 28–44.

Kuhn, Thomas S. (1962), *The Structure of Scientific Revolutions*, Chicago: University of Chicago Press.

Kyburg, H.E. and H.E. Smokler (eds) (1964), *Studies in Subjective Probability*, New York: Wiley.

Lakatos, I. (1977), *Proofs and Refutations*, Cambridge: Cambridge University Press.

Lane, Rose Wilder (1933), *Let the Hurricane Roar*, New York/Toronto: Longmans Green and Co.

Lange, Oscar (1938), 'The rate of interest and the optimum propensity to consume', *Economica*, 5 (1), 12–32.

Lawlor, Michael S., William A. Darity, Jr and Bobbie L. Horn (1987), 'Was

Keynes a Chapter Two Keynesian?', *Journal of Post Keynesian Economics*, 9 (Summer), 516–28.

Lawson, T. (1985), 'Keynes, prediction and econometrics', in T. Lawson and H. Pesaran (eds), *Keynes' Economics: Methodological Issues*, Armonk, NY: M.E. Sharpe pp. 116–133.

Lawson, T. and H. Pesaran (eds) (1985), *Keynes' Economics: Methodological Issues*, Armonk.

Leijonhufvud, Axel (1968), *On Keynesian Economics and the Economics of Keynes*, London: Oxford University Press.

Lerner, A.P. (1936), 'Mr. Keynes' *General Theory of Employment, Interest and Money*', *International Labour Review*, 34 (3), 435–54.

Lerner, A.P. (1938), 'Alternative explanations of the Theory of Interest', *Economic Journal*, 48 (2), 211–30.

Lerner, Max (1937), 'Introduction', in Adam Smith, *The Wealth of Nations*, New York: Modern Library, pp. xxiii–lvi.

Levitan, Sar. (1948), 'Review of Lorie Tarshis (1948), *The Elements of Economics: An Introduction to the Theory of Price and Employment*', *Political Science Quarterly*, 63, 301.

Mackintosh, W.A. (1940), *The Economic Background of Dominion–Provincial Relations*, Study for Royal Commission on Dominion–Provincial Relations, Ottawa: King's Printer.

Mackintosh, W.A. (1966), 'The White Paper on employment and income in its 1945 setting', Canadian Trade Committee in S.F. Kaliski (ed.), *Canadian Economic Policy since the War*, Montreal: Private Planning Association of Canada, pp. 9–21.

Marshall, Alfred (1890; 8th ed. 1920), *Principles of Economics*, London: Macmillan.

Marshall, Alfred (1926) *Official Papers*, London: Macmillan for the Royal Economic Society.

Mason, Edward S. (1982), 'The Harvard Department of Economics from the beginning to World War II', *Quarterly Journal of Economics*, 97 (3), 383–434.

McCann, Charles R., Jr (1994), *Probability Foundations of Economic Theory*, London: Routledge.

McCormick, Brian (1992), *Hayek and the Keynesian Challenge*, London: Harvester-Wheatsheaf.

Meade, J.E. (1937), 'A simplified model of Mr Keynes' system', *Review of Economic Studies*, 4 (1), 98–107; (rpt 1988) in Susan Howson (ed.), *Employment and Inflation*, Vol. 1 of *The Collected Papers of James Meade*, London: Allen & Unwin.

Meltzer, Allan H. (1988), *Keynes's Monetary Theory: A Different Interpretation*, Cambridge: Cambridge University Press.

Merleau-Ponty, M. (1967), *The Structure of Behavior*, Boston: Beacon Press.

Michie, J. and J. Grieve Smith (eds) (1995), *Managing the Global Economy*, Oxford: Oxford University Press.

Milgate, Murray (1982), *Capital and Employment: A Study of Keynes's Economics*, London: Academic Press.

Mills, Richard Charles and Frederic Benham (2nd ed., 1925), *The Principles of Money, Banking, and Foreign Exchange and their Application to Australia*, Sydney: Angus & Robertson.

Mini, P. (1974), *Philosophy and Economics*, Gainesville, FL: University Presses of Florida.

Minsky, H.P. (1975), *John Maynard Keynes*, London: Macmillan.

Minsky, H.P. (1982), *Inflation, Recession and Economic Policy*, Brighton: Wheatsheaf.

Modigliani, Franco (1944), 'Liquidity preference and the theory of interest and money', *Econometrica*, 12 (1 January), 45–88.

Moggridge, D. (ed.) (1977), *Activities 1940–1944 Shaping the Post-War World: The Clearing Union, The Collected Writings of John Maynard Keynes*, Vol. XXV, London/Basingstoke: Macmillan and New York: Cambridge University Press for the Royal Economic Society.

Moggridge, D. (1992), *Maynard Keynes: An Economist's Biography*, London: Routledge.

Moggridge, D. (and E.A.G. Robinson) (eds) (1973–), *Collected Writings of John Maynard Keynes*, Vols 11–14 and 19–30, London/Basingstoke: Macmillan and New York: Cambridge University Press for the Royal Economic Society.

Moore, G.E. (1903), *Principia Ethica*, Cambridge: Cambridge University Press.

Naim, M. (1995), 'Latin America the morning after', *Foreign Affairs*, 74 (4, July–August), 45–61.

Newman, P. (1987), 'Frank Plumpton Ramsey', in J. Eatwell, M. Milgate and P. Newman (eds) ([1987], 1990), New York: Norton.

[Notice of] *An Economic Program for American Democracy* (1939), *American Economic Review*

O'Donnell, Rod M. (1989), *Keynes: Philosophy, Economics, and Politics*, London: Macmillan and New York: St Martin's Press.

O'Donnell, Rod M. (1991), 'Keynes's weight of argument and its bearing on rationality and uncertainty', in Bradley W. Bateman and John B. Davis (eds), *Keynes and Philosophy: Essays on the Origin of Keynes's Thought*, Aldershot/Brookfield, VT: Edward Elgar, pp. 69–88.

Ohlin, Bertil (1937a), 'Some notes on the Stockholm theory of savings and investment. Part I', *Economic Journal*, 47 (1), 53–69.

Ohlin, Bertil (1937b), 'Some notes on the Stockholm theory of savings and investment. Part II', *Economic Journal*, 47 (2), 221–40.

Owram, D. (1986), *The Government Generation – Canadian Intellectuals and the State, 1900-1945*, Toronto: University of Toronto Press.

Palma, G. (1995), 'UK lending to the Third World from the 1973 oil shock to the 1980s debt crisis: on financial "Manias, Panics and (Near) Crashes"', in P. Arestis and V. Chick (eds), *Finance, Development and Structural Change: Post Keynesian Perspectives*, Aldershot: Edward Elgar.

Pareto, Vilfredo (1935), *The Mind and Society*, Arthur Livingston (trans.), New York: Harcourt-Brace.

Parker, I.C. (1977), *Studies in the Economics of Communication*, Yale University PhD dissertation New Haven, CN: Yale University.

Parker, I.C. (1994), 'Myth, telecommunications and the emerging global informational order', in E. Comor (ed.), *The Global Political Economy of Communication*, New York: St Martin's Press, pp. 37–60.

Patinkin, Don (1948), 'Price flexibility and full employment', *American Economic Review*, 38, 543–64; (rev. ed. 1951), in Friedrich A. Lutz and Lloyd W. Mints (eds), *Readings in Monetary Theory*, New York: American Economic Association – Blakiston, pp. 252–83.

Patinkin, Don (2nd ed. 1965), *Money, Interest, and Prices: An Integration of Monetary and Value Theory*, New York: Harper & Row.

Patinkin, Don (1981), *Essays on and in the Chicago Tradition*, Durham: Duke University Press.

Patinkin, Don (1990), 'On different interpretations of the *General Theory*', *Journal of Monetary Economics*, 26 (2), 205–43.

Patinkin, Don (1993a), 'Meltzer on Keynes', *Journal of Monetary Economics*, 32, 347–56.

Patinkin, Don (1993b), 'On the chronology of the *General Theory*', *The Economic Journal*, 103 (3 May), 647–63.

Patinkin, Don and J. Clark Leith (eds) (1977), 'Keynes as seen by his students in the 1930s (i) Robert B. Bryce; (ii) Walter S. Salant; (iii) Lorie Tarshis', in *Keynes, Cambridge* and The General Theory, London: Macmillan, pp. 39–63.

Patinkin, Don and J. Clark Leith (eds) (1977), *Keynes, Cambridge and* The General Theory, London: Macmillan.

Peano, Guiseppe (1973), *Selected Works*, Hubert C. Kennedy (ed. and trans.), Toronto: University of Toronto Press.

Peirce, C.S. (1955), *Philosophical Writings of Peirce*, New York: Dover.

Pigou, A.C. (1927a), *Industrial Fluctuations*, London: Macmillan.

Pigou, A.C. (1927b), 'Wage policy and unemployment', *Economic Journal*, 37 (September), 355–68.

Pigou, A.C. (1933), *The Theory of Unemployment*, London: Macmillan.

Pigou, A.C. (1937), 'Real and money wages in relation to unemployment', *Economic Journal*, 7 (3), 405–22.

Pigou, A.C. (1941), *Employment and Equilibrium*, London: Macmillan.

Ploix, Helene (1994), 'Postface', in C.P. Kindleberger (ed.), *Histoire mondiale de la speculation financiere* [French translation of (1989), *Manias, Panics and Crashes*] Paris: Editions PAU, pp. 337–41.

Polya, G. (1945), *How to Solve It*, Princeton, NY: Princeton University Press.

Raiffa, H. (1970), *Decision Analysis*, Reading, MA: Addison-Wesley.

Ramsey, Frank P. ([1926] 1931), 'Truth and probability', in [Frank P. Ramsey] *The Foundations of Mathematics and Other Logical Essays*, R.B. Braithwaite (ed.) London: Routledge & Kegan Paul; in (1990), D.H. Mellor (ed.), *F.P. Ramsey: Philosophical Papers*, Cambridge: Cambridge University Press.

Ramsey, Frank P. (1931), *The Foundations of Mathematics and Other Logical Essays*, R.B. Braithwaite (ed.), London: Routledge & Kegan Paul.

Rawls, John (1971), *A Theory of Justice*, Cambridge, MA: Belknap Press of Harvard University Press.

Richardson, J. Henry (1939), 'Real wage movements', *Economic Journal*, 49 (September), 425–41.

Robbins, Lionel (1971), *Autobiography of an Economist*, London: Macmillan.

Robertson, D.H. (1936), 'Some notes on Mr Keynes' General Theory of Employment', *Quarterly Journal of Economics*, 51 (1), 168–91.

Robertson, D.H. (1937), 'Alternative theories of the rate of interest', *Economic Journal*, 47 (3), 4.

Robertson, D.H. (1940), *Essays in Monetary Theory*, London: P.S. King.

Robinson, Abraham (1966), *Non-Standard Analysis*, Amsterdam: North-Holland Publishing Co.

Robinson, Joan (1937), *Introduction to the Theory of Employment*, New York: The Macmillan Company.

Rosenberg, Nathan (1975), 'Problems in the economist's conceptualization of technological innovation', *HOPE*, 7 (4), 456–81.

Rueff, Jacques (1979), *Oeuvres completes de Jacques Rueff*, Paris: Plon, t. 2.

Ruggles, Richard (1940), 'The relative movements of real and money wage rates', *Quarterly Journal of Economics*, 55 (November), 130–49.

Ruggles, Richard (1941), 'Rejoinder', *Quarterly Journal of Economics*, 55 (August), 697–700.

Runde, Jochen (1991), 'Keynesian uncertainty and the instability of beliefs', *Review of Political Economy,* 3 (2), 125–45.

Runde, Jochen (1994), 'Keynesian uncertainty and liquidity preference', *Cambridge Journal of Economics*, 18 (2, April), 129–44.

Russell, Bertrand, see Whitehead.

Rymes, Thomas K. (1987), *Keynes's Lectures, 1932–35: Notes of Students*, Ottawa: Department of Economics, Carleton University.

Rymes, Thomas K. (1989), *Keynes's Lectures, 1932–35: Notes of a Representative Student*, London/Basingstoke: Macmillan and Ann Arbor: University of Michigan Press.

Sacco, Pier Luigi (1990), 'On the fragility of reputational equilibria under systematic uncertainty: what is wrong with rational expectations', *Banca Nazionale del Lavoro Quarterly Review*, 175 (December), 459–74.

Sachs, J. (ed.) (1989), *Developing Country Debt and Economic Performance*, Chicago: University of Chicago.

Sachs, J. (1994), 'Beyond Bretton Woods: a new blueprint', *The Economist*, 333, (1, October), 23–4.

Salant, Walter S. (1976), 'Alvin Hansen and the Fiscal Policy Seminar', *Quarterly Journal of Economics*, XC (1), 14–23.

Salant, W.S., E. Despres, L.B. Krause, A. Rivlin, W.A. Salant and L. Tarshis (1963), *The United States Balance of Payments in 1968*, Washington, DC: Brookings Institution.

Samuelson, Paul A. (1946), 'Lord Keynes and *The General Theory*', (rpt. 1983) in John Cunningham Wood (ed.), *John Maynard Keynes: Critical Assessments*, London: Croom-Helm, 4 vols, pp. 190–202.

Samuelson, Paul A. (1948; 2nd ed. 1952; 3rd ed. 1955; 4th ed. 1958; 5th ed. 1961; 6th ed. 1964; 7th ed. 1967; 8th ed. 1970; 9th ed. 1973; 10th ed. 1980), *Economics: An Introductory Analysis*, New York: McGraw-Hill Book Co.

Samuelson, Paul A. (1972), 'Jacob Viner 1892–1970', *Journal of Political Economy*, 80 (1), 5–11.

Samuelson, Paul A. (1976), 'Alvin Hansen as a creative economic theorist', *Quarterly Journal of Economics*, XC (1), 24–31.

Samuelson, Paul A. (1997), 'Credo of a lucky textbook author', *The Journal of Economic Perspectives*, 11 (2, Spring), 153–60.

Savage, Leonard J. ([1954] 1972), *The Foundations of Statistics*, New York: Dover.

Schumpeter, Joseph A. (1934), *The Theory of Economic Development*, Cambridge, MA: Harvard University Press.

Schumpeter, Joseph A. (1954), *A History of Economic Analysis*, New York: Oxford University Press.

Selgin, George (1988), *The Theory of Free Banking*, Totowa, NJ: Rowan & Littlefield.

Sexton, Robert L., Philip R. Graves and Dwight R. Lee (1993), 'Lowering the age requirement for adult courts: an analytical framework', *Atlantic Economic Journal*, 21 (4, December), 67–70.

Shionoya, Y. (1991), 'Sidgwick, Moore and Keynes: a philosophical analysis of Keynes's "My Early Beliefs"', in Bradley W. Bateman and John B. Davis (eds), *Keynes and Philosophy: Essays on the Origin of Keynes's Thought*, Aldershot/Brookfield, VT: Edward Elgar, pp. 6–29.

Simon, Herbert A. (1957), *Models of Man: Social and Rational. Mathematical Essays on Rational Human Behaviour in a Social Setting*, New York: Wiley.

Simon, Herbert A. (1982), *Models of Bounded Rationality*, Cambridge, MA: MIT Press.

Simons, Henry C. ([1934] 1949), *A Positive Program for Laissez Faire. Some Proposals for a Liberal Economic Policy*, Public Policy Pamphlet, 15, Chicago: University of Chicago Press.

Skidelsky, Lord Robert (1983), *John Maynard Keynes: A Biography*, London: Macmillan, 2 vols; (rpt. 1994), *John Maynard Keynes*, New York: Penguin/ Viking, 2 vols.

Slater, David W. (1995), *War, Finance and Reconstruction: The Role of Canada's Department of Finance 1939–1945*, limited ed., Ottawa: David Slater.

Smith, Adam ([1759; 1766] 1896), *Lectures on Justice, Police, Revenue and Arms*, Oxford: Clarendon Press.

Smith, Adam (11th ed.,1808), *The Theory of Moral Sentiments*, Edinburgh: Bell & Bradfute, 2 vols.

Soloman, R. (1989), 'International monetary reform: the future is not what it used to be!', in O. Hamouda, R. Rowley and B. Wolf (eds), *The Future of the International Monetary System*, Aldershot: Edward Elgar, pp. 10–16.

Solow, Robert M. (1986), '"What is a nice girl like you doing in a place like this?", macroeconomics after fifty years', *Eastern Economic Journal*, 12 (3), 191–8.

Spero, Joan Edelman (1980), *The Failure of the Franklin National Bank*, New York: Columbia University Press.

St Hill, R. (1991), *A Post Keynesian Analysis of Commercial Bank Regulation* (mimeo), Lincoln, UK: Lincoln University.

Staples, Robert (5th ed., 1994), *The Black Family: Essays and Studies*, Belmont, CA: Wadsworth Publishing.

Stein, Herbert S. (1968), *The Fiscal Revolution in America*, Chicago: University of Chicago Press; (rpt. 1990), Washington, DC: The American Enterprise Institute Press.

Stigler, George J. (1988), *Memoirs of an Unregulated Economist*, New York: Basic Books.

Strange, S, (1986), *Casino Capitalism*, Oxford: Blackwell.

Strange, S. (1994), 'From Bretton Woods to the casino economy', in S. Corbridge, R. Martin and N. Thrift (eds), *Money, Power and Space*, Oxford: Blackwell.

Swedberg, Richard (1990), (Interview with) 'George A. Akerlof', *Economics and Sociology*, Princeton, NJ: Princeton University Press, pp. 61–77.

Szenberg, Michael (ed.) (1992), *Eminent Economists. Their Life Philosophies*, Cambridge: Cambridge University Press.

Tarshis, Lorie (see his major writings listed after the Introduction to this volume).

Tarski, A. ([1941] 1965), *Introduction to Logic*, New York: Oxford University Press.

Taussig, Frank William (1911; 3rd ed. 1929), *Principles of Economics*, New York: Macmillan, 2 vols.

Thomas, Dorothy S. (1926), 'An index of British business cycles', *Journal of the American Statistical Association*, 21 (March), 60–63.

Tobin, James (1939), *Money Wages and Employment*, thesis (AB, Honours), Cambridge, MA: Harvard University.

Tobin, James (1978), 'A proposal for international monetary reform', *Eastern Economic Journal*, 3, 153–9.

Tucker, R.C. (ed.) (1978), *The Marx–Engels Reader*, New York: Norton.

United Nations Monetary and Financial Conference ([1944]), *Articles of Agreement* n.p, Bretton Woods, NH: International Bank of Reconstruction and Development.

Van Wijnbergen, S. (1991), 'Mexico's external debt restructuring in 1989/90: an economic analysis', *Economic Policy*, 12, 13–56.

Veblen, T. (1915), *Imperial Germany and the Industrial Revolution*, New York: Viking.

Veblen, T. (1934), *Essays in Our Changing Order*, New York: Viking.

Von Neumann, J. and O. Morgenstern ([1944] 1953), *Theory of Games and Economic Behavior*, Princeton, NJ: Princeton University Press.

Von Wright, G.H. (1951, 1960), *A Treatise on Induction and Probability*, Paterson, NJ: Littlefield, Adams.

Whitehead, Alfred Norton and Bertrand Russell, *Principia Mathematica*, Cambridge: The University Press, 3 vols.

Wicksell, K. ([1898] 1936), *Interest and Prices*, London: Macmillan.

Williams, John H. (1947), 'Reflections on Keynesian Economics', Lectures presented at The Harvard Fiscal Policy Seminar, Cambridge, MA.

Williams, John H. (1952), 'An economist's confessions', *American Economic Review*, 42 (March), 1–23.

Williams, John H. (1976), 'Tribute in Hansen's memory in the symposium to Hansen', *Quarterly Journal of Economics*, XC, (1), p. 8.

Williamson, J. (1992), 'International monetary reform and the prospects for economic development', in J. Teunisson (ed.), *Fragile Finance: Rethinking the International Monetary System*, The Hague: FONDAD.

Williamson, J. (1995), 'Reform of the international financial institutions',

Paper presented at 'Canada and the 1995 G7 Halifax Summit: Developing Canada's Positions', Ottawa, ON.

Wittgenstein, L. (1953), *Philosophical Investigations*, Oxford: Basil Blackwell.

Wittgenstein, L. (1956), *Remarks on the Foundations of Mathematics*, Cambridge, MA: MIT Press.

Wolfe, D.A. (1978), 'Economic growth and foreign investment: a perspective on Canadian economic policy, 1945–1957', *Journal of Canadian Studies*, 13 (1, Spring), 3–20.

Wood, George Henry (1910), *The History of Wages in the Cotton Trade during the Past Hundred Years*, London: Sherratt & Hughes.

Young, Warren (1987), *Interpreting Mr Keynes: The IS/LM Enigma*, Oxford: Polity.

Young, Warren and Frederic Lee (1993), *Oxford Economics and Oxford Economists*, London: Macmillan.

Index